PLANTERS and PIONEERS
Life in Colonial Virginia

PLANTERS and

For the first few years of Virginia's settlement, colonists lived in a triangular palisade, called James Forte. Church, guardhouse, and storehouse are surrounded by fifteen dwellings. *Painting by John Hull for A. H. Robins Company, Inc.*

PIONEERS

Life in Colonial Virginia

The story in pictures and text of the people who settled England's first successful colony from its planting in 1607 to the birth of the United States in 1789

by Parke Rouse, Jr.

HASTINGS HOUSE *Publishers*   New York

For my Wife
Betsy Gayle Rouse

Published simultaneously in Canada
by Saunders, of Toronto, Ltd.,
Don Mills, Ontario

Library of Congress Catalog Card Number: 68-17650

Printed in the United States of America

Contents

Acknowledgments

This book is a companion to *Virginia: The English Heritage in America*, which I wrote in 1966. Here I have tried to depict how Virginians lived in colonial times, whereas the earlier book dealt with their political and military exploits. It is in part a result of research I have undertaken as executive director of The Jamestown Foundation, which maintains the exhibit area known as Jamestown Festival Park for the Commonwealth of Virginia. Many of the illustrations result from a search of English sources made possible through a grant from the Old Dominion Foundation.

It is impossible to thank adequately the many people who have kindly helped. Many sources are indicated in the captions of illustrations and in the bibliography. However, I should like to thank Mrs. Jacqueline Chapman, my secretary, for her generous voluntary assistance. Mrs. Evelyn Danner of Williamsburg did useful research, and Mrs. Frances Bemiss Mason of Richmond read most of the text and made helpful suggestions.

The following provided useful information:

Mrs. Louise Catterall, Richmond; Hill Carter, Shirley Plantation, Charles

City County, Virginia; Sidney E. King, Milford, Virginia; Erle Prior, Richmond; Mrs. Mildred F. Councilor and William Francis Smith, Alexandria; Mrs. Segar Cofer Dashiell, Smithfield, Virginia; Commander Walter Raleigh Gilbert, Devon, England; Miss Susie Ames, Pungoteague, Virginia; William Dunn, Lynchburg; the Reverend Howard McK. Wilson, Staunton; the Rev. John Byerly, Jr., the Rev. John H. Grey, and the Rev. Thomas Pugh, Williamsburg; Lewis Kirby, Convent, N.J.; Mrs. Joyce Lindsay, Richmond; Noel Currer-Briggs, London; Mrs. Mary Black, New York; Mrs. Philippa Bruce Shepperson, Charlottesville; Thomas L. Williams, Williamsburg; Lewis A. McMurran, Jr. and Richard Epes McMurran, Newport News; Mrs. Elizabeth Von Schilling, Surry County, Virginia; and Thomas W. Wood, Williamsburg.

Assistance is also acknowledged from the following and their organizations:

Mrs. Blanche Kenney Bosher, the Latrobe Theater, Richmond; Orland Wages, Bridgewater College, Bridgewater, Virginia; John S. Lanahan, Richmond Hotels, Richmond; James F. McInteer, Jr., Virginia Commission of Game and Inland Fisheries, Richmond; Mrs. Dorothy Robertson, *The Times-Dispatch*, Richmond; Mrs. Ruth S. Bentley, Waterford Foundation, Inc., Waterford, Virginia; John Melville Jennings and Mrs. Mary S. Southall, Virginia Historical Society, Richmond; Norman G. Beatty, Miss Marguerite Gignilliat, Mrs. Eileen Newman, Mrs. Jean Sheldon, Mrs. Rose Belk, Mrs. Mary Mordecai Goodwin, Miss Jane Carson, Mrs. Joan Dolmetsch, George Reese, and Milo Naeve, Colonial Williamsburg; Douglas B. Fugate, Virginia Department of Highways, Richmond; Paul Hulton, the British Museum, London; Robert F. Williams, Virginia Education Association, Richmond; H. M. Brimm, Union Theological Seminary, Richmond; Miss Josephine L. Harper, Wisconsin Historical Society, Madison, Wisconsin; Woodford B. Hackley, Virginia Baptist Historical Society, Richmond; Francis L. Berkeley, Jr., the University of Virginia, Charlottesville; Chester Bradley, Fort Monroe Casemate Museum, Old Point Comfort, Virginia; Miss Jean Hildreth, the Abby Aldrich Rockefeller Folk Art Collection, Williamsburg; Miss Elizabeth Harrell and William Francis, Virginia Museum of Fine Arts, Richmond; Daniel M. Hawks, Hampden-Sydney College, Hampden-Sydney, Virginia; Mrs. Betty Gray Gibson, the Valentine Museum, Richmond; Jack R. Hotaling, Sigma Alpha Epsilon Fraternity, Evanston, Illinois; Thomas Moore Carruthers, Michie Tavern, Charlottesville; Ben Belchic, Winchester-Frederick County Historical Society, Winchester, Virginia; Mrs. Agnes Brabrand, Mrs. Belinda Watkins, Robert Burgess, and John Lochhead, Mariners Museum, Newport

News; Frank J. Gilliam, Ollinger Crenshaw, Allen W. Moger, and Rupert Latture, Washington and Lee University, Lexington, Virginia; Louis B. Wright, Folger Shakespeare Library, Washington; Miss Alice O. Gilmer, Russell County Public Library, Lebanon, Virginia; Ben C. McCary, Harold L. Fowler, Wayne Kernodle, Richard K. Newman, Jr., Herbert Ganter, Ross Weeks, Jr., Miss Margaret Cook, Miss Suzanne Foley, and Miss Marie Ellis, the College of William and Mary, Williamsburg; Robert K. Heimann, American Tobacco Company, New York; William B. Hill, Prestwould Foundation, Clarksville, Virginia; Charles E. Hatch, Jr. and J. Paul Hudson, Colonial National Historical Park, Yorktown, Virginia; Mrs. Katherine M. Smith and William J. Van Schreeven, Virginia State Library, Richmond; Mrs. Elizabeth Emmerson, Mrs. Margaret Grey, Pembroke Thomas, and Gordon Perkins, the Jamestown Foundation, Jamestown.

Finally, I would like to acknowledge my wife's encouragement during the research and writing. I hope it was not in vain.

PARKE ROUSE, JR.

Jamestown, Virginia

Captain Christopher Newport enters the James River with the Virginia colonists in 1607. Crewmen fill casks from a spring at Newport News. *Mural by Allan D. Jones in Newport News Public Library*

London Town, from the south bank of the Thames, when England's colonizers were striking roots at Jamestown. *Jamestown Foundation*

Lastly and chiefly the way to prosper and achieve good success is to make yourselves all of one mind for the good of your country and your own, and to serve and fear God the Giver of all Goodness, for every plantation which our Heavenly Father hath not planted shall be rooted out.

from *Instructions By Way of Advice,*
from the *Virginia Company of London*
to the settlers of Virginia, 1606

Prologue

It is late afternoon on May 13, 1607. Three sailing ships wind slowly up the James River in Virginia. The smaller ship pushes ahead to test the depth, while her crew and passengers scan the shore for a suitable mooring. Then the captain of the lead ship sights a peninsula jutting into the channel and noses his ship toward its shore, signaling the others to follow.

By such means the *Discovery* led the *Susan Constant* and *Godspeed* to Virginia 360 years ago. In the unearthly glow of sunset, they tied their bows to overhanging trees and prepared to land their 104 passengers and cargo next day. England's flag — the red Cross of Saint George on a white field — brightened the gloom of the pine forest.

Thus was born "King James His Towne," later known as Jamestown. Small as it was, it was to be remembered as the beginning of England overseas. Lord Bryce, British statesman of the early twentieth century, called it one of the epic events in the life of man. It was the beginning of the American era of world history.

The securing of the beachhead was no easy achievement. Thousands of

Englishmen lost their lives to establish a foothold in the swamp. Its career was the commencement of the American success story: from crude infancy to world power. The settlement of Virginia was the beginning of Act I of the American dream.

This book tells the story of the men and women who came from the green fields of England to people that dream. It is the story of John Smith and his fruitless efforts to find gold, of John Rolfe and his timely planting of tobacco, of Governor Sir George Yeardley and his first legislative assembly in America in 1619. Bacon the rebel and Berkeley the Governor are here, followed by a lusty crop of tobacco planters who divided Tidewater into great estates crowned by Georgian houses like those of the country squires of England.

But Virginia was not only the province of Englishmen. It grew also from the sweat of thousands of Negro slaves, brought in chains from Africa. Germans and Poles came in the early years to blow glass, and two hundred French Huguenots in 1700 fled to the James River valley to escape the axe of their Catholic king. Scottish merchants settled in its port towns. Then, in Virginia's second century, came a flood of Scotch-Irish and Germanic settlers in the Valley of Virginia. The Highlanders' story is a triumph of courage in a blue-green Eden where Shawnees lurked, determined to halt, with fire and tomahawk, the ever-moving tide of western settlement.

But if so many died, why did so many come?

Call it "the Virginian fever," as Ben Jonson did. Call it hope or ambition. Whatever you call it, it was man's eternal search for a better life. Like most human ventures, the migration had elements of both idealism and the desire for gain. Hemmed in by class distinctions in the old country, men like Rolfe wanted the freedom that Virginia offered. But more than that, Virginia's settlers wanted to own land, to make money, to bring up children with hope of a brighter future.

To the middle-class Englishman or Scotsman who came, the passage to Virginia seemed a ticket in a vast lottery. He had so much to gain in that boundless and abundant country. The Virginia Company investors looked for profit, too. With such vast natural wealth in Virginia, it should be easy to produce many profitable articles that England needed. Thus Virginia's was a planned economy from the beginning. Gold and silver must be sought first. Then ship's masts, ship's stores, and such new luxury articles as glass, silk, wine, and tobacco, all of which England wanted. In return for Virginia's products, of course, her settlers must take English manufactures.

So it was that tobacco became synonymous with Virginia. In fact, the honey-colored leaf soon was Virginia's currency, for lack of adequate English

Beginnings of self-government. Governor Sir George Yeardley convenes the Virginia Assembly, first legislative body in America, in Jamestown's wooden church, July 30, 1619. *Diorama, National Park Service, Jamestown*

coinage. But the colony's dependence on one luxury export put Virginians increasingly at the mercy of the merchants of London. Around the tables of the Virginia and Maryland Coffee House, a handful of tobacco buyers could set the prices for a whole year's work on all Virginia's plantations. Thus, in the building of empire, the colonist has always been at the mercy of the mother country.

As England's holdings grew, Virginia became a pawn in her ceaseless contest with European rivals. It was the Navigation Acts, first passed in 1651, which began to disillusion the planters and pioneers along the James. Never again could American colonists trade freely with the Dutch or other Europeans. From fourpence a pound in 1650, the price of Virginia tobacco dropped by 1667 to a mere halfpenny. Though Virginia had remained loyal to the Stuart kings throughout the Cromwellian revolution, Charles II refused her plea for relief when he came to power. Virginia was not to forget his ingratitude.

Hope was reborn in Virginia with the accession of the more democratic monarchs King William and Queen Mary, in 1689. Lacking the Stuart kings' arrogant belief in their divine right to rule, they showed greater interest in their colonial subjects. More Scotsmen, Presbyterians, and farmers now helped to make British policy. The Whig party began to curb the power of Tory merchant princes. With the support of William and Mary, Parliament passed a Toleration Act which allowed wider freedom of worship. As a result, Vir-

(*Left*) The Reverend James Blair. (*Right*) Dr. Henry Compton, Lord Bishop of London, first English church official to seek improvement in Virginia's spiritual life. *National Portrait Gallery, London*

ginia became a haven for Quakers, Presbyterians, Huguenots, Baptists, and other Protestants of democratic outlook. The colony got its second wind in the fruitful reign of "the Whig monarchs."

It was during the rule of William and Mary that England first showed an interest in the spiritual life of colonists. The Bishop of London sent the Reverend James Blair to direct the growth of the Church of England in Virginia, and Blair obtained the monarchs' charter for a college. The birth of the College of William and Mary was the colony's most hopeful augury since its Assembly began in 1619. From the beginning of Williamsburg's reign as capital, the pulse of Virginia beat faster. The vigorous logic of Europe's Enlightenment was the stimulus of Virginia's golden age. Colonists were beginning to think for themselves.

Then, in a few short decades, Virginia's joyous confidence was reined in again by new dictates from London. To pay the cost of her war to dislodge France from North America, Britain under George III began to impose added taxes on the American colonies. This time Virginians had the power to resist. The freedom and prosperity which they had intermittently enjoyed gave them a passion to be free.

In England, arch-Tory Samuel Johnson warned of danger ahead. "When the Whigs of America are thus multiplied," he predicted in 1775, "let the Princes of the earth tremble in their palaces." It was too late. In 1776, thrones began to shake.

How was it that Virginia grew to such strength and political insight from 1607 to 1776? How did the handful of men who made up the garrison at Jamestown increase and spread inland for 500 miles when the Revolution came? It was indeed a remarkable upsurge of the human spirit. The Virginia born at Jamestown was medieval in its small scale and narrow aspirations. In contrast, the Virginia which in 1788 reared its Jeffersonian temple on Richmond's Capitol Hill was a society of broad and humane interests.

No longer was man a mere means to his monarch's glory. Man was an end in himself, entitled at birth to life, liberty, and the pursuit of happiness. To this growth no colony had contributed more than Virginia.

William and Mary, England's liberal-minded monarchs, enthroned 1689. Virginia named its new capital, Williamsburg, in the King's honor. Engraving by R. de Hooge. *The British Museum*

Jamestown made its own tools and utensils. Above, the Potter molds pitchers and cups, fires them in his stove. Below, the Blacksmith forges horseshoes and scythes. Two drawings illustrating *Orbis Sensualis*, published in the seventeenth century. *The British Museum*

I tell thee, gold is more plentiful there [Virginia] than copper is with us; and for as much red copper as I can bring, I'll have thrice the weight in gold. Why, man, all their dripping pans and their chamber pots are pure gold; and all the chains with which they chain up their streets are massy gold; all the prisoners they take are fettered in gold; and for rubies and diamonds, they go forth on holidays and gather 'em by the seashore . . .

from
Eastward Ho!
by John Marston and Ben Jonson, 1605

1

The Search for Gold

The chief object of Virginia's settlement was to find the "treasure" that England needed to build ships and to pay armies, as Spain had done. In the Virginia charter of 1606, it was specified that a fifth of the gold and silver found should belong to the King, with the rest going to the company and the founders. Settlers scoured the Tidewater earth, but the supposed ore they sent by Newport's second return voyage in 1608 proved to be only fool's gold.

No better luck rewarded their second object, which was to find a water-course westward through North America and thence to Cipangu and Cathay, later known as Japan and China. This had been reported by Ralph Lane and quoted in Hakluyt's *Voyages,* published in 1599. Admiral Newport in 1607 sailed his three ships as far up Virginia's westernmost river as he could, but the fall line forced him back to Jamestown.

Undaunted, John Smith probed each creek and river for the next two years, but no westward passage materialized. To England's dismay, the Dutch and Portuguese continued to drain off the gold of the East Indies unchallenged.

"Gold fever" so seduced the minds of most early settlers that Jamestown nearly died for lack of food. It led the gentlemen adventurers who made up half of the settle-

Glassblowing factory was built near Jamestown in 1608. Germans and Poles were sent from England to man it, but the effort failed. *National Park Service*

ment to spend their energy in fruitless search instead of fishing or raising crops.

Except for a few realists like Smith, John Rolfe, and Sir Thomas Dale, Jamestown would have died of starvation. The effect on Virginia Company investors was quickly demoralizing. The Spanish ambassador in London reported to his government that "This plantation has lost much ground, as it was sustained by companies of merchants, who were disappointed at finding no gold nor other silver mines, nor the passage to the South Sea which they had hoped for."

Fortunately, England needed other raw materials abounding in Virginia. Timbers for ships' masts were sent back by the returning *Susan Constant* and *Discovery*, and lumber thereafter remained an important export throughout Virginia's history. True, the colony was not able to supply the olive oil, citrus fruits, and wine that the Bristol merchant William Parkhurst had glowingly predicted in 1582. Neither could it produce the salt, sugar, grains, and hides that Spain was importing from her Latin American colonies; nor the exotic spices, porcelain, Japan work, and lacquer that Portugal and the Netherlands were extracting from the Indies.

England also wanted her own supply of glass and raw materials — tar, pitch, timber, and soap ashes — that the Muscovy Company had imported from Russia and Poland. Virginia could and did produce these. Glass was first blown there in 1608, and such staples as wheat, Indian corn, barrels, boats, and pitch and tar for caulking hulls and tarring rigging were produced.

Besides its desire for gold, the Virginia Company hoped to produce certain luxury goods in Virginia to compete with the Orient's. Most of England's wealth was in the hands of city merchants and nobles, who passionately desired the exotic imports from China and Japan. Luxury goods for this class were highly saleable, for it had "ready money." The Virginia Company encouraged settlers to produce them. Wrote the poet James Cathorne in his "Essays on Taste":

Of late, 'tis true, quite sick of Rome and Greece,
We fetch our models from the wise Chinese.

For the luxury trade, Virginia made trial from 1608 to 1620 of various commodities. When Captain George Yeardley arrived in Virginia in 1618 as deputy governor, he was directed by the company to promote the growing of flax to make linen. However, the plant did not take to Virginia's soil, and the effort was abandoned. More desirable still was silk, which was in high fashion in Europe. English promoters believed silkworms would flourish in Virginia's climate, and mulberry trees were planted at Jamestown to feed them. King James himself encouraged this project in the desire to supply European silk weavers who set up silk manufactures in 1608 at Spitalfields and Morefields, near London.

At Virginia's first Assembly in 1619, the Burgesses enacted into law a Virginia Company proposal that each settler plant six mulberry trees for seven years. Instructions for growing mulberry leaves and feeding the silkworms were prepared for the colony by the head of the Royal Silk Establishment, and an expert grower was sent to Jamestown with a supply of worms from Spain and Italy. Some silk fibre was returned to England, but the infant industry was destroyed in the massacre of 1622.

Another luxury product which the company encouraged was wine. Since the Norman Conquest in 1066, Englishmen had fancied European wines, but wars and customs duties limited the supply. In all Europe only Portugal, which was usually allied with England against France and Spain, was a dependable supplier. The Portuguese vintners' sherry, port, and madeira became English standbys. Nevertheless, England tried to reproduce French and Italian vintages for 300 years in her colonies. Virginia's native scuppernong and fox grapes were pressed and fermented from 1609 onward, but English gourmets were not enthusiastic.

Wine-making was endorsed in 1619, in the deliberations of the first Virginia Assembly at Jamestown. The Virginia Company in that year sent French growers to Jamestown with grape rootings from Lanquedoc, but settlers derided both the workmen and their efforts. The wine that they sent back

Husbandry.   XLVI.   *Agricultura.*

The Plow-man 1.
yoketh Oxen 3.
to a Plough, 2.
and holdeth the Plow-stilt, 4.
in his left hand,
and the Plow-staff 5.
in his right hand,
with which he removeth
clods 6.
he cutteth the Land,
(which was manured afore
with Dung 8.)
with a Share, 7.
and a Coulter,
and maketh furrows 9.
Then he soweth *the*
Seed 10.
and harroweth *it in with a*
Harrow. 11.
The Reaper 12.

Arator, 1.
jungit Boves 3.
Aratro, 2.
& tenens lævâ Stivam, 4.

dextrâ Rallum 5.

quâ amovet
Glebas, 6.
terram scindit
Vomere,
& Dentali, 7.
anteà Fimo 8.
Surcoratam,
facitque Sulcos. 9.
Tum seminat
Semen 10.
& innoccat Occa, 11.

Messor 12.
(sheareth

Methods of farming in England followed by Virginia's settlers. A page from *Orbis Sensualis*. *The British Museum*

to London and Bristol was so poor that they were accused of sabotage. After the 1622 massacre, the neglected vineyards were despoiled by deer. Wine-making was often tried in later years, and Italian vintners were brought to Albemarle by Thomas Jefferson, but Virginia's soil and climate rarely produced an acceptable product.

England's economic ambitions in Virginia were finally gratified by a product which was infinitely better suited than mining or manufacturing to the colony's rich soil and its limited labor supply. This was tobacco. First having been known to Europeans during Columbus' discovery of the West Indies in 1492, it had in the next hundred years spread through fashionable circles on the continent. Its introduction in the court of Queen Elizabeth was credited to Sir Walter Raleigh and to Ralph Lane, his colleague in the ill-fated Roanoke Island settlement in North Carolina in 1584. By the time Virginia was settled in 1607, pipe-smoking had become a mark of urbanity, and tobacco shops had sprung up in England's port towns.

Offended by tobacco smoke and its taste, effete King James I tried to discourage the "stinking weed." He declared it "loathesome to the eye, hateful to the nose, harmful to the brain," and "dangerous to the lungs." In a proclamation in 1604 he imposed a fine on users, complaining that "by

Spanish-type tobacco was the source of Virginia's slowly improving economy after 1612. First grown in central America, it was popularized in Europe by explorers and traders. *Jamestown Foundation*

immoderate taking of tobacco the health of a great number of our people is impaired, and their bodies weakened and made unfit for labor." However, many Englishmen continued to consider it a cure for all ailments. One described it as an "antidote to all poisons; that it expelled rheums, sour humors, and obstruction of all kinds, and healed wounds better than St. John's wort." Even apothecaries sold it and demonstrated its use.

In the early seventeenth century, tobacco leaves were spun on spinning wheels into thin ropes, which were coiled into acorn-shaped mounds for convenient sale to pipe smokers. Pictures of coiled tobacco and Negro slaves were shown on English tobacconists' signs and on printed tobacco labels to signify Virginia tobacco.

Virginia's settlers found the Indians smoked tobacco but it was far less palatable than the Spanish. The shipments of Indian leaf they sent to London and Bristol accordingly found few buyers until settler John Rolfe in 1612 obtained seeds of the Spanish leaf and grew the first saleable crop in Virginia. Where and how Rolfe obtained the seed is unknown, for Spain prohibited its sale; perhaps it was from Don Fernando de Berrio, governor of Trinidad, who in 1612 was fined for "trading with the enemy." All that is known certainly is that William Strachey, the colony's secretary, recorded in 1612 that Rolfe's seeds came from Trinidad, then a Spanish possession. Presumably a Dutch or English seaman had smuggled them thence to Jamestown.

Rolfe's Spanish tobacco was the desirable large-leaf variety known as *Nicotiana tabacum,* from which the modern tobacco plant has evolved. Its growth had originated in pre-Columbian South America and spread by trade between prehistoric Indian tribes. Cultivation of this variety by 1492 had reached the West Indies, where it was discovered by Columbus. Meanwhile, a smaller-leafed tobacco, called *Nicotiana rustica*, had spread by 1607 over a much wider area, reaching as far northward as the present New Brunswick. This was the bitter-tasting leaf grown by the Indians when Virginia was settled in 1607. The area of its cultivation through the New World was almost identical with that of corn, another South American plant which had been spread by Indian trade.

Rolfe's shipment late in 1612 or 1613 for England changed England's reaction to the Virginia leaf. Here at last was good news from Virginia, for England had been buying tobacco from Spain and worsening her trade balance. In 1615 some 2,300 pounds were shipped out, and the following year 20,000 pounds were exported. Thereafter, except during the Indian massacres in 1622 and 1644, the crop grew in size almost yearly until the European market was denied to Virginia by England's Navigation Act of 1651. This and subsequent acts in 1660 and 1663 caused a decline in price from fourpence a pound in 1650 to halfpenny in 1667, but even at this low price, plantations with slave labor could make a profit.

Tobacco culture set the pattern for life in lowland Virginia from 1613 until after the Civil War. The Company's early vision of farms and cottage industries clustering around the ports of Jamestown, Kecoughtan, York, and Norfolk — in James City, Charles City, and Elizabeth City — vanished as settlers claimed their 50 acres (100 for those who came before 1616) on creeks and rivers and spread rapidly westward toward the fall line. Indian clearings, known as "old fields," were grabbed up because they re-

quired no ground-clearing. Land fronting on deep water was also valued because ships could dock at bankside, as at Jamestown. Even the largest ocean-going cargo ships in the seventeenth century drew no more than twelve feet of water.

For ease in handling, Virginians packed tobacco in barrels called hogsheads. These were rolled by men or pulled by oxen or horses over "rolling roads" to plantation docks, there to be loaded aboard ship and stacked on end. To prevent the export of inferior leaf, the Burgesses in 1619 ordered that tobacco be examined before shipment by four viewers and the worst destroyed. By 1632 the Burgesses felt that additional inspection posts and warehouses were needed at Denbigh plantation on the lower James, at Shirley Hundred on the Upper James, at Southampton River, and at Chiskiack plantation on the York. Other warehouses were later built at other points, one of which survives at Urbanna, Virginia, today. Throughout the colonial era, Virginia sought Maryland's aid to sustain the price of tobacco by controlling the size and quality of the crop. However, the effort had little effect against the massive force of English mercantilism.

Rolfe's tobacco was known as Oronoco or Oronoko, for the Orinoco River basin in Venezuela, from which it came. Other early varieties were Trinidado, named for the West Indies Island off the Venezuelan coast; and Varinas, which took its name from a South American town. The most desirable variety of all was Sweet-Scented, and especially that grown on Edward Digges' plantation, Chiskiack, now within the Naval Weapons Station at Yorktown. Digges' "York River" label brought a higher price than any other Virginia product. Its quality was attributed to the richness of the river-bank soil, for tobacco was a heavy feeder. England took all of Virginia's Sweet-Scented output, while sharing the Oronoko with Continental buyers.

Ignorant of soil chemistry, colonial farmers repeated tobacco plantings in the same field each year until the soil was exhausted. They were then forced to shift to wheat or corn, which required less nourishment, or to let their fields lie fallow and clear new land for tobacco. This constant need for new fields hastened the spread of settlement upland along the tidal peninsulas in the seventeenth century to the fall line of the James, the York, the Rappahannock, and the Potomac rivers.

Tobacco also made heavy demands on the grower. It required constant care from

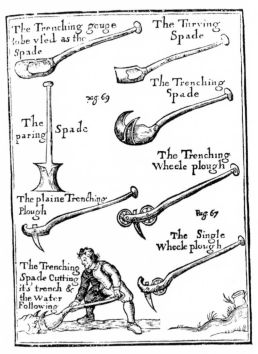

The Trenching gouge to be vsed as the Spade

The Turving Spade

Pag. 69

The Trenching Spade

The paring Spade

The Trenching Wheele plough

The plaine Trenching Plough

Pag. 69

The Single Wheele plough

The Trenching Spade Cutting it's trench & the Water Following

Plows and spades, such as those used in early Jamestown, described for the planter in *The English Improver Improved*, 1652. *The Guildhall Library, London*

March, when the tiny seeds — ten thousand to a spoonful — were sifted into an outdoor seedbed, until late fall, when the cured leaf was placed in hogsheads to await shipment. In May the seed germinated, and in June rows of plants were set in hillocks in cleared fields. One hard-working man could cultivate about 10,000 plants, occupying three or four acres.

If the weather smiled, the plants were large enough by July to be topped, to limit each plant to no more than a dozen large leaves. Then the farmer must remove the "suckers," or offshoots from the main stem, and cut off the "lugs," or coarse bottom leaves. Full growth was reached by September. The plants were then cut down and allowed to wilt before being dried.

The first planters let tobacco cure in the sun, but they soon improved the process by tying stalks in "hands" and suspending them from rafters in curing houses, or barns. Sweet Scented tobacco dried in three weeks, while the heavier Oronoko took six. The grower then waited until a rainy day when the dried leaf was pliable and piled the hands beneath a cloth cover to let it "sweat" by absorbing moisture. Sometimes the grower performed the further step of removing the stem from each leaf.

In late fall the leaves were layered into a hogshead, compressed under force, and the barrel sealed, weighed, and marked with the owner's initials and insignia. Since handling and shipping costs were computed by hogshead, planters packed them tightly. If a dock was nearby, the hogsheads were rolled there. If not, they were floated by flatboat or sloop to the nearest dock, or, after 1619, to the public warehouse for inspection and for shipment. Before the first Navigation Act was passed in 1651, tobacco could be

The smuggling into Virginia of Spanish type tobacco seed from Trinidad in 1612 saved the colony's economy. Settlers scattered over Tidewater to grow the green leaf. Painting by Sidney King. *National Park Service*

shipped aboard the first merchantman to call at the dock. However, after tension with the Netherlands and France increased, English merchant ships were required by law to sail from Chesapeake Bay in convoy, protected by warships against enemy raiders and pirates.

Early shipments were directed by the planter to an English consignment merchant, accompanied by the planter's bill of lading and instructions. Throughout this long and tedious course to market, the planter bore all risks. He could lose his crop through shipwreck, piracy, pilferage, or failure to sell. Once safely in a British port, however, the tobacco was usually examined for quality by the consignment merchant and sold. The merchant then deducted freight and storage charges and his commission — 2½ or 3 per cent — and deposited the remainder to the planter's account. From this fund the merchant drew the cost of goods which the planter wished in return.

British merchants had every advantage in this trade. Concentrated in London, Bristol, and smaller "outports," they controlled the market price. Around the tables at the Virginia and Maryland Coffee House in London they agreed on what to buy and how much to pay. Moreover, in buying for the planters they charged a healthy commission and often advanced the purchase price. Meanwhile the planters, living 3,000 miles and six weeks from London, never knew how accounts stood. Because of shipping hazards and agents' avarice, they were often insolvent. Too few took the precaution of William Fitzhugh of Stafford County, who conditioned his purchases with the proviso, "if my money will reach to it, but rather leave some out than bring me a penny in debt."

War between England and the Netherlands in 1664 added to the hardships of Virginia's economy. Ever since Dutch ships began to trade with England's colonies, ambitions of the two nations had headed toward the conflict. England's enactment of

The popularity of Virginia tobacco in Great Britain is evident in the emphasis on Virginia in these labels used by early English tobacconists. *From the Ingham Foster Collection of the Imperial Tobacco Company, Bristol, England*

the Navigation Acts had shut the door on that trade and incensed the Netherlands. When the Anglo-Dutch war broke out, England's Privy Council in 1665 directed Governor Sir William Berkeley in Virginia to require all ships leaving Chesapeake Bay to sail in convoy. Tobacco growers thereafter faced longer delays and greater hazards than before as tobacco ships gathered in lower Chesapeake Bay to inaugurate the convoy system. For several years after 1665, tobacco convoys were permitted to depart the Virginia Capes only on March 24, June 24, and September 24.

Reprisal against the convoy system was quickly taken by the Dutch. In 1667 four of their men-of-war and two fireships entered the Bay and burned an English frigate and five of the tobacco fleet assembled off Celey's plantation, at Newport News. The Dutch then sailed away with their prize of 13 British merchant vessels. Again in 1672 eight Dutch men-of-war sailed through the Capes and took or destroyed eleven of the

40 tobacco ships making up a convoy there, despite the defense of two English men-of-war. Trade with England was so disrupted that colonist Philip Ludwell feared "mutiny and confusion."

But peace with the Netherlands and the accession of the Dutch prince William of Orange and his wife, Mary, in 1689 brought Virginia prosperity again. By 1700 Virginia had grown to 58,000 inhabitants. The 70,000 hogsheads of tobacco which left Chesapeake Bay each year enriched England's treasury by £300,000 a year. Tobacco convoys grew huge. Each fall and spring several hundred ships loaded cargo at plantation docks and then gathered, like flocking ducks, near Cape Charles, to sail in convoy. In April, 1706, about 300 ships were required to carry the crop.

The union of England and Scotland in 1707 strengthened Virginia's trade links with the principal Scottish port of Glasgow. From a ten per cent share of Great Britain's tobacco trade in 1738, the Glasgow "tobacco lords" by 1769 had captured more than half. This was partly because canny Scottish traders kept shipping costs lower than England's. It was also due in part to Glasgow's location, which was a week closer to Virginia by sail than were London, Bristol, or Liverpool.

In 1750 the Scots revolutionized the tobacco trade by sending out factors, or agents, to the American colonies and buying tobacco on the spot. While the grower might thus receive less in the long run, he was spared the delay and risks of the consignment system. The result was that many growers deserted English consignment merchants for Scottish factors.

Typical of the factors was the firm of William Cuninghame and Company, which had eight offices in Virginia along the James, York, Rappahannock, and Potomac. There they bought not only tobacco but wheat, corn, and iron. For his goods, the colonist would receive a bill of exchange, similar to a check, denoting the amount of his credit. Against this balance he bought such supplies as clothing, furniture, sugar,

wines, and slaves. So successful was factoring that by 1774 more than 50 Glasgow factors were in Virginia. Both Scotland and England were now in hot pursuit of Virginia's trade; 2,000 merchants were in Virginia when the Revolution came, most of them British.

Such competition for their products led to a vast overextension of Virginians' credit. John Wayles warned in 1766 that planters were ordering items like "turkey carpets" and fine furniture instead of paying for what they had. A debt of £1,000 had seemed large in 1740; now, Wayles said, some planters owed ten times that. The Virginia Assembly attempted to discourage the factors' over-easy credit terms by making bankruptcy easy, but these laws were vetoed by the Crown. Thus mercantilism concentrated an empire's wealth into favored hands.

British currency controls limited the circulation of sterling outside the British Isles and inflicted untold hardships on colonial commerce. The colony's domestic trade as a result had to depend instead on tobacco notes, for Virginia was not permitted to is-

sue a currency of her own. These notes transferred ownership of hogsheads from one man to another. Even the salaries of clergymen were specified in tobacco; a Sweet Scented parish was preferred by a cleric to an Oronoko parish because it paid more. The relatively few coins which filtered in were so needed for trade that they were cut into eight pie-shaped "bits," giving rise to the colloquial value of "two bits."

Next to tobacco, wheat and corn were Virginia's chief exports. Wheat was the chief crop of the uplands, above the fall line. Its cultivation increased steadily after Scotch-Irish and Germans began settling the Valley of Virginia in the eighteenth century. The light upland soil was better suited to grains and to pasturage than to tobacco, with its voracious appetite. Swift-flowing Valley of Virginia streams turned the paddlewheels of flour mills, and Britain and her West Indies colonies afforded a ready market. Corn and cornmeal were traded to the West Indies and to the Northern colonies, but Britons never acquired a taste for this New World product.

As the eighteenth century progressed, Britain continued to frustrate the aspirations of Virginia's economy. Governor Sir William Gooch protested in 1740 that the "Board of Trade sent me so many queries to

Tobacco shops in Britain used the carved figure of a blackamoor in grass skirt. The Virginia planter and the Indian also appeared in many labels. *From the Ingham Foster Collection of the Imperial Tobacco Company, Bristol, England*

answer, that I have been obliged to write almost a history of this part of the world . . ." Under British policy, nearly all American manufacturers were discouraged. And although the Valley of Virginia afforded ideal sheep grazing, Britain's Wool Act in 1699 made it clear that Americans should produce neither wool nor anything else that England could.

One of the few manufactures encouraged was the making of pig iron, which Alexander Spotswood encouraged at Germanna after his retirement from the governorship in 1722. The industry grew a little, but it was hamstrung by the Board of Trade's insistence that it make no finished products. Gooch assured England in 1732 that the four small ironworks then in Virginia produced only pig iron except — he apologized — a few pots, firebacks, and andirons.

England's commercial policy from 1607 to 1776 forced Virginia into a one-crop economy. And while the plantation system generally prospered when England was at peace, it suffered intensely when trade between England and the colonies was constricted by war.

What was worse was Virginia's inability — thanks to selfish British policy — to develop a middle class of tradesmen and artisans. In a colony where tobacco-growing was all, craftsmen who emigrated from England almost always abandoned their craft and raised tobacco. Some of these men prospered. Some founded dynasties which produced a Jefferson or a Madison. But more were crushed in the boom-and-bust tobacco market. An untold number emigrated westward. The slow trickle out of colonial Virginia became a torrent after the Revolution. With it went many of the future leaders of the republic.

Bermuda Hundred, August 12, 1767

JUST imported, by the way of *Antigua*, a cargo of choice genuine MADEIRA WINE, which we will sell very reasonably for cash, hemp, tobacco, wheat, corn, or pease. We have also a quantity of choice cordage, twine, log and lead lines, nails of all sorts, single and double tobacco screws, *Newcastle* coals, fine *Durham* mustard, and all sorts of ship chandler wares, and fine salt.

DANIEL L. HYLTON, & CO.

Virginia's dependence on trade with England is evident in this merchant's card in the *Virginia Gazette* of 1767

Windmills and tidemills were built to grind corn and wheat. This tidemill in Mathews County survived until the twentieth century. *Photo by Milton Murray II from The Mariners Museum*

"Peuples de Virginie" were portrayed in a 17th century French volume, *Description de l'Univers. The Victoria and Albert Museum, London*

Unless we bang the Indians stoutly, and make them fear us, they will never love us, nor keep the peace long with us.

John Bartram, 1750

2

Brave Lewis, our Colonel, an officer bold
At the mouth of Kanawha did the Shawnees behold
On the tenth of October, at the rise of the sun
The armies did meet and the battle begun.

Like thunder from heaven our rifles did roar
Till twelve of the clock, or perhaps something more
And during this time the Shawnees did fly,
Whilst many a brave man on the ground there did lie.

From a popular song celebrating the victory of
General Andrew Lewis over the Shawnee warriors
of Chief Cornstalk at Point Pleasant, 1774.

The Indians

When the three ships bringing English settlers first touched Virginia, on April 26, 1607, an exploring party went ashore at Cape Henry. They were entranced by what they saw. But danger lurked in the midst of beauty. Out of the pine woods that rimmed Chesapeake Bay darted naked Indian warriors. Before the Englishmen could flee in their shallop, the savages had wounded settler Gabriel Archer and sailor Mathew Morton.

This was the Englishmen's first meeting with the tribesmen who had lived along Virginia's shores since the shadowy centuries before Columbus discovered the New World. It was a symbolic meeting. Many

Englishmen would die before Virginia was truly won. And, in spite of the settlers' lurking sense of guilt, they would kill or displace most of Virginia's tribes before the land was theirs.

The English expected to find Indians as mild as the indolent Caribs of the West Indies. They knew that Spanish conquistadors had killed and enslaved the South American tribes, but they ascribed this to cruelty. Their instructions from the Virginia Company were to befriend the Indian, obtaining his help in finding gold and the westward passage to the South Sea. They expected even to create Indian schools and to convert the natives to Christianity,

Tidewater Indians lived along rivers and creeks, housed in arbors covered with reeds and skins. They grew corn, beans, pumpkins, and gourds. This village near Roanoke Island, North Carolina, was sketched in 1587 by John White. *Arents Collection, New York Public Library*

cause they occupied the coastal and Tidewater areas, east of a line running south from the District of Columbia through Fredericksburg, Richmond, Petersburg, and then along the Blackwater River and into North Carolina as far south as the Neuse River. They also held the territory on the Eastern Shore which is now Accomac and Northamptom Counties.

Archeologists surmise that the Algonquins pushed down into this area from the north hundreds of years before the English came. By 1607 they had been organized into a confederacy of more than thirty tribes, with Wahunsonacock — known to colonists as Powhatan — as their great chief. Six of these tribes — the Powhatan, Arrohattoc, Appomattox, Mattaponi, Pamunkey, and Youghtanund — he had inherited. The others he had won over by force or threat.

Captain John Smith, in his *Travels & Works* lists thirty-two tribes of the Powhatan confederacy, but he shows 36 "king's houses" on his map of Virginia. Throughout these provinces, Smith identifies 161 Indian villages. Over these people, who numbered about 9,000 in 1607, Powhatan had power of life and death.

Beneath him, heading each of the thirty-two subtribes, was a local chief or werowance who gave his allegiance and paid tribute to Powhatan. By tacit agreement, each tribe hunted and fished in its circumscribed area. Tribute was collected annually like taxes, and Powhatan visited nearby tribes to collect it: corn and beans, turkey and deer, skins and copper, and beads and pearls. Distant tribes sent their tribute by chiefs. Each, according to colonist William Strachey, paid to Powhatan "eight parts of ten tribute of all the commodities which their country yieldeth."

as faithful subjects of the King. They suffered from the romantic delusion that man in his native state was a "noble savage." Yet they ended by exploiting the Indians, just as they themselves were exploited by British colonial policy.

When the Jamestown settlers arrived, the present area of Virginia was inhabited by a large number of tribes from three linguistic stocks: Algonquin, Iroquois, and Sioux. Of these, the Algonquins were in most constant contact with the settlers be-

How Europe viewed America's Indians. A startled Amerigo Vespucci alarms a buxom Indian female while in the background natives roast human limbs on a spit. Engraved by Theodore Galle after painting by Stradanus, circa 1580. *The British Museum*

When Virginia was settled, Powhatan's chief camp was at Werowocomoco, on the York River in what is now Gloucester County. There John Smith visited him in 1608 and found him "a tall, well-proportioned man, with a sour look, his head somewhat gray, his beard so thin that it seemeth none at all, his age near sixty, of a very able and hardy body to endure any labor." In 1609, Powhatan moved his chief camp westward to Orapax, in present New Kent County, to be farther from the English intruders. There he ruled until his death in 1618, when he was succeeded by the vengeful Opechancanough.

The earliest aborigines in Virginia were nomadic tribesmen who had ventured eastward across North America years since the Ice Age, some 10,000 to 12,000 years before the birth of Christ. Archeological evidence indicates that all the Indians of North and South America were descendants of Mongol tribesmen who crossed the Bering Strait from Siberia to Northern Alaska, in the unknown past. Moving gradually southward in pursuit of big game, such as mammoths and bison, the tribesmen over thousands of years were separated into distinct cultures. Some ventured southward into Central and South America. The highest of these were

The Indians encountered by the Jamestown settlers were tall, muscular people. They were similar in appearance and dress to the natives of North Carolina's Roanoke Island, whom the English settler John White painted about 1585. *The British Museum*

the Aztec and Mayan civilizations, destroyed by the Spanish in Central America.

The finding in Virginia of spear points which archeologists believe to be 10,000 years old indicates that primitive men stalked Virginia's forests long before the English first saw them at Cape Henry. Through successive millenia, their nomadic life gradually gave way to a more settled existence. About 500 or 600 years before 1607, the savages had become so proficient in growing food and in catching fish that they established more and larger villages. Population expanded, and some tribes agreed on boundaries, though hunger or blood-lust often prompted marauders to invade enemy territory.

It was during this period, designated by archeologists as the Woodland period of pre-history, that Virginia's Algonquin Indians acquired from neighboring southern tribesmen the seed of tobacco and of maize, or corn. The cultivation of corn and beans in village clearings now gave more certainty to Indian life. The 9,000 tribesmen whom Powhatan ruled in 1607 were a relatively peaceable and stable society, who tended such plots beside tidal streams. They also hunted with bows and arrows, caught fish with nets, traps and spears, and traded with nearby tribes for beads and shells.

The religion of the Powhatan Indians was pantheistic; sun, stars, thunder, lightning and other natural phenomena were thought to be great spirits. An idol called Okee was worshipped, and posts were carved with men's faces and planted in circles for ceremonial dances. Besides the solace of tobacco, Powhatan's people drank a wine made from fermented persimmons; the distillation of corn liquor was a skill they learned from white settlers later. For about

400 years before Jamestown was settled, the Algonquins had been burying their dead in large pits or ossuaries.

The tribal order that had emerged among the Virginia Algonquins in some respects resembled European monarchical rule. The great chief, or Powhatan, had absolute authority over his subjects. Men were required to fight on order of the chief, and culprits could be put to death on his order. The heads or scalps of victims became sacrificial offerings, and war captives were sometimes retained as slaves. The tendons of their feet were often cut to prevent their easy escape.

The paintings of John White at Roanoke Island and the accounts of John Smith and William Strachey at Jamestown give an interesting picture of the Indian's domestic life. Lodges or wigwams were built of saplings set in the ground in circles or rectangles and bent and tied together at the top with deer thongs. The sides were then cov-

Colonists in the pinnace *Discovery* fighting Indians in 1608. An early print. *Maryland Historical Society*

ered with bark or reed mats, and the top with skins to keep out rain. A wide shelf around the inside wall provided seats and beds, and a fire was kept burning at the center to cook food and furnish warmth in winter.

Around their villages, the Powhatan women grew pumpkins, beans, sunflowers, gourds, and tobacco in clearings hewn with stone axes, or celts, and then burned clear of stumps and roots. "Their houses," wrote John Smith, "are in the midst of their fields or gardens, which are small plots of ground." As in most other primitive societies, women did much of the heavy work. "The men bestow their times in fishing, hunting, wars, and such man-like exercise," John Smith wrote, "scorning to be seen in any woman-like exercise, which is the cause that the women be very painful [fatigued] and the men often idle. The women and the children do the rest of the work. They make mats, baskets, pots, mortars, pound their corn, make their bread, prepare their victuals, plant their corn, gather their corn, bear all kinds of burdens, and such like."

Powhatan's tribesmen were handsome people. Inured to cold, they wore animal

Powhatan in council, drawn by Captain John Smith for his Map of Virginia. *Colonial Williamsburg*

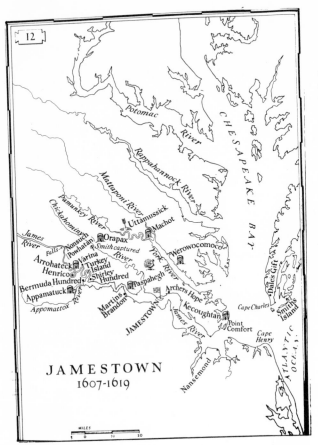

Tidewater villages of Powhatan's tribesmen among spreading English plantations. *Colonial Williamsburg*

skins winter and summer. Chiefs and priests had deerskin mantles embroidered with white beads or copper, or painted bright colors. Others wore mantles of turkey feathers. The higher one's rank, the more he wore.

To toughen boys for a warrior's life, they were isolated in the woods for a period of nine months between the ages of ten to fifteen. During this ordeal they were not permitted to speak. Tribal leaders taught them religious lore and some became "priests and conjurers." The practice was similar to the "husquenawing" followed by the Sioux tribesmen south of Virginia, as described by John Lawson a century later:

. . . Most commonly, once a year, at farthest, once in two years, these people take up so many of their young men as they think are able to undergo it and husquenaugh them, which is to make them obedient and respective to their superiors, and, as they say, is the same to them as it is to us to send our children to school, to be taught good breeding and letters. This house of correction is a large, strong cabin, made on purpose for the reception of the young men and boys that have not passed the graduation already; and it is always at Christmas that the husquenaugh their youth, which is by bringing them into this house and keeping them dark all the time, where they more than half starve them.

Besides, they give the pellitory bark, and several intoxicating plants, that make them go raving mad as ever were any people in the world; and you may hear them make the most dismal and hellish cries and howlings that ever human creatures expressed; all which continues about five or six weeks. . . .

Now, when they first come out, they are as poor as ever any creatures were; for you must know several die under the diabolical purgation. Moreover, they either really are, or pretend to be, dumb, and do not speak for several days; I think twenty or thirty, and look so ghastly and are so changed that it is next to an impossibility to know them again, although you were ever so well acquainted with them before. . . .

. . . Now the savages say if it were not for this they could never keep their youth in subjection; besides that, it hardens them ever after to the fatigues of war, hunting, and all manner of hardship, which their way of life exposes them to. Beside, they add that it carries off those infirm, weak bodies that would have been only a burden and disgrace to their nation and saves the victuals and clothing for better people than would have been expended on such useless creatures.

Despite English efforts to coexist peaceably, the Powhatans were resentful of the intruders. Hostages were traded as insurance against attack, but both peoples committed wanton cruelties. John Rolfe's marriage to Powhatan's daughter, Pocahontas, in 1614, brought peace until the great chief died in

A reconstructed arbor of the Powhatan Indians at Jamestown Festival Park shows fireplace and earthen pot, a handhewn log canoe, and a shelf for sitting and sleeping. Raccoon skins and baskets hang against the walls of woven rushes. A descendant of the Rappahannock tribe stands at right. *Photo by Thomas L. Williams for The Jamestown Foundation*

1618. Then, on Good Friday in 1622, the Algonquins fell upon the scattered English farms and murdered 347 of the 1,250 settlers. One of these was Pocahontas' widowed husband; their son Thomas Rolfe was in England and escaped.

After 1622, the English treated the Indians with greater severity, waging war against them until 1636. A second massacre in 1644 permanently estranged the two peoples. Opechanconough was captured and killed, and the dwindling tribes were confined to reservations. By 1665 Powhatan's people were dependents of the English.

Despite Rolfe's example, few settlers married Indians. English policy discouraged it, though occasionally such union was permitted. Efforts to use Indian labor came to naught, for they were unused to domestic routine and desired little that the settlers offered except for baubles or firearms and alcoholic liquors, which the English were loath to trade them.

Northward of Virginia's Algonquins lived several tribes of the hostile Sioux language group. Above the falls of the James, in the present Goochland and Powhatan Counties, lived the Monacans, whom Smith

Indians hollowed canoes with fire and stone hatchets from tree trunks. English settlers followed a similar design in their Chesapeake Bay canoes, using adze and axe. *Virginia Department of Highways*

discovered in 1607 and Captain Christopher Newport visited the next year. Another Sioux tribe, the Manahoacs, were found by Smith along the upper Rappahannock River in 1608. Smaller Sioux tribes were the Saponi, near the present Charlottesville; the Nahyssan, near Amherst; the Tutelo, near Salem; and the Occoneechee near Clarksville, in Mecklenburg County. Little was known of these upcountry tribes until Governor Sir William Berkeley sent John Lederer to explore the area in 1670.

Bloody as Jamestown's Indian massacres had been, they seemed mild compared with the cruelties which the Cherokee and Shawnee inflicted on white settlers in the Piedmont and the Valley after 1700. "His method of making war is never open and manly," wrote J. B. Witherow of the Indian of that day. "He skulks in ravines, behind rocks and trees; he creeps out in the night and sets fire to houses and barns; he shoots down, from behind a fence, the ploughman in his furrow; he scalps the women at the spring and the children by the roadside, with their little hands full of berries."

The second century of Virginia's growth began ominously in 1701 when the Assembly at Williamsburg passed an "Act for the Better Strengthening the Frontiers and discovering the Approaches of the Enemy." Generous grants were offered settlers who would establish upland forts. Immediately, Indians of that region recognized a threat. By treaty of 1684 between Virginia and the Iroquois Confederacy, tribesmen of the Six Nations had been permitted to venture as far east as the Piedmont, though not to the mouths of its rivers. Now the English were claiming this tribal range.

In 1722 the red men were forced even farther west when they reluctantly signed a new treaty at Albany, New York, promising not to cross the Blue Ridge into eastern Virginia without written pass. They could still hunt and journey over their ancient Great Warrior's Path from Maryland to North Carolina, for royal governors promised to prohibit white settlement west of the Blue Ridge. However, this agreement was likewise breached by an influx of settlers, and a third treaty was concluded, at Lancaster, Pennsylvania, in 1744, in which Virginia frankly claimed "all lands within the said colony as it is now or hereafter may be peopled or bounded."

Outraged at the settlers' greed for land, the Indians now opened attacks on white outposts. In an effort to reach agreement, colonial officials met at Winchester in 1753 with a hundred aggrieved chiefs from Virginia's western lands. For eight days in September the village was overrun with frowning Iroquois leaders of Great Lakes tribes — Mohawks, Oneidas, Senecas, Ondagas, Cayugas, and Tuscaroras — plus the neighboring Delawares, Wyandotts, Twightwees, and ever-vengeful Shawnees. Emigration of Scotch-Irish and Germans abruptly ceased as war loomed. Many frontier Virginia and Pennsylvania settlers fled into North Carolina.

The murderous Shawnees of western Virginia were subjugated by settlers led by General Andrew Lewis at Point Pleasant, 1774. A nineteenth century artist's idea of Indian warfare. *The Jamestown Foundation*

Citizens of Winchester, on Virginia's frontier, sought George Washington's protection against Iroquois tribesmen in 1753. *Winchester-Frederick County Historical Society*

The Winchester peace was momentary. In 1754, tribesmen from Pennsylvania southward to Virginia launched bitter war against settlements. Then, joining with the French in the Ohio River valley, they clashed with English forces under General Edward Braddock in a series of bloody battles along the disputed frontier. The defeat of Braddock near Fort Duquesne, now Pittsburgh, in 1755, brought the French and Indian War to a boil and catapulted George Washington to fame. At Fort Loudoun, on the Great Philadelphia Wagon Road near Winchester, Washington made his headquarters and fought off the threat to Virginia.

Though England won the French and Indian War in 1763, the threat of the Indians did not end. The very next year Chief Pontiac of the Ottawas renewed the fight to exterminate the white man. Again Shawnees ravaged the Valley, annihilating a settlement on the Greenbrier River and ravaging others on Kerr's Creek. Wrote Francis Parkman: "The country was filled with the wildest dis-

may. The people of Virginia betook themselves to their forts for refuge. But those of Pennsylvania, ill supplied with such asylums fled by thousands . . ."

Deprived of their historic homeland, the Indians made a last stand against the tide of settlement in 1774. Their atrocities against Ohio River settlers spurred Governor Lord Dunmore to raise a force of 1,000 militiamen in Northern Virginia and to meet Colonel Andrew Lewis of Augusta County with a similar force. Lewis' fighting Scotch-Irishmen encountered the Shawnees under Chief Cornstalk at Point Pleasant, at the mouth of the Kanawha River, and defeated them. This victory drove the Indians west of the Ohio River and encouraged settlers to cross the mountains into Kentucky and West Virginia.

Except for sporadic Indian alliances with Tory forces in the Revolution, Dunmore's was the last Indian war in Virginia. However, the displaced Shawnees and Cherokees remained a threat. As late as 1784, a band of Indians massacred a family at Abb's Valley in Tazewell County, capturing the courageous Mary Moore, who at length escaped from them. Another Southwestern heroine was Fanny Dickenson Scott, who survived capture by Indians in Lee County in 1785 and roamed the forest a month before reaching home.

By the time of the Revolution, Virginia's once-great Indian civilization was in fragments. The Powhatans had been reduced to two tribes, the Pamunkey and Mattaponi, whom Jefferson numbered at only fifteen men. Other tribes had emigrated or lost identity through Negro intermarriage. The Cherokees, once lords of the Appalachians, were forced onto a reservation in North Carolina.

However, the chief cause of Indian decline was neither war nor emigration, but illness and demoralization. Not having immunity to diseases of Europeans, Indians died readily of smallpox, tuberculosis, and pneumonia. Even worse, the Indian was unable to cope with the environment which Europeans forced on him. Unlike the easy-going African, he would not work on settlers' farms. Inept and demoralized, many redmen took to drink. "For their strong drink," wrote Robert Beverley in 1705, "they are altogether beholding to us, and are so greedy of it that most of them will be drunk as often as they find an opportunity . . ."

To his colonial contemporary, the Indian seemed an inferior being, unworthy of human treatment. Yet John Smith called Pocahontas the "nonpareil" of Virginia, and young Chanco saved the Jamestown settlement in 1622 by forewarning his benefactor Richard Pace of the coming massacre. So hopeful were Englishmen of civilizing the Indian that trustees of the estate of scientist Robert Boyle gave the College of William and Mary £200 for an Indian school, which operated with indifferent success from 1723 till 1779. However, young braves fled classes each spring when nature beckoned.

Statesmen continued to argue the Indian could be taught to live peaceably, but the average Virginian disbelieved it. As the tide of settlement rolled steadily forward, colonial governors repeatedly defined Indian tribal preserves, but eventually most tribes were forced westward. William Byrd II, whose father had traded through Cherokee middlemen in prehistoric Kentucky, urged humane treatment. So did Jefferson and Henry, who was appointed by the Continental Congress in 1774 to win Indian sup-

Austenaco was a chief of the Cherokees, one of the Iroquois tribes forced from Virginia's Appalachian mountains to a reservation in North Carolina. Engraving from the *Royal Magazine*, 1762. *The Smithsonian Institution*

port for Americans in the Revolution. However, most Indians fought for the British, who seemed the lesser evil.

Thus ended England's early hope of "Christianizing the salvages" in Virginia. It had been an unrealistic one, for no stone-age civilization could co-exist for long with gun-toting Europeans. Outclassed, outnumbered, and out-maneuvered, the Indian could only fall back on deceit and savagery. Far from proving to be the "noble savage" Rousseau expected the Indian to be if undefiled by society, he fought Virginians with every wile and weapon as they moved west.

The Indians [39]

THE FIRST SETTLERS OF JAMESTOWN

BELOW ARE LISTED THE NAMES OF THOSE WHO REMAINED WHEN THE SHIPS RETURNED TO ENGLAND IN 1607 AS RECORDED BY CAPTAIN JOHN SMITH

Henry Adling (or Adding), gentleman

Jeremy (or Jerome) Alicock, gentleman

Captain Gabriel Archer, gentleman

John Asbie

Benjamin Beast, gentleman

Robt. Behethland (or Betheland),Gent.

Edward Brinto, mason, soldier

Edward Brookes, gentleman

John Brookes, gentleman

Edward Browne, gentleman

James Brumfield, boy

William Bruster (or Brewster), Gent.

Andrew Buckler

John Capper

George Cassen (or Cawsen), laborer

Thomas Cassen, laborer

William Cassen, laborer

Ustis (or Eustace) Clovill, Gent.

Samuell Collier, boy

Roger Cooke, gentleman

Thomas Couper (or Cowper), barber

Richard Crofts, gentleman

William Dier (or Dye)

Richard Dixon, gentleman

John Dods, laborer, soldier

Ould Edward, laborer

Thomas Emry, carpenter

Robert Fenton, gentleman

George Flower, gentleman

Robert Ford, gentleman

Richard Frith, gentleman

Stephen Galthorpe, gentleman

William Garret, bricklayer

George Golding (or Goulding), laborer

Thomas Gore, gentleman

Anthony Gosnoll, gentleman

Captain Bartholomew Gosnoll, Gent.

Thomas Gower, gentleman

Stephen Halthrop, gentleman

Edward Harrington, gentleman

John Herd, bricklayer

Nicholas Houlgrave, gentleman

Robert Hunt, master, preacher, Gent.

Thomas Jacob, sergeant

William Johnson, laborer

Captain George Kendall, councilor

Ellis Kingston (or Kinistone), gentleman

William Laxton, carpenter

John Laydon, laborer, carpenter

William Loue (or Love), tailor, soldier

Captain John Martin, councilor

John Martin, gentleman

George Martin, gentleman

Francis Midwinter, gentleman

Edward Morish, gentleman, corporal

Mathew Morton, sailor

Thomas Mounslie

Thomas Mouton

Richard Mutton, boy

Nathaniel Pecock, boy, sailor, soldier

John Penington, gentleman

George Percy, master, gentleman

Dru Pickhouse (or Piggase), gentleman

Edward Pising, carpenter

Nathaniell Powell, gentleman

Jonas Profit, sailor, fisher, soldier

Captain John Ratcliff, councilor

James Read, blacksmith, soldier

John (or Jehu) Robinson, gentleman

William Rods (or Rodes), laborer

Thomas Sands, gentleman

John Short, gentleman

Richard Simons, gentleman

Nicholas Skot (or Scot), drummer

Robert Small, carpenter

William Smethes, carpenter

Captain John Smith, councilor

Francis Snarsbrough, gentleman

John Stevenson, gentleman

Thomas Studley (or Stoodie), Gent.

William Tankard, gentleman

Henry Tavin (or Tauin), laborer

Kellam Throgmorton, gentleman

Anas Todkill, soldier

William Vnger (or Unger), laborer

John Waller, gentleman

George Walker, gentleman

Thomas Webbe, gentleman

William White, laborer

William Wilkinson, surgeon

Edward Maria Wingfield, master, councilor, president

Thomas Wotton, gentleman, surgeon, a Dutchman

with diverse others, to the number of 105.

Of the 105 settlers who set out from London in 1606 for Virginia, the names of these 92 were mentioned in the narratives of Captain John Smith. Most of them died before 1611. Only two of the first 105 — Robert Behethland and William Spencer, whose name escaped Smith — are known to have descendants today. *National Park Service*

Such preferment hath this country [Virginia] rewarded the industrious with, that some, from being wool-hoppers and of as mean and meaner employment in England, have there grown great merchants and attained to the most eminent advancements the country afforded.

3

John Hammond, 1656

People are the real strength and riches of a country . . .

Charles Davenant, 1697

The First Families

A half-century of prosperity under Queen Elizabeth had raised England's population to 5,500,000 people in 1600. Of these, 180,000 were in bustling London, home office of the Virginia Company. Chief rivals for London's trade were Bristol, bordering Wales, and Plymouth, which looked across the Channel from the Devon coast to France and the New World. Because Plymouth investors were colonizing New England, the ports of London and Bristol continued to concentrate on Virginia.

All of England sent settlers to Virginia, but the earliest came from the West Country around Bristol. Many families from this area had invested in the Virginia Company

of London in 1606. In Virginia's formative years before 1680, this rural gentry sent many younger offshoots to Virginia. Crop failures and the decline in West Country mining and manufacture were incentives. However, the West Countrymen had always been in love with the sea. John Cabot had sailed from Bristol, while Sir Francis Drake, Sir Walter Raleigh, and Sir Humphrey Gilbert were all from nearby Devon. It was natural for young men reared in the maritime counties of Gloucester, Somerset, Dorset, Devon, and Cornwall to catch the "Virginian fever."

The accents of southwest England became the typical speech of Tidewater Vir-

The arrival of 90 "maids to be wives" at Jamestown in 1620 strengthened the colony. The Virginia Company also encouraged young families to emigrate. *Drawing by Howard Pyle from Radio Times-Hulton, London*

ginia in these early years and remained so. In a study of Virginians' dialect, the late Bennett W. Green found countless survivals of southwestern English speech: "Cyar" for "car," "Warick" for "Warwick," "gret" for "great," and the like. "Virginia English is the southwestern," Green concluded. "Virginia English is not a development of the American soil, but a survival of archaic English forms that have been lost in England."

In the 1660s many Loyalists from northern England fled to Virginia and named their Northern Neck counties for the Lancaster, Northumberland, and Westmoreland they left behind.

Of the 10,000 people who left Bristol for America during the years 1654-1685, about half went to Virginia; the remainder went to the other mainland colonies and to British Islands in the West Indies. In a typical year, 1662, 510 of the 842 Bristol sailings were for Virginia. In return, Virginia sent most of her tobacco to Bristol. London's sailings drew settlers from such East Anglian counties as Norfolk, Suffolk, Essex, and Kent.

The large number of "gentlemen adventurers" who came to Virginia to find gold diminished when no tangible results were found. The majority of settlers thereafter were of the middle class known as yeomen or franklins. These were landowners of free but not noble birth, ranking in England below the gentry. To pay for passage to Virginia, those who lacked money signed a contract to work for seven years, known as an indenture. Such emigrants were listed as "servants," but in a truer sense they were employees. On completion of their indenture, they could claim the 50 acres offered each settler. Many who came as indentured servants rose to become men of substance, like Adam Thoroughgood or Captain Abraham Wood, who lived at the present site of Petersburg.

So democratic was early Jamestown's political structure that when the first Assembly was convened in 1619, voting was open to all adult males. It was only after the development of a class structure based on land that the right to vote was qualified by land ownership, as in England.

Normal family life was impossible in the the years when Jamestown was a military garrison. As Francis Bacon wrote in his essay on plantations: "When the plantation grows to strength, then it is time to plant with women as well as with men, that the plantation may grow from generation, and not be ever placed from without." However, the arrival of Mistress Forrest and her maid, Anne Burras, in 1608, was the beginning of a native Virginian home life. Anne's marriage to John Laydon in 1608 produced the first white child to be born in Virginia in 1609.

Women busied themselves in early Virginia with sewing and spinning. *The Guildhall Library, London*

With the arrival of the "shipload of maids" in 1620, the English began to sink roots in American soil. Settlers began to think of Virginia as a lifetime home. The enthusiastic acceptance of the first 90 women encouraged the emigration of other "young, handsome, and chaste maidens" whose fare was paid by the settler who chose her to wife.

In the factionalism between King Charles I and the Cromwellian Roundheads from 1649 to 1659, many loyalists or Cavaliers came to Virginia, concentrating in the Northern Neck and Princess Anne County. Later, after the Stuart restoration of Charles II, many of Cromwell's adherents fled to Virginia. Covenanters from Scotland and Protestants from southwest England came later.

Some criminals were transported under lifetime indenture, but these were relatively few; Virginia was no dumping ground. Wrote Thomas Jefferson: "Only 2,000 felons came to Virginia from the earliest settlement until 1787, one thousandth of the population, a negligible quantity."

The demand for English laborers was great until slave-trading destroyed it. From 1640 to 1700, some 1,500 to 2,000 Englishmen came over each year. By the end of the

Jamestown farmers built ice houses to keep meat, eggs, and dairy products. Oxen were used to draw plows and carts. Their strength was necessary in clearing forests for tobacco fields. *Painting by Sidney King for National Park Service*

first century, about 68,000 white settlers and 16,000 Negroes were in Virginia. The number would have been greater had not many died of disease, starvation, and Indian massacre.

Dispersion of the Powhatan Indians after the 1644 massacre made Virginia a more attractive place for settled families. Increasingly, after midcentury, the pattern of English country life was followed. Governor Sir William Berkeley about 1645 built "Green Spring," the first sizeable plantation house. Under his encouragement, the emigration of Cavaliers gave a higher tone to the colony beginning about 1649. About Berkeley's palatial estate near Jamestown gathered such gentlemen as Colonel Henry Norwood, Major Francis Moryson, Richard Fox, Francis Cary, Captain Ralph Wormeley, Sir Thomas Lunsford, Sir Henry Chicheley, and Sir Philip Honeywood. "Virginia was the only city of refuge left in His Majesty's dominions in those times for distressed Cavaliers," one Loyalist wrote.

The English in Virginia had always respected social gradations, though impatiently. In church, families were seated according to rank, as in England. Under Berkeley's administration, a planter class emerged which emphasized such distinctions. No longer could a servant move readily into the class of freeholders. The small farmer found himself unable to compete effectively with the planters' Negro labor. The price which Virginia paid for her splendid plantations was the near-loss of her middle class.

Some of the planters had risen from the yeomen's ranks through hard work. Others came to Virginia equipped with wealth and education. Among these families, the use of coats of arms on silver, china, tombstones, and other hereditaments was usual. Entitled to such arms were the early families of

Bacon, Berkeley, Bland, Byrd, Bolling, Beverley, Bennett, Burwell, Claiborne, Cary, Cole, Cocke, Clayton, Digges, Ferrar, Fitzhugh, Kingsmill, Lee, Ludwell, Ludlow, Milner, Page, Parke, Robinson, Randolph, Spencer, Thoroughgood, Throckmorton, Thurston, Tucker of Lower Norfolk County, Willoughby, Woodhouse, Washington, Booth, Batte, Chichely, Calthrope, Fleet, Jennings, Lunsford, Peyton, West, Wyatt, and a few others.

The term "esquire" was used after the name of a man of highest rank. Gentlemen were addressed as "Mr.," for "Master." The term "planter" by the year 1700 had come to denote social rank and was interchangeable with "gentleman." Lesser persons were occasionally addressed as "Goodman" or "Goodwife."

The gulf between the planter aristocracy and the plain folk was clear. The Reverend Devereux Jarratt, a native of Dinwiddie who became a prominent Anglican clergyman, recalled in his old age:

We were acustomed to look upon what were called gentle folks as being of a superior order. For my part, I was quite shy of them and kept off at an humble distance. A periwig in those days was a distinguishing badge of gentle folk, and when I saw a man riding the road near our house with a wig on, it would so alarm my fears and give me such a disagreeable feeling that I dare say I would run off, as for my life. Such ideas of the difference between 'gentle' and 'simple' were, I believe, universal among all of my rank and age.

As in England, land was the key to eminence and office. In each county, the Governor looked to a few leading landholding families to preserve the peace and the status quo. From these he chose his councilors. By virtue of their leadership, they were also selected as county lieutenants and as colonels of the county militia units.

By such criteria, Lyon Gardiner Tyler concluded that the first families of colonial Virginia were:

Allerton, Armistead, Ballard, Bassett, Beale, Berkeley, Beverley, Blair, Bland, Bray, Bridger, Browne of "Four Mile Tree," Burwell, Byrd, Carter, Cary, Churchill, Claiborne, Corbin, Custis, Cole, Dawson, Digges, Eppes, Ferrar (Farrar), Fitzhugh, Fairfax, Gooch, Grymes, Harrison, Jenings of "Ripon Hall," Kemp, Lewis, Littleton, Ludwell, Lee, Lightfoot, Mathews, Nelson, Page, Perry, Parke, Randolph, Robinson, Scarborough, Smith of Gloucester County, Spotswood, Taylor, Thoroughgood, Thornton, Warner, West, Whiting, Willoughby, Willis, Wormeley, and Yeardley.

Most of these settled below the fall line of the rivers, extending from the James River northward to the Potomac. This was Tidewater's heartland.

Wealthy families arranged marriages of sons and daughters to add distinction and fortify their leadership. Planters wanted enough land to be able to seat each son on his own estate. In English fashion, the eldest son inherited parental estate or "home place." Others received lesser portions, while daughters were given a dowry at marriage.

So lordly were some of the planter families that an Englishman observed, "Truly, these Virginians worship themselves. I believe if one were introduced to the Queen, he would feel it no honor."

Wealthy widows were pursued with indecent ardor; second marriages often were made almost before the corpse was decently buried. This was in contrast with England, where a year's wait was considered proper. Diarist John Aubrey perhaps explained this when he wrote in 17th-century England: "It is still accounted undecent for widows to marry within a year, I think, because in that time the husband's body may be presumed to be rotten." Anne Fairfax Washington, widow of Colonel Lawrence Washington, married Colonel George Lee only five months after her husband's death. George Washington married the wealthy Martha Custis seven months after her hus-

The one-room cottages that sheltered most settlers in 1670 had kitchen and dining room at one end and bedroom at the other. This shows the wide medieval fireplace and bake oven, homemade trestle table and benches, and high storage shelf. *Jamestown diorama by National Park Service*

Opposite the kitchen end of the early Virginia cottage were sleeping quarters. The fireplace surrounded with Delft tiles and the small, diamond-paned windows were typical of houses built in seventeenth century Virginia as well as in rural England. *Jamestown dioramas by National Park Service*

band's death. Two days after Samuel Jordan died, the Reverend Greville Pooley proposed to his widow.

Said William Byrd II: "An old maid or an old bachelor are as scarce among us and reckoned as ominous as a blazing star." He described his 19-year-old daughter Evelyn as the most "antique virgin" he knew.

The dependency of wife upon husband was advocated by church and by law. Guided by Saint Paul's dictum that "the head of every man is Christ; and the head of the woman is the man . . ," the laws of England and Virginia subjected a wife to her husband as soon as she said "I do." No longer had she will or property of her own. She could neither bring suit, make contracts, execute deed, dispose of her estate by will, or administer any property left to her. These became her husband's duties.

Under Virginia law, there was no easy end to marriage. The Anglican church recognized no divorce. Separate maintenance was sometimes granted, but the husband in-

variably had custody of the children. Thus locked in wedded torment, many couples lived in a state of war. To his secret diary, William Byrd II confessed on May 23, 1710: "I had a great quarrel with my wife, in which she was to blame, altogether; however, I made the first step to reconciliation to [which] she with much difficulty consented." Byrd advised one of his overseers to correct his wife "in virtue of his conjugal authority."

But some wives did not submit. In her marriage to the Rev. James Blair, Commissary (deputy) of the Bishop of London, Sarah Harrison replied to the admonition to love, honor, and obey, "No obey!" After the third attempt, the embarrassed clergyman proceeded. Mrs. John Custis of Arlington, on the Eastern Shore, rarely exchanged a word with her husband. At the height of exasperation, he drove their carriage into Chesapeake Bay. "Where are you going, sir?" she said. "To hell, madam," he replied. "Drive on," she retorted.

Life at Jamestown was simple and arduous. But long winter nights gave time to read, spin, weave, play games, and teach the children their letters. *Painting by Sidney King for National Park Service*

When Custis died, he had his tomb inscribed:

Beneath this Marble Tomb lies the Body
of the Hon. John Custis, Esq.

* * * * *

Aged 71 years, and yet lived but seven years,
which was the space of time he kept
a bachelor's home at Arlington
on the Eastern Shore of Virginia

Large families were usual among all classes. Pregnancy was expected of "wives who love their husbands," even though repeated child-bearing took a heavy toll. Lord Adam Gordon observed that Virginia women were "great breeders." A popular toast was:

Our land free
Our men honest
Our women fruitful.

Families of twelve to fifteen children were usual. Governor John Page had twelve by one wife and eight by another. Major Lewis Burwell had fifteen. William Byrd III had five by his first wife and ten by his second. Patrick Henry had six by his first, and eleven by his second. Exhausted wives entrusted wet nursing and other duties to Negro slaves. The Negro nurse, or mammy, became a fixture.

An early tomb is inscribed:

Underneath lies what was mortal of Mrs. Margaret Edwards, Wife of Mr. John Edwards, Merchant of this place. Daughter of Mr. Alexander Perronneau, Gent. She Died in Travail with her Tenth Child, aged 34 years and 4 months. A sincere, modest and humble Christian . . . She committed her soul to Him whom she ardently loved and died without fear or a groan, Augt. 27th, 1772.

The dynastic attitude of English life was very evident. Parents sought to build up

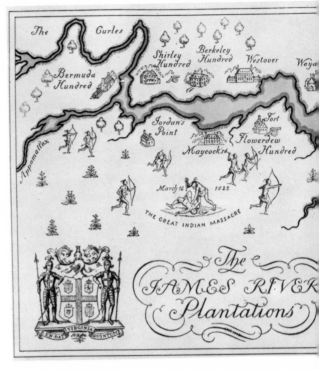

ABOVE: James River lands westward from Jamestown to the fall line were the first to be settled by English colonists in Virginia, beginning in 1607. Most of the great houses were built after 1700. *Map by Eric M. Simon from American Heritage*

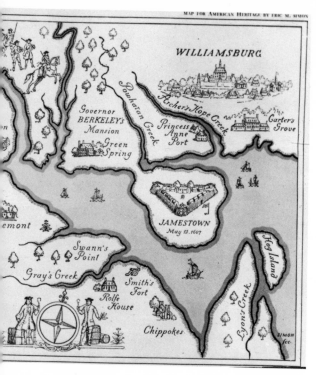

BELOW: By 1650 Jamestown was a village of 35 houses and a brick church whose tower served as a lookout against Indians. Its life was similar to that of an English village. *Colonial Williamsburg*

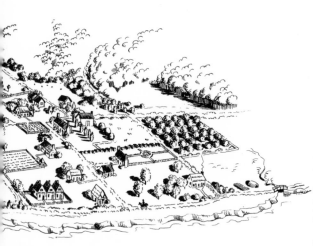

wealth and distinctions for their children. Fathers sought to pass on political offices to sons, and the Governor's Council became a sort of House of Lords for entrenched Tidewater oligarchy. No paid office was too small to be sought; between 1670 and 1691, every official position in Henrico County was held by a member of the Randolph, Cocke, or Ferrar families.

By the end of the seventeenth century, one in every four families in Virginia owned from 500 to 20,000 acres. The largest land holdings of this period were owned by the Fairfaxes, Carters, Byrds, Ludwells, Eppeses, Randolphs, Beverleys, Armisteads, Allens, Harrisons, Pages, Bassetts, Washingtons, Lees and Spencers.

To strengthen their dynasties, landholders made use of primogeniture and entail, by which the bulk of a family estate was directed by law to each eldest son, in succession. Although Virginians usually left "the home place" to the eldest son, they did not favor one child to the exclusion of the others, as the English often did, because the colony had no system of legal nobility, as England had. Furthermore, Virginia offered few opportunities in professions or trades to which disinherited younger sons could turn; one must plant or go poor. Thomas Jefferson obtained repeal of the Virginia law of entail in 1776.

The dynastic character of early Virginia shows up in such families as the Randolphs, who were prominent in every aspect. John and Mary Isham Randolph, of Turkey Island, have been called the Adam and Eve of Virginia society, though early Lees, Carters, and Pages might make equal claim. Randolph came to Virginia about 1673, the son of Richard and Elizabeth Randolph of Bedfordshire, England. Through intermarriage,

The First Families [49]

Tazewall Hall, original home of the Randolphs in Williamsburg, as reconstructed in 1966 at Newport News. Sir John Randolph, first Virginian to be knighted, built it in 1732; Peyton Randolph, president of the first Continental Congress, and John Randolph, the Tory who returned to England during the Revolution, lived in it. *Virginia Museum of Fine Arts*

the Randolphs were eventually connected with nearly every powerful family in the colony. Jefferson and John Marshall were a part of it, through their mothers, as were Peyton Edmund and John Randolph. The family was closely allied to such James River dynasties as the Harrisons, Eppes, Amblers, Flemings, Jaquelins, Burwells, and Carys.

In colonial times, the Randolphs numbered three members of the Governor's Council, five burgesses, two treasurers of Virginia, one Speaker of the burgesses, two clerks of the burgesses, two attorneys general, and the president of the Continental Congress, Peyton Randolph. Over the years, Randolph descendants became presidents, governors, justices, and clergymen, scholars, lawyers, and judges beyond number. Early Randolph estates were located along the James, beginning with Turkey Island, and

including Curles Neck, Varina, Wilton, Tuckahoe, Dungenness, Chatsworth, and Bremo, as well as in Williamsburg and Richmond.

Fortunately for Virginia, the eighteenth century brought new emigrants to widen the scope of the Tidewater plantocracy. First came Huguenots to settle in 1700 above the falls of the James, on the site of a Monacan Indian village (now Manakin), in present Powhatan County. These French farmers had been granted asylum by the Protestant monarchs William and Mary after Louis XIV revoked the Edict of Nantes in 1685. Some 800 settled on 10,000 acres of James River farmland, under the Reverend Benjamin de Joux.

A few Huguenots had preceded them to Virginia as early as 1619, to attempt wine cultivation. Others had come in 1632 to produce silk, and a few as clergymen of the

Church of England, having taken holy orders in England. However, the heaviest emigration followed King Louis' withdrawal of Huguenot freedom in 1685.

Scattered through Virginia after 1700, as a result, were such Huguenot names as d'Aubigne (Dabney), Bernard, Boissieux, Battaille (Battle), Durant, DuPuy, Duval, Dashiell, Latane, Larus, DeLanoue (Delano), Fontaine, Foushee, Guerrant, Gilliam, Maury, Maupin, Jerdone (Jordan), Gerow, Fourquerean, Huger, Bondurant, Remy, Barraud (Barrow), Minitree, Fauntleroy, Flournoy, Michaux, Lewis, Norman, Noel, Paul, Perdue, Perrot, Pettit (Poteat), Moncure, Munford, Robin, Ravanel, Rozier, Revell, Royall, Sully, Sorrel, Taliaferro, and Valentine. They are reminders of the Huguenots' part in building America.

Encouragement of Protestant settlement became royal policy under William and Mary. Dutchmen came to the Eastern Shore and Welshmen to Northern Virginia. Germans came in large numbers beginning in 1710 with the movement of 2,000 from the Rhenish Palatinate, first in Stafford County and then in Madison, Culpeper, Orange, and Fauquier.

Unlike the English in Tidewater, the Germans grew little tobacco and bought few slaves. They lived a puritanical life, growing wheat and living peaceably on church-centered farmlands. They concentrated in Page, Shenandoah, and Rockingham counties, along the Massanutten Mountains, with lesser numbers in Madison, Rappahannock, Prince William, Botetourt, and Culpeper. Strasburg — named for the capital of Alsace — Luray, Newmarket, and Harrisonburg were trading centers. Most were members of the Lutheran or United Brethren Churches. A few were Mennonites.

The Germans' valley wheat was ground at mills in Alexandria and Richmond and sold throughout the colonies. The Valley became the "granary of the world." Although many German names were Anglicized, German speech and folkways persisted.

Among early Germanic settlers were the families of Strickler, Rhodes, Brubaker, Souder, Stone, Bomgarner (Baumgardner), Berry, Root, Holman, Blosser, Miller, Good, Heiston (Heistand), Alger, Lineweaver, Gochenour, Funk (Funck), Grove, Burner, Berry (Burry), Bowman (Bauman), Hendrick, Grabill, Spangler, Weaver, Eberly, Rhodes (Rhoads), Mauck, Kauffman, (Coffman), Stauffer (Stover), Kagey, Shank (Schenck), Ruffner, Musselman, Comer, Rinehart, Grove, Hoover (Huber), Hite, Heatwole, Showalter, Burkholder, Kyser (Keiser), Conrad, Swank, Driver, Frank, Pennypacker, Ruebush, Nisewanger, Brenneman, and Barnhart.

On the heels of the Germans came Scotch-Irish settlers, who had also entered America through Philadelphia and then moved south to take up land in the Valley. "The northern men are fond of buying land there," said William Beverley "because they can buy it for six or seven pounds per hundred acres cheaper than they can take up land in Pennsylvania, and they don't care to go as far as Williamsburg" to obtain grants.

Like the Germans, the Scotch-Irish sought religious liberty. Originally Scottish and northern English, they had settled in Ireland after 1611 in support of King James I's policy of establishing Protestantism more strongly there. Being industrious, they had quickly created a linen and wool industry. This aroused rival English manufacturers, who in 1698 obtained laws inimical to Ire-

The Great Planters began to develop in the late seventeenth century. Founders of four leading Virginia families are shown here. At the upper left are Colonel and Mrs. Richard Lee, who lived first at Gloucester Point and then in Northumberland County. At lower left are Matthew Page and Mary Mann Page of Timberneck in Gloucester

County. At upper right are William and Mary Isham Randolph of Turkey Island, on the James River in Henrico County. At lower right are John Wickham and Elizabeth Selden McClurg Wickham of Richmond.

Lee portraits from Mrs. Cazenove Lee; Randolph from Virginia Historical Society; Page from the College of William and Mary; and Wickham from the Valentine Museum.

land. The Presbyterian faith of the Scotch-Irish also came under attack. To escape discriminatory laws, large numbers of transplanted Scots, usually called "Scotch-Irish," began emigrating from Ireland to America in 1719.

While the Scots accused Tidewater landholders of using them as a barrier against the Indians, they did not object to a fight. The story of Virginia is full of their bravery. Through successive migrations, they filled the western Valley before spreading into southwest Virginia and the future Kentucky and West Virginia. Like the Germans, they grew wheat, corn, sheep, and cattle. Others moved south into the Carolinas, Georgia, and territory which became Tennessee.

Among the Scotch-Irish were the families of Breckenridge, Brown, Graham, Alexander, Lewis, White, Reid, Houston, Paxton, McClure, McCrum, Preston, Blair, Campbell, Pickens, Stuart, McDowell, Johnston, and Rutledge. They centered in the counties of Augusta, Rockbridge, Bath, Highland, Allegheny, Botetourt, and the lands to the southwest. From this stock were to spring such Virginians as General Andrew Lewis, Cyrus McCormick, George Rogers Clark, Edgar Allan Poe, Sam Houston, General Winfield Scott, Thomas "Stonewall" Jackson, Woodrow Wilson, and Ellen Glasgow.

Scotsmen also entered Tidewater in increasing number in the 1730s. The port of Alexandria was founded by Scotsmen in 1749 and named for John Alexander, a Scotsman. Wherever tobacco was sold and shipped — at Richmond, Norfolk, Petersburg, Dumfries, Port Royal, Falmouth, Fredericksburg, and other ports — Scottish merchants set up shop. The towns of Winchester, Staunton, Lexington, Fincastle, and Abingdon were largely Scotch-Irish.

The Scots differed strongly with Tidewater's Englishmen, and their differences often were bitter. The Scotch-Irish referred to the English as "Tuckahoes" — a root eaten by Indians; the English called the highlanders "Cohees," from their use of "quoth he" for "said he." The planter differed from the democratic Scotsman on every major issue except the Revolution. In 1863 it proved to be the Scotch-Irish of western Virginia who led the secession from Virginia.

The conflict of English and Scottish ways in the early frontier towns — Winchester, Lexington, Charlottesville, Lynchburg — led to bitter party battles. However, from this Valley battleground came an unusual number of leaders from the mid-eighteenth century onward.

Along with their conflicts, the English and the Scottish had complementary virtues. The English were organizers. They had a genius for order, which sometimes necessitated compromise. Their strong middle class had forced English kings and nobles to accept representative government. Moreover, they had created a magnificent literature. Milton did not exaggerate when he asked his countrymen: "Consider what nation it is whereof ye are: a nation not slow and dull, but of quick, ingenious and piercing spirit; acute to invent, subtile and sinewy to discourse, not beneath the reach of any point that human capacity can soar to."

In contrast, the Scots were prickly and dogmatic — the English called them "dour" or "crafty." Theirs was an austere nature, but what they lacked in dash they made up in solidarity. Glasgow merchants required their Virginia agents to remain single so they could live cheaply and work around the clock. No people had greater reverence for learning. Their schools were Europe's best. Under the tutelage of stern parsons, they produced a harvest of scholars, scientists, physicians, clergymen, and theologians. To the English sense of beauty and balance, the Scots added thoroughness and perseverance. To Virginia they brought good heads, strong backs, and stubborn determination.

An early observer of the Scot's quirks found them to be:

. . . an economy and even parsimony of words, which does not always betoken a poverty of ideas; an insuperable dislike to wear his heart upon his sleeve, or make a display of the deeper and more tender feelings of his nature; a quiet and undemonstrative deportment which may have great firmness and determination behind it; a dour exterior which may cover a really genial disposition and kindly heart; much caution, wariness, and reserve, but a decision, energy of character, and tenacity of purpose; . . . a very decided practical faculty which has an eye on the main chance, but which may co-exist with a deep-lying fund of sentiment; a capacity for hard work and close application to business, which, with thrift and patient persistence, is apt to bear fruit in considerable success; in short, a reserve of strength, self-reliance, courage, and endurance which, when an emergency demands, . . . may surprise the world.

The stream of Anglo-Saxon settlement which entered America at Jamestown was a triumph for England's middle class, which had fought its way up since the Reformation. These hardy freeholders wanted a new life. They seized it enthusiastically.

Then, after the English had firmly anchored their colonies, King William and Queen Mary felt safe to admit other Protestants: Huguenots, Germans, Scotch-Irish, Dutchmen, and Swiss. In Virginia's second century, they joined the English in claiming the waiting west.

OVERLEAF: The planter families of Tidewater intermarried to create a wealthy governing class. This chart by Benjamin B. Weisiger III illustrates the relationships between the families of George Washington, "King" Carter, Lewis Burwell, John Marshall, Edmund Randolph, and other leaders. *Virginia State Library*

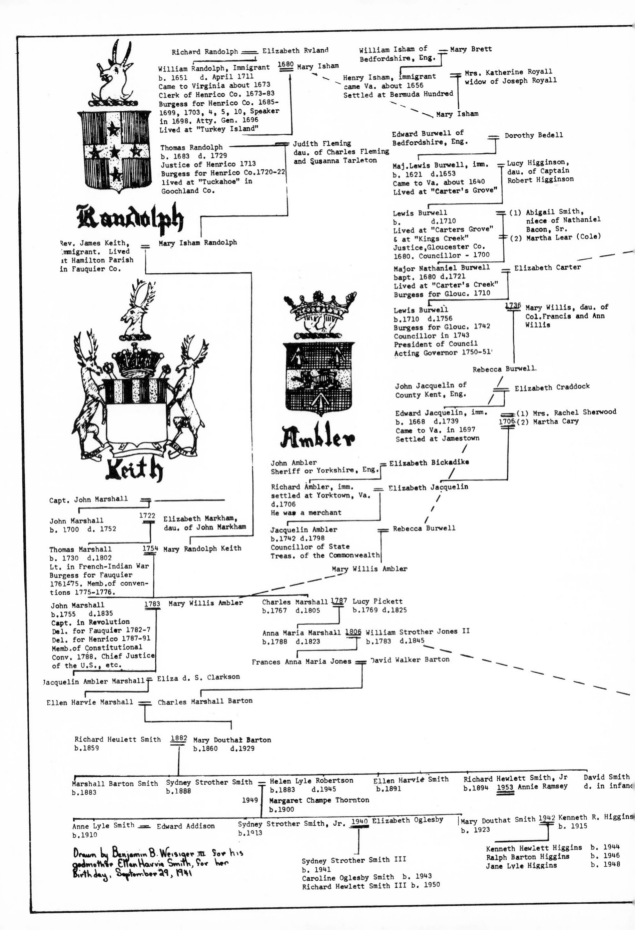

Richard Randolph ══ Elizabeth Ryland

William Randolph, Immigrant ══1680══ Mary Isham
b. 1651   d. April 1711
Came to Virginia about 1673
Clerk of Henrico Co. 1673-83
Burgess for Henrico Co. 1685-
1699, 1703, 4, 5, 10, Speaker
in 1698. Atty. Gen. 1696
Lived at "Turkey Island"

William Isham of ══ Mary Brett
Bedfordshire, Eng.

Henry Isham, immigrant ══ Mrs. Katherine Royall
came Va. about 1656   widow of Joseph Royall
Settled at Bermuda Hundred

Mary Isham

Thomas Randolph ══ Judith Fleming
b. 1683 d. 1729   dau. of Charles Fleming
Justice of Henrico 1713   and Susanna Tarleton
Burgess for Henrico Co.1720-22
lived at "Tuckahoe" in
Goochland Co.

Edward Burwell of ══ Dorothy Bedell
Bedfordshire, Eng.

Maj.Lewis Burwell, imm. ══ Lucy Higginson,
b. 1621   Came to Va. about 1640   dau. of Captain
Lived at "Carter's Grove"   Robert Higginson

Randolph

Lewis Burwell ══ (1) Abigail Smith,
b.   d.1710   niece of Nathaniel
Lived at "Carters Grove"   Bacon, Sr.
& at "Kings Creek"   ══ (2) Martha Lear (Cole)
Justice,Gloucester Co.
1680. Councillor - 1700

Rev. James Keith, ══ Mary Isham Randolph
immigrant. Lived
at Hamilton Parish
in Fauquier Co.

Major Nathaniel Burwell ══ Elizabeth Carter
bapt. 1680 d.1721
Lived at "Carter's Creek"
Burgess for Glouc. 1710

Lewis Burwell ══1736══ Mary Willis, dau. of
b.1710 d.1756   Col.Francis and Ann
Burgess for Glouc. 1742   Willis
Councillor in 1743
President of Council
Acting Governor 1750-51'

Rebecca Burwell

John Jacquelin of ══ Elizabeth Craddock
County Kent, Eng.

Edward Jacquelin, imm. ══ (1) Mrs. Rachel Sherwood
b. 1668 d.1739   1706 (2) Martha Cary
Came to Va. in 1697
Settled at Jamestown

Ambler

John Ambler ══ Elizabeth Bickadike
Sheriff or Yorkshire, Eng.

Richard Ambler, imm. ══ Elizabeth Jacquelin
settled at Yorktown, Va.
d.1706
He was a merchant

Jacquelin Ambler ══ Rebecca Burwell
b.1742 d.1798
Councillor of State
Treas. of the Commonwealth

Keith

Capt. John Marshall ══

John Marshall ══1722══ Elizabeth Markham,
b. 1700 d. 1752   dau. of John Markham

Thomas Marshall ══1754══ Mary Randolph Keith
b. 1730 d.1802
Lt. in French-Indian War
Burgess for Fauquier
1761-775. Memb.of conven-
tions 1775-1776.

Mary Willis Ambler

John Marshall ══1783══ Mary Willis Ambler
b.1755   d.1835
Capt. in Revolution
Del. for Fauquier 1782-7
Del. for Henrico 1787-91
Memb.of Constitutional
Conv. 1788. Chief Justice
of the U.S., etc.

Charles Marshall ══1787══ Lucy Pickett
b.1767 d.1805   b.1769 d.1825

Anna Maria Marshall ══1806══ William Strother Jones II
b.1788 d.1823   b.1783 d.1845

Frances Anna Maria Jones ══ David Walker Barton

Jacquelin Ambler Marshall ══ Eliza d. S. Clarkson

Ellen Harvie Marshall ══ Charles Marshall Barton

Richard Heulett Smith ══1882══ Mary Douthat Barton
b.1859   b.1860   d.1929

Marshall Barton Smith   Sydney Strother Smith ══ Helen Lyle Robertson   Ellen Harvie Smith   Richard Hewlett Smith, Jr   David Smith
b.1883   b.1888   b.1883 d.1945   b.1891   b.1894 ══1953══ Annie Ramsey   d. in infancy
                                1949 Margaret Champe Thornton
                                b.1900

Anne Lyle Smith ══ Edward Addison   Sydney Strother Smith, Jr. ══1940══ Elizabeth Oglesby   Mary Douthat Smith ══1942══ Kenneth R. Higgins
b.1910   b.1913   b. 1923   b. 1915

Drawn by Benjamin B. Weisiger III for his
godmother Ellen Harvie Smith, for her
Birthday, September 29, 1941

Sydney Strother Smith III
b.1941
Caroline Oglesby Smith b. 1943
Richard Hewlett Smith III b. 1950

Kenneth Hewlett Higgins b. 1944
Ralph Barton Higgins   b. 1946
Jane Lyle Higgins   b. 1948

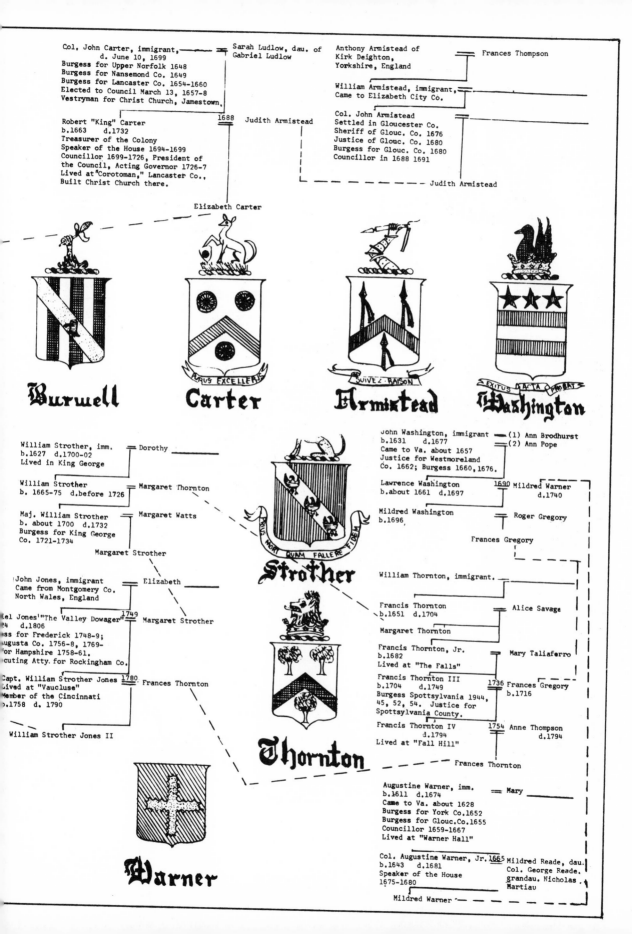

Col. John Carter, immigrant, ═ Sarah Ludlow, dau. of
d. June 10, 1699   Gabriel Ludlow
Burgess for Upper Norfolk 1648
Burgess for Nansemond Co. 1649
Burgess for Lancaster Co. 1654-1660
Elected to Council March 13, 1657-8
Vestryman for Christ Church, Jamestown.

Anthony Armistead of   ┌─── Frances Thompson
Kirk Deighton,
Yorkshire, England

William Armistead, immigrant, ═
Came to Elizabeth City Co.

1688 Judith Armistead

Robert "King" Carter
b.1663   d.1732
Treasurer of the Colony
Speaker of the House 1694-1699
Councillor 1699-1726, President of
the Council, Acting Governor 1726-7
Lived at "Corotoman," Lancaster Co.,
Built Christ Church there.

Col. John Armistead
Settled in Gloucester Co.
Sheriff of Glouc. Co. 1676
Justice of Glouc. Co. 1680
Burgess for Glouc. Co. 1680
Councillor in 1688 1691

─── Judith Armistead

Elizabeth Carter

Burwell   **Carter**   *FLORUS EXCELLENS*   **Armistead**   *SUIVEZ RAISON*   **Washington**   *EXITUS ACTA PROBAT*

John Washington, immigrant ═ (1) Ann Brodhurst
b.1631   d.1677   ═ (2) Ann Pope
Came to Va. about 1657
Justice for Westmoreland
Co. 1662; Burgess 1660, 1676.

William Strother, imm. ═ Dorothy _____
b.1627 d.1700-02
Lived in King George

Lawrence Washington   1690 Mildred Warner
b.about 1661 d.1697   d.1740

William Strother   ═ Margaret Thornton
b. 1665-75 d.before 1726

Mildred Washington   ═ Roger Gregory
b.1696

Maj. William Strother ═ Margaret Watts
b. about 1700 d.1732
Burgess for King George
Co. 1721-1734

Frances Gregory

Margaret Strother

Strother   *PRIUS MORI QUAM FALLERE FIDEM*

William Thornton, immigrant.

John Jones, immigrant   ═ Elizabeth
Came from Montgomery Co.
North Wales, England

Francis Thornton   ═ Alice Savage
b.1651 d.1704

...el Jones "The Valley Dowager" 1749 ═ Margaret Strother
..4   d.1806
...ess for Frederick 1748-9;
...ugusta Co. 1756-8, 1769-
...or Hampshire 1758-61.
...cuting Atty. for Rockingham Co.

Margaret Thornton

Francis Thornton, Jr. ═ Mary Taliaferro
b.1682
Lived at "The Falls"

Capt. William Strother Jones 1780 ═ Frances Thornton
Lived at "Vaucluse"
Member of the Cincinnati
..1758 d. 1790

Francis Thornton III   1736 Frances Gregory
b.1704   d.1749   b.1716
Burgess Spottsylvania 1944,
45, 52, 54. Justice for
Spottsylvania County.

William Strother Jones II

Francis Thornton IV   1754 Anne Thompson
        d.1794   d.1794
Lived at "Fall Hill"

Thornton

─── Frances Thornton

Augustine Warner, imm. ══ Mary _____
b.1611 d.1674
Came to Va. about 1628
Burgess for York Co.1652
Burgess for Glouc.Co. 1655
Councillor 1659-1667
Lived at "Warner Hall"

Col. Augustine Warner, Jr. 1665 Mildred Reade, dau.
b.1643   d.1681   Col. George Reade.
Speaker of the House   grandau. Nicholas
1675-1680   Martiau

Mildred Warner

Warner

John Paul Jones was born in Scotland and lived in Fredericksburg before becoming the most successful naval commander of the American Colonies. *Portrait owned by Hugh Watson. The Mariners Museum*

O, a hundred years aint a very long time
On the Eastern Sho'
O-way-o
Look out, gal, I'm comin' home
To the Eastern Sho'
O-way-o

4

Early Chesapeake Bay chantey

In the name of the Father, Son, and Holy Ghost . . . Amen . . . Being by
God's grace bound for England and knowing the frailty and uncertainty
of man's life . . . [I] do now ordain, constitute, and appoint this my last
will and testament.

William Fitzhugh, in his will written in 1700
before embarking from Stafford County for England

Sea Lanes to England

The need to produce raw materials for England dominated Virginians' thinking until the Revolution. During those 169 years, therefore, Virginia faced eastward, toward the sea lanes to London, Bristol, and Glasgow. The interlacing rivers that flowed into Chesapeake Bay and the Atlantic Ocean provided readymade highways to the plantations of Virginia and Maryland. One writer called Virginia "A sylvan Venice." Because waterways were numerous and roads few, shipping dominated the thinking of the Tidewater colonists.

As one contemporary put it, "'Tis the blessing of this country . . . and fits it extremely for the trade it carries on, that the planters can deliver their commodities at their own back doors, as the whole colony is interflowed by the most navigable rivers in the world." Added the Reverend Hugh Jones in 1722, "No country is better watered for the conveniency of which most houses are built near some landing place; so that anything may be delivered to a gentleman there from London, Bristol, etc. . . ."

It was the prospect of a northwest passage, from the Chesapeake to the Pacific, which brought the English to the James River in the first place. And though the passage never materialized, the protected harbors which were found at Jamestown, Kecoughtan, and York proved ideal for the

Several ships were built at early Jamestown. Sloops and schooners for coastal and West Indies service were produced at Norfolk, Hampton, and Gosport (later Portsmouth), in the eighteenth century. *Engraving by Peter Van der AA in Voyagien, 1606-7*

small craft — seldom over 300 tons — which carried most English commerce in the seventeenth century. They were the first Virginia ports. Then, in the eighteenth century, larger ships required larger harbors. By the time of the Revolution, Virginia's shipping was concentrated at Norfolk, with lesser ports at Alexandria, Petersburg, Hampton, and Richmond. In the interim, Virginians developed a vigorous maritime trade.

The *Susan Constant* and *Godspeed*, which the Virginia Company leased from the Muscovy Company in 1606 for the settlement voyage, were typical merchantmen of the earlier period. The *Susan* was a vessel of 100 tons displacement, with a length of 76 feet at the waterline and a draft of 11 feet. The 40-ton *Godspeed* had a waterline length of 48 feet and drew 7 feet of water. To provide maximum space for cargo, they were built with broader beam than fighting ships. Hence they were slower and less maneuverable.

What the square-rigger lost in speed, it made up in stability. Because of its deep draft and immense weight, it could stay afloat in rough weather. Since the Middle Ages, Europe's shipbuilders had clung to the belief that a ship should be shaped like a whale, with broad bow trailing off to narrow stern. In the tradition of Roman galleys of Nero's time, they continued to elevate the captain on a high quarterdeck astern, from which he could direct his crew in storm or battle. As protection against pirates or privateers — privately owned ships authorized by the king to harry enemy commerce — they carried a few guns.

One deck below the captain's castle was the main deck, where the crew was quartered. Below the main deck, in the dark and stinking hold, were stowed the cargo and passengers. While passengers were permitted abovedeck in good weather, fear of the "rheumy" night air drove them below to sleep. Rations were cooked on deck over a brick galley, but hardtack and corned meat or gruel enlivened with alcoholic spirits was substituted in foul weather.

Logs of voyages to Virginia are filled with entries of illness and death. Passengers and crew contracted scurvy or dysentery from unbalanced diet or spoiled food. The miasmic stench arising from the bilges caused other illness. No sanitary facilities were provided except the open latticework head, as the forepeak of the vessel was called. If worse came to worst, the victim was buried at sea. William Bradford wrote in his *Plymouth Plantation* of a Virginia-bound vessel which lost 130 of its passengers. On another Virginia voyage, a passenger wrote: "Betwixt decks, there can hardly a man fetch his breath by reason there arises such a funk in the night that it causes putrefaction of blood and breedeth disease much like the plague."

Many ships disappeared at sea and after due interval were declared legally lost. Shipwreck was commonest in the shoal waters of the British Isles and of the North American coast, particularly in the Cape Hatteras area off North Carolina. Virginia herself offered hospitable harbor; Governor Sir William Berkeley declared that "fewer

The *Susan Constant*, flagship of the Virginia Company of London, was similar to this English merchantman of 1600, sketched for the National Maritime Museum at Greenwich, England, by Gregory Robinson. *National Maritime Museum*

An old print shows Christopher Newport boarding the pinnace *Discovery* at Jamestown. *Virginia State Library*

ships miscarry going to Virginia than to any port at that distance in the world," and Robert Beverley wrote in 1705, "a bolder and safer course is not known in the universe."

At the first of the 17th century, voyagers to Virginia followed the South Atlantic route which Captain Christopher Newport took in his first voyage of 1606-07 and the four supplies he made for the Virginia Company before 1611. While much longer, it avoided the rough North Atlantic weather. Furthermore, it broke the voyage with watering stops in the Canary Islands and the West Indies. Its chief drawback was the danger of being becalmed in the horse latitudes between Africa and South America. Four to five months were required for the outward passage, but favoring westerly winds shortened the return. It usually took no more than seven weeks.

To guide him, the colonial mariner had charts compiled since Columbus' day. As navigational aids, he had a quadrant, an astrolabe, a cross staff, a backstaff, a compass, a nocturnal for taking the height of stars at sea, and a sandglass for measuring the time on each course and thus reckoning his position. To assure his speed and thus determine, with the sandglass, the distance covered, he streamed a knotted rope in the water; the faster his speed, the more knots were exposed.

After the mid-17th century, some English captains sailed the northern route, which brought them due west to Newfoundland and thence down the coast to Virginia. This avoided storms off Cape Hatteras. As the century progressed, ships became slimmer and longer, giving greater speed; they were moving toward the sleek clipper-ship design of the nineteenth century. In 1688 William Byrd I crossed from Land's End, England, to Cape Henry in twenty-eight days.

Voyages improved after the northern route prevailed. Except on crowded slave-ships, passengers had better food and cleaner air. One slaving vessel arrived in Virginia in 1702 from Guinea with a loss of 100 of its 230 Negroes. Half the crew were dead, and the others were "yellow in their faces." Crews loathed the slave voyages, with their overcrowded cargoes of frightened natives, moaning and dying.

Just as the first settlers sailed to reach Virginia at wheat-planting time, in April, so later voyages were scheduled to avoid arrival in the hot summer, when illness was greatest. A Dutchman reported in the 1630s that new arrivals succumbed easily to the heat of June, July, and August. Early fall came to be the preferred arrival time, permitting the ship to haul the newly-cured tobacco crop on her return.

There were other hazards besides shipwreck and illness. A Mrs. Browne, bound from London to Virginia in 1754-55, reported that a passenger lost overboard a live sheep, two pigs, eight turkeys, and six ducks.

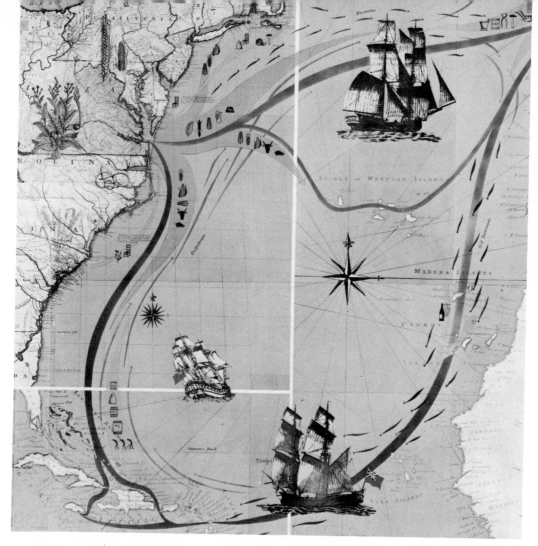

Dutch ships exchanged European products in the Caribbean for sugar and rum, and exchanged these in Virginia for tobacco and other goods. England's Navigation Acts stopped this triangular trading. *Colonial Williamsburg*

She herself lost 30 gallons of brandy that leaked into the scuppers. The Swiss botanist Francis Louis Michel wrote in 1701 that the *Nassau* carried to Virginia 45 pigs, a calf, 3 sheep, some 20 turkeys, 14 geese, and more than 100 chickens to supply the captain's table. "Englishmen pay much attention to good eating and drinking, but especially to meat," he observed with astonishment.

What happened when food ran out was described by a passenger on the *Virginia Merchant:*

Women and children made dismal cries and grievous complaints. The infinite number of rats that all the voyage had been our plague, we now were glad to make our prey to feed on; and as they were ensnared and taken, a well-grown rat was sold for sixteen shillings as a market rate. Nay, before the voyage did end, a woman great with child offered 20 shillings for a rat, which, the proprietor refusing, the woman died.

Dutch merchantmen were frequent visitors from the time one of them brought the first twenty Negroes in 1619 until forty years thereafter. The Netherlanders sailed a triangular route, bringing goods from Europe to the West Indies and trading part of it for rum, molasses, and sugar for American ports. England determined to stop this trade with her Navigation Acts beginning in 1651. Other acts in 1660 and in 1663 were more vigorously prosecuted, bringing an end to Dutch trade with the colonies and inciting war between England and the Netherlands.

Denied the European market, Virginians' tobacco after 1661 rotted in fields and warehouses. Virginians protested — and traded when they could with the enemy. However, King Charles II was determined to enforce the law. A station ship or guardship was posted at the entrance to Chesapeake Bay to prevent Dutch entry, and the governors of Virginia and Maryland were instructed in 1666 to order English-bound vessels to gather in convoys to protect each other against Dutch marauders.

The following June a fleet of six Dutch warships retaliated by entering the bay and surprising the station ship, *H.M.S. Elizabeth*, off Newport News. After burning the *Elizabeth* and five tobacco ships awaiting convoy, the Dutch captured thirteen other ships and sailed before Governor Berkeley's troops could come from Jamestown and Yorktown. Five years later the Dutch repeated the attack and took or destroyed eleven of the forty tobacco ships awaiting convoy at Lynnhaven Bay.

The old free-and-easy days of triangular trading were over. After 1665, merchant ships from Virginia to England usually sailed under protection of warships. Some 150 to 200 merchantmen for each convoy loaded individually at plantation docks and then proceeded to anchorages within the Capes until the commodore made signal to sail. But rarely in any year were these sufficient ships to haul the whole crop, even though some hogsheads were put aboard convoying

During Britain's eighteenth century maritime wars, tobacco ships sailed with protective convoys to and from Virginia. This print of 1773 shows Dover Castle and shipping on the English Channel. *The Mariners Museum*

warships. For lack of ships, freight rates soared. By 1703 more than half the tobacco crop annually remained in Virginia and Maryland for want of cargo ships. This was the price Virginia paid to support British mercantilism.

The convoy's departure was set by the captain of the man-o-war and communicated to the governors of Virginia and Maryland. Notices were posted on church and courthouse doors, and newspapers carried it in advertisements. Collectors and naval officers along each river passed the information and prodded laggard planters to deliver their hogsheads. On the appointed sailing day, the commodore summoned shipmasters and gave them sailing orders.

Signals were provided so that the commodore's orders could be passed through the ranks. The commodore directed speeds, courses, maneuvers, and when to anchor. Battle formation was adopted when attack threatened. Flags, guns, sail adjustments, cannons, bells, and drums were all used to pass the word.

In large convoys, the tobacco ships were divided into three sections commanded by the admiral-in-chief, a vice-admiral, and a rear-admiral. As soon as a "prosperous wind" sprang up, the commodore signalled his brood, and they streamed between Cape Henry and Cape Charles into the dark Atlantic. At night, the flagship burned lightwood in a cresset at the fantail. When fog enveloped her, a gun was discharged every minute so the fleet could follow.

Convoying reduced losses, but it broke down when England went to war and needed her ships in battle. During King George's War, Virginia shipping suffered especially great depredation. In 1748, a number of armed French privateers dared

Typical of coastal galleys that plied Chesapeake Bay is this vessel docked at London's Custom House in 1714. *Archives of the Custom House, The Mariners Museum*

to enter Chesapeake Bay and capture ships within sight of the English garrison at Fort George, at Old Point Comfort. Under such hazards, insurance rates rose too high for planters. Virginians learned to expect losses if they grew tobacco.

Ships bound for the West Indies usually sailed alone. They were preyed upon by Spanish and French privateers and by pirates, but the potential profit in untaxed French goods made it worth the risk.

A few planters owned ships, most of them small sloops, schooners, or brigs engaged in coastal or Caribbean trading. Some of these were built in Virginia from the earliest days at Jamestown. Other shipways operated at Norfolk, Hampton, Accomac,

Large sailing ships were built in colonial Virginia for trade with the English colonies in North America. Some shippers defied the Navigation Acts to buy and sell in Dutch and French islands of the West Indies. *From a diorama at The Mariners Museum*

and on the Chickahominy River near Williamsburg. Governor Sir Edmund Andros noted in 1697 that Virginia had recently built eight ships, eleven brigantines, and fifteen sloops, using carpenters brought from England. However, the colony lacked the incentive of New England's fisheries to stimulate seafaring. A few Virginia vessels reached 250 tons — big enough to haul tobacco to England — but not many colonials had enough capital to become ship-owners. This deepened their dependency on England.

The fast and maneuverable schooner was the jack-of-all-trades in Chesapeake commerce. It was used as a pilot boat in the eighteenth century bay and for smuggling, privateering, and trade with other colonists in North America, Barbados, Antigua, the Bahamas, St. Christopher, Nevis, Anguilla, Montserrat, and Bermuda. It became famous in the Revolution as "Virginia-built schooner" and in the War of 1812 as the "Baltimore clipper."

Two other popular Virginia vessels were the Chesapeake log canoe, a fore-and-aft rigged vessel of Indian derivation, carved from three, five, or seven logs; and the skipjack or bugeye. The colonists adapted the crude technique to produce fishing and oystering vessels called "coastal canoes." A later outgrowth was the bugeye, whose hull was hewn from large logs. Many were painted bright Elizabethan colors.

Virginia might have developed global seafaring had not mercantilism discouraged it. The few ocean-going vessels built in the 17th century were nearly all lost to privateers and enemy warships by 1708. Then, for nearly 60 years after Britain defeated France in Queen Anne's War, ending in 1713, Chesapeake planters built vessels again in an effort to assure transport of their tobacco. So many were built in America that England's master of shipwrights informed the king in 1724 that England's own shipbuilding had "very much decayed." When the Revolution halted these shipments, the larger ships rotted away in disuse; the smaller sloops, schooners, and brigs saw service as the "mosquito fleet" in the Revolution.

Foremost among Virginia shipowners were the Scottish seaport merchants. On a smaller scale were such planters as the Washingtons, Carters, Byrds, Harrisons, Custises, Braxtons, and Fitzhughs. In the number of vessels they owned, Virginians ranked behind Massachusetts, Rhode Island, New Hampshire, Connecticut, and New York. However, Virginia ships were larger because they were designed to haul bulky tobacco hogsheads.

Bristol vied with London as Virginia's chief customer until 1685. Thereafter London was the major destination until Glasgow became a strong contender about 1725. Heavy trade was also carried on throughout colonial times between Chesapeake Bay and the West Indies. Virginians exchanged their corn, wheat, flour, iron, lumber, barrel staves, tar, pitch, and salted pork and beef for the Indies' rum, molasses, sugar, cocoa, and indigo. The chief hazard to this trade was French and Spanish privateering in the Indies.

Virginia-bred mariners were few. As Governor Sir Edmund Andros wrote home, English sailors in Virginia "leave the sea wholly" to be planters. The Governor could impress seamen from other ships to fill vacant billets on an English man-o-war, while merchant shippers came to depend on Negro slaves and freedmen for crews. Norfolk and Portsmouth were home ports of most mariners, while others came from Hampton, the Eastern Shore, Gloucester, Mathews, Isle of Wight, and Nansemond.

As Virginia's chief eighteenth-century port, Norfolk attracted many shippers like Niel Jamieson and merchants like Moses Myers, who built handsome town-houses. It was also close to the forests of the Dismal Swamp, whose oak and cypress were used in shipbuilding. After the 1730s, it attracted most ocean-going vessels, whose draft was too deep for the upriver harbors. It also dominated the shipping of upper North Carolina and the South Atlantic trade with the West Indies. By 1775 it had grown to 3,000 population. Baltimore was growing even faster.

The bugeye was an all-purpose sailing vessel developed in Chesapeake Bay during colonial times. *Photo by Percy E. Budlong from The Mariners Museum*

Sea Lanes to England [67]

Typical of the British ships that protected Virginia commerce in the eighteenth century were *HMS Success* and *HMS Norwich*. Illustration from the journal of their voyage to Nova Scotia and Virginia, 1754-1756. *The Mariners Museum*

Commanding a ship required harsh discipline. Many shipmasters had much in common with Captain Bligh. William Byrd II expressed a typical view:

They are commonly men of no aspiring genius, and their understanding rises little higher than instinct. When they go out of their ships they are out of their element. They are most of them arrant sea calves, and the tritons that swim under the water are just as wise as those that sail upon it. The most they can be brought to do, is, sometimes deliver a letter, and if they happen to have superior parts, they may be instructed to call for an answer. One may as soon tutor a monkey to speak or a French woman to hold her tongue as to bring a skipper to higher flights of reason.

There were exceptions, however. One was Captain Robert Necks of Norfolk, whose death was reported in the *Virginia Gazette* of September 29, 1774:

He was a commander in the Virginia trade for many years, and few were more generally esteemed. The many passengers that have crossed the Atlantic with him will always venerate his memory, for that more than ordinary kindness and attention he payed to all under his care, as well as for his constant good humor and gaiety.

Another Virginia captain, John Booth, died at sea in 1748 at the age of 34. His epitaph read in part:

Whilst on this variant stage he rov'd.
From port to port on shipboard drove.
Sometimes the wished-for haven reached,
But twice his bark was stranded on the beach.
No other coffin but the ship, the sea his grave
But God, the merciful and just,
Has brought him to the haven safe in dust.

. . . .

His sails unfurled, his voyage 'tis o'er,
His anchors gone, he's safe on shore.

The scattered plantations were easy prey to seaborne attack. For this reason, the bay promontory known as Point Comfort was fortified in 1609 as Fort Algernon to keep watch over traffic into the James and York Rivers. Renamed Fort George in 1728, it remained in service until 1749, when a hurricane destroyed it. Thereafter the bay was usually patrolled by a guardship or station ship to intercept enemy warships, privateers, or pirates which played havoc with coastal shipping from the time of the Navigation Acts to the Revolution. Such guardships were rotated between the American and West Indies colonies, breaking the monotony with convoy duty.

Guardships had to be ready at all times for battle. The earliest of them sent to the colony were shallow-draft sloops which could chase smugglers up creeks. These proved too small to battle pirates, and the Royal Navy at length sent a larger ship. H.M.S. Shoreham, which arrived in 1700, was a frigate of 30 guns and 100 men. When the French pirate Louis Guittar sailed confidently into the Chesapeake Bay in La Paix soon after the Shoreham's arrival, he was surprised when the large ship appeared and gave chase. La Paix lost 39 of her crew before she went aground and surrendered. Three pirates were hanged and the rest deported to England.

One of the Shoreham's casualties was buried in Pembroke churchyard, at Hampton. Governor Sir Francis Nicholson, who chanced to be aboard, erected a tombstone there reading:

In memory of Peter Heyman, Esq., grandson to Sir Peter Heyman of Summerfield in the

To protect the colony and its commerce, Point Comfort was fortified in 1609 as Fort Algernon. Rebuilt and renamed Fort George a hundred years later, it continued as harbor defense and dockyard. This drawing of the fort in 1609 is by W. D. Rogers. *Casemate Museum, Fort Monroe*

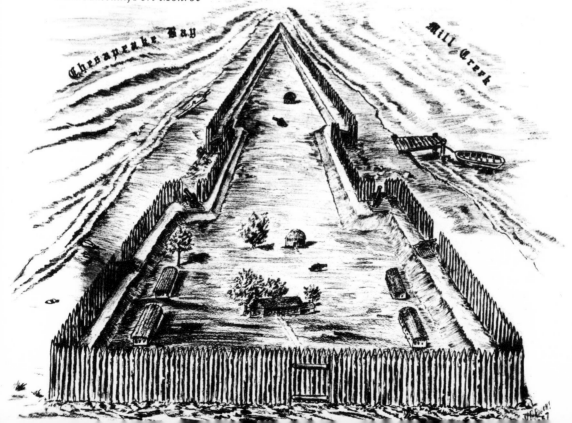

county of Kent. He was collector of customs in the lower district of James River and went voluntarily on board the king's ship Shoreham in pursuit of a pirate who greatly infested this coast. After he had behaved himself seven hours with undaunted courage, was killed with a small shot the 29th day of April, 1700. In the engagement he stood next the Governor, upon the quarterdeck, and was here honorably interred by his order.

Piracy was a serious threat for much of the colonial era. Barbadian rum was widely smuggled into the Southern colonies to avoid import duties. Virginia tobacco was shipped in return to the French and Dutch West Indies, violating Navigation Acts provisions against trade with foreign nations. Such goods found ready carriers in the pirates, who held meetings frequently on the Eastern Shore. In 1682 the English pirate William Dampier and twenty men spent months in Virginia disposing of hides, cocoa, brandy, and European goods taken in the Caribbean. Edward Davis and John Cook joined Dampier at Accomack in 1683 and prepared for a pirate voyage around Cape Horn to Peru and the South Seas. Western shoremen, unsympathetic with the Navigation Acts, readily traded food to the buccaneers for brandy.

Davis returned to Virginia in five years aboard the *Batchellour's Delight*, loaded with South Pacific booty. He and his cronies, John Hinson and Lionel Delawafer, were persuaded by Governor Sir Francis Nicholson in 1688 to accept immunity in return for endowing the new College of William and Mary with £300 of their plunder. In 1699 the colorful John James, known as Captain Kidd, captured a Bristol ship, the *Maryland Merchant*, in Lynnhaven Bay. However, the county militia were alerted, and Kidd sailed with only a little plunder.

Blackbeard the pirate preyed on Virginia and Carolina shipping until slain by Lieutenant Maynard at Ocracoke, North Carolina. *New York Public Library*

From islands in the Caribbean and along North Carolina's Outer Banks, pirates preyed on Virginia-bound commerce. One of the best-known was Stede Bonnet, of Barbados, who was driven by unhappy marriage to the "humor of going a-pirating." In 1717 he captured several merchant ships off the Capes, plundering and burning them and sending their crews ashore. Bonnet later joined the notorious Edward Teach, called Blackbeard, who terrorized the coast from Virginia to South Carolina. Half-hidden by a fierce beard which stretched from eyes to waist, Teach went into battle with matches smoking beneath his hat and three brace of pistols slung from his shoulders.

Teach responded to a proclamation of immunity by King George I to surrender to Governor Eden of North Carolina and swear allegiance to the Crown. But the sea called again, and Teach left his thirteenth wife, aged 16, and joined forces with Bonnet. He sailed to his old hideout at Charleston, South Carolina, and enforced exorbitant demands for booty by holding leading citizens as hostages. Then, offering Governor Eden part of his plunder, he returned to Ocracoke Inlet immune to punishment. North Carolina's shippers called for aid, and Governor Alexander Spotswood promptly dispatched two Royal Navy sloops from Virginia to bring Blackbeard to Williamsburg, dead or alive.

In one of the sea's bloodiest battles, the brave Lieutenant Robert Maynard of *H.M.S. Pearl*, fought Blackbeard hand-to-hand after twelve of Maynard's crew had been killed and twenty-two wounded. Felled at last with twenty-five wounds, Blackbeard was decapitated and his head nailed to Maynard's bowsprit. The Hampton shore on which the head was hung was named Blackbeard's Point. Fifteen members of Blackbeard's captured crew were tried in Williamsburg, and thirteen were hanged there on Pirate Road as an example to others that British power reigned supreme.

Equipped with larger ships, the Royal Navy gradually subdued the pirates and reduced illicit trade. The chief violators were Norfolk merchants who could buy sugar and molasses more cheaply in the French islands of Martinique, Guadaloupe, and Santo Domingo than in the British colonies. However, by 1763, Governor Sir Francis Fauquier could assure the Board of Trade that British regulations were "pretty effectual to suppress illegal trade" in Virginia. "The men-of-war stationed on our coast think it hardly worth watching," he wrote.

Another requirement of Chesapeake shipping was pilotage. The bay and its estuaries were pocked with shoals which could wreck an unwary ship. Between Baltimore channel, which led Potomac-bound ships past Cape Charles, and Norfolk channel, which brought vessels past Cape Henry into Virginia, lurked the menace of Middle Ground. Shippers in 1720 advocated a lighthouse at Cape Henry, but construction was not begun until 1774.

Pilots were authorized by the colony beginning in 1661, and their little boats have been familiar sights on the bay ever since. Each major river also had pilots, who charged £1 from Cape Henry to Hampton Roads, £2 to Yorktown, £3 to Urbanna, and £5 to Smith's Point at the Potomac's mouth.

The threat of British invasion of the Chesapeake in the Revolution brought a frantic renewal of Virginia shipbuilding. Notices appeared in the *Virginia Gazette* for ship's carpenters, and private vessels were purchased and armed by Virginia. A Board of Naval Commissioners was appointed in May, 1776, to direct naval activities under Colonel Thomas Whiting of Hampton, and a fleet of 70 "mosquito ships" was raised to stand off the Royal Navy. One writer thus described them:

They were probably the fastest sailers in the world, except the lateens of the Mediterranean. Then they were of such light draft that they were perfectly at home in the shallow inlets. . . . The fleet included frigates, brigs, brigantines, schooners, sloops, galleys, and armed pilot boats and barges. Some were row-galleys, one-half decked over and provided with high and strong bulwarks. These galleys looked like huge water spiders, being broad and flat and usually rigged as schooners with two or three masts. They were used as lookouts or flying sentinels as well as for transports for troops, each being large enough to carry a company with 68 men with arms and baggage . . .

The most celebrated mosquito fleet captains were James and Richard Barron of

Hampton, whose father had commanded Fort George at Old Point. They went to sea early in life, rising through the ranks to be pilots and merchant skippers. When war with England became imminent, they began to prey on British shipping and caused the grounding and burning of the *H.M.S. Otter* at Hampton Creek in 1775. In reprisal, the British appeared at Hampton with six armed sloops. The town was saved by its militia and 100 Culpeper Minutemen sent there by Virginia's Committee of Safety. James Barron was made one of three commodores of Virginia's Revolutionary navy and in 1779 became commander-in-chief of all armed forces of the Commonwealth.

Other merchant captains who served the Virginia Navy were Richard Taylor of Orange County, Edward Travis of James City, and Thomas Lilly of Gloucester. Lilly captured and brought into Hampton late in December, 1776, a British vessel captured en route from Tortola to London. Her cargo of rum and sugar was valued at about £6,000 sterling. But the British blockaded Chesapeake Bay in October, 1780, with a fleet of fifty-four ships which were to protect Cornwallis' army.

Virginia's greatest naval hero, however, was the brooding bachelor, John Paul. Born to a large, poor family in Scotland, he worked his passage to Fredericksburg at an early age, to live with his older brother. But the sea was in his veins, and he shipped out again as captain of slave ships. After he was charged with the death of a crewman in Tobago, he adopted the incognito John Paul Jones. When the Revolution broke out, he volunteered to the Continental Congress and won great victories as captain of the *Providence*, the *Ranger*, and the *Bonhomme Richard*. It was Jones who defied his foe with the cry: "I have just begun to fight!"

Had Virginia not been influenced by geography and by British policy to be a rural economy, she might have developed transatlantic shipping that survived the Revolution. As it was, she lacked the necessary concentration of capital in port cities. When the smoke of the Revolution cleared, it was the shippers of Boston, New York, Providence, and Philadelphia who successfully competed for much of the trade that the British had carried. Virginians, like Cincinnatus of yore, beat their swords into plowshares and went back to the soil.

Pilot boats met incoming ships at Cape Henry from Virginia's early days. This print from *The Naval Chronicle, 1815*, shows the lighthouse built in the late eighteenth century. *The Mariners Museum*

There is nothing which has yet been contrived by man, by which so much happiness is produced as by a good inn.

Samuel Johnson

5

Houses, Roads, Ferries, and Inns

The tobacco economy of Virginia changed little from 1607 until after the Revolution. As a result, the mode of life on farms and plantations was essentially unchanged from the time of Jamestown's settlement until well after Cornwallis' surrender in 1781 at Yorktown. Most goods continued to move by water, while the cart paths which were cut from one clearing to another on "the Main" were gradually extended.

The former Indian trail leading from Jamestown across the isthmus inland became known as the Great Road to the West. Skirting the glass factory built in 1608, it thrust through pine forests to a point be-

tween the James and York Rivers, where Middle Plantation was cleared in 1632. From there, the road passed over Queen's Creek to Chiskiack plantation and on to York and thence, in stages, through marshland to Kecoughtan and the coast-watching station at Fort Algernon. Meanwhile, other cart roads were developing elsewhere in the colony.

Newly-arrived settlers chose land on creeks and rivers to afford dockage to tobacco ships. By 1617 "the Colony dispersed all about, planting tobacco." Sir George Yeardley, who arrived as governor in 1619, brought word that each "Ancient Planter" who had come before 1616 would have 100

The first Jamestown dwellings were houses of wattle-and-daub, covered with thatched roofs. To house the 104 settlers, 15 were built inside James Fort. *Photo by Thomas L. Williams for the Jamestown Foundation*

acres. Settlers thereafter were given fifty acres and an additional fifty for each person they brought with them.

The convening of the first Virginia Assembly in 1619 brought a sense of permanence that had not existed before. At Jamestown, the fort was deserted as settlers built along the "High Way" and the "Back Street" which flowed into the Great Road. Huts of wattle-and-daub were replaced with brick and clapboard cottages with one or two ground-floor rooms and a sleeping loft. Casement windows with small glass planes replaced the shuttered openings of the first houses, though they were so small that rooms remained dark. A few houses had basements for cold storage of food.

Narrow row-houses were built, affording the economy of common walls and the comfort of close neighbors. Like European houses of the Middle Ages, they had steep roofs, exposed beams, and sparse furnish-ings. Floors were of brick or tile, and fire-places were roomy enough for tea-kettles, meat spits, and long-legged iron "spider" skillets for cooking over flames.

Because Jamestown was swampy, ditches were cut between houses. Into these, house-wives threw garbage and broken pots, dishes, and bottles. Dogs, horses, and even occasionally human beings were buried in these middens to save high ground for roads and gardens.

By 1625, settlement had grown to twenty-seven plantations, scattered thinly along the James, the York, and the Eastern Shore. No doubt it would have been greater but for the 1622 Indian massacre. The census of 1625 listed only 175 people at Jamestown, nine of them Negroes. In Jamestown and its mainland "suburbs" there were only thirty-three households. In an effort to enlarge the village, the House of Burgesses in 1637 of-fered a "portion of land for a house and garden" to every person who built, but this produced only twelve houses in two years. In 1639 the first brick church was begun, and in 1662 the Assembly encouraged brick homes to avoid the ever-present fires, but with little effect.

It was soon clear that the four original "corporations" which had been planned as towns were developing as rural shires. So the Assembly in 1634 yielded to the inevi-table and decreed that James City, Elizabeth City, Charles City, and Henricus were counties, at the same time adding Accomack, Charles River, Warrosquyoake (later Isle of Wight), and Warwick River. These were patterned after England's shires, for which most of them were named. Thereafter Vir-ginia expanded by the creation of counties.

King Charles II was chagrined at Vir-ginians' refusal to congregate in towns, and at his behest the Assembly in 1662 again called for a town at James City, even though it was not needed. The king was "resolved, as soon as storehouses and conveniences can be provided, to prohibit ships trading [in Virginia] to load or unload but at certain fixed places." Thus the contest between city-minded England and rural Virginia continued.

But no matter how good its harbors, Virginia needed roads. Planters first cut rolling roads so that tobacco hogsheads could be pushed to docks. They also wanted to go by horse to church and to county courts, which made county laws and heard law suits. The Assembly therefore ordered in 1632 that "highways shall be laid out in such convenient places as are requisite according as the Governor and Council or the commissions for the monthly courts shall appoint, or according as the parishioners of every parish shall agree."

Despite this, roads grew slowly. The few that did were narrow, usually over Indian trails, and unsuited to vehicles. In 1657 the Assembly tried again, ordering "that

Early Jamestown houses were one-room cottages. This conjectural painting by Sidney King shows the thatched roof and wide-bottomed chimney, which cooked food and heated the house. *National Park Service*

surveyors of highways and maintenance for bridges be yearly kept and appointed in each county court," and "that all general ways from county to county and all churchways [are] to be laid out and cleared yearly . . ." Even so, roads were few before 1700.

By 1640 brick houses were built at Jamestown. Row houses copied those of English towns and gave residents a feeling of security against Indians. *Painting by Sidney King photographed by Thomas L. Williams*

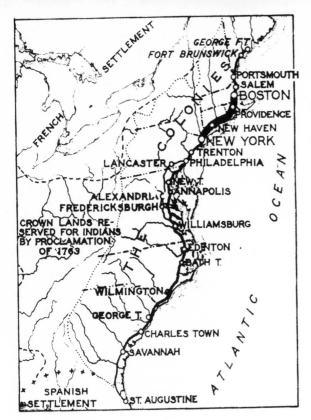

By the year 1763, a muddy "post road" connected Virginia with the other colonies and with Spanish-held Florida. It took four weeks for a letter to move from Williamsburg to Boston. *U.S. Bureau of Public Roads*

A few stage wagons had begun to carry mail and passengers in Virginia and nearby colonies when the Revolution came. At left is a post house. From *Travels Through the States of North America.* (*London, 1799*)

Most goods moved by water, and humans by horse. The Swiss traveller Francis Louis Michel noted that everyone rode horseback. "Going to church means at some places a trip of more than thirty miles," he observed, "but . . . it is not a great hardship because people are well-mounted . . . Horses, which are hardly used for anything else but riding, are half deers. They run always in a fast gallop."

It was 1693 before the colony provided post riders. Soon, beginning in 1717, a post-rider departed Williamsburg every two weeks for Philadelphia, where he made connection with New York and beyond. It required more than a month for a letter from Virginia to reach Boston, while service to the south was even slower. The rider to Charleston, South Carolina, departed only when a bagfull had accumulated. The Williamsburg office of William Parks' *Virginia Gazette* was the center of Virginia's postal service. To it, post riders brought news for the *Gazette*'s columns from other weekly papers and by incoming ships from abroad.

As the mails grew heavier, stage coaches were required. In 1738 Postmaster General Spotswood granted to William Parks a com-

Few wagons could be used in early Virginia for lack of roads. This is a late seventeenth century English vehicle. From Loggan's *Oxonia Illustrata*. *The British Museum*

mission to "carry on a stage" across Burwell's Ferry to Hog Island on the James River, and thence through Nansemond Courthouse and Norfolk to North Carolina's capital at Edenton. To build roads that that stage coaches required, turnpike companies were chartered. The first in the United States was the Fairfax and Loudoun Turnpike Road Company, in 1795.

Taverns offered bed and board to travellers from Governor Yeardley's day onward. Jamestown had public houses during most of its ninety-two years as capital. Local centers of gaiety and gossip were the Raleigh Tavern in Williamsburg, the Borough in Norfolk, the Rose and Crown in Hampton, the Rising Sun in Fredericksburg, and Gadsby's in Alexandria. Simpler fare than these taverns' was offered by ordinaries, like Sewell's near Gloucester Point or Dragon Run Ordinary in upper Gloucester. "Ordinary" denoted that visitors ate whatever was ordinarily served at the host's table.

The uncouth simplicity of early inns was satirized by Ebenezer Cook in his poem, "The Sot-Weed Factor; or a Voyage to Maryland," published in 1708:

Soon after hearty Entertainment
Of Drink and Victuals without Payment;
For Planters Tables, you must know,
Are free for all that come and go.

While Pon and Milk, with Mush well stoar'd,
In Wooden Dishes grac'd the Board;
With homine and Syder-pap
(Which scarce a hungry dog would lap)

Well stuff'd with Fat from Bacon Fry'd,
Or with Mollossus dulcify'd.
Then out our Landlord pulls a Pouch
As greasy as the Leather Couch

On which he sat, and straight begun
To load with Weed his Indian Gun ...
His Pipe smoak'd out, with aweful Grace,
With aspect grave and solemn pace,

The reverend Sire walks to a Chest ...
From thence he lugs a Cag of Rum
. . . .
Not yet from Plagues exempted quite,
The Curst Muskitoes did me bite;
Till rising Morn and blushing Day
Drove both my Fears and Ills away; ...

A tavern or ordinary was usually found near a courthouse for accommodation of the justices of the peace and lawyers at court time. After Williamsburg became

Houses, Roads, Ferries, and Inns [77]

Ferries transported colonists across creeks and rivers. Most were rowed, but some were moved by rope or sail. Rates were fixed by county courts for transporting people, live-stock, and vehicles. Engraving from Benson J. Lossing's *The Hudson. The Mariners Museum*

Virginia's capital, several inns catered to officials and their families attracted by the annual Public Times. Washington, Jefferson, and Patrick Henry were patrons of Anthony Hay's Raleigh, of Mrs. Vobe's King's Arms, or of Mrs. Campbell's Coffee House. Stabling and servants' quarters were provided by each.

Minimum rates for taverns were set by counties. The Bath County court in 1791 established a price of 21¢ for dinner, 12½¢ for "cold supper," 6¢ for lodging, 8¢ for a quart of cider, and 4¢ for a gallon of corn whiskey.

Ferry boats were numerous, for creeks and rivers were Virginia's streets; what gondolas were to Venice, ferries were to the Old Dominion. Fifty-one of these were operating in the colony by 1700. The James and York Rivers each had 17, while the Rappahannock had nine, and the Potomac,

the Mattaponi, the Pamunkey, and Hampton Roads had two each. The earliest were free, but eventually a table of authorized fares was set by the colony. As carriages increased, ferry-keepers were admonished to provide "convenient boats for the transportation of coaches, carts, and wagons" and "other wheel-carriages."

Later travelers often cursed ferries, but the leisurely colonials seem to have enjoyed them. Lord Adam Gordon, visiting Virginia in 1755, wrote that "the ferries, which would retard in another country, rather accelerate." Ferrymen, he said, "assist . . . all strangers with their equipages in so easy and kind a manner, as must deeply touch a person of any feeling."

Most ferries were flat-bottomed scows or barges, up to 30 feet, with sloped ends and upright sides to keep horses from going overboard. Even so, nervous steeds might break a leg getting in or out. The ferryman poled or rowed; if the passage were narrow he might pull across by rope. On the broad waters of Hampton Roads or Chesapeake Bay a "passage boat" or "packet sloop" was used, propelled by sail. Such vessels sailed from Hampton to Sewell's Point and to Northampton, as well as from Queen Mary's Port at Williamsburg to Clay Bank on the York.

By the end of the colonial period, two principals roads had been cut through Virginia. The first, paralleling the coast, had been hacked by the tidewatermen to connect them with the Carolinas and Maryland. This route ran from Edenton, North Carolina, along the Dismal Swamp to Norfolk, thence across Hampton Roads to Hampton, and northward through Yorktown, Williamsburg, Bowling Green, Fredericksburg, Falmouth, Alexandria, Georgetown, and to Baltimore.

The second trail was blazed by German and Scotch-Irish settlers who pushed southward in Virginia from Philadelphia after 1730. This was the Great Philadelphia Wagon Road, also called the Wilderness Road. It ran from Martinsburg (now West Virginia) southward through Winchester, Harrisonburg, Staunton, Lexington, Salem, Christiansburg, Wytheville, and Marion.

The sluice-gate through which this road emptied into the west was Cumberland Gap, discovered in 1774 at the present western tip of Virginia. Explorers like Abraham Wood, William Byrd I, and Daniel Boone had traversed the area, but until the Revolution it remained too hazardous to attract many settlers. After victory was won in 1781, Cumberland Gap led thousands of pioneers into the territory which became Kentucky and West Virginia.

The James and Rappahannock were the chief links between eastern and western Vir-

Michie Tavern was frequented by upland travellers for many years after 1784. Built 20 miles northwest of Charlottesville on the road from Richmond westward to the Valley of Virginia, the tavern was moved in 1927 and re-located near Monticello.

The oldest brick house in America was built by Adam Thoroughgood in Princess Anne County near Norfolk in 1634. *Virginia Chamber of Commerce*

ginia. Each penetrated the Piedmont almost as far west as the Blue Ridge. Boats could traverse the James from Westham, five miles above Richmond, for about 125 miles upriver to Lynchburg. From there, it was only a short distance to the Wilderness Road. On the Rappahannock, many passengers were landed at Falmouth for the brief trip to the Valley. The Potomac tobacco ports of Dumfries and Alexandria welcomed many Scottish emigrants to America.

Newly arrived settlers built houses much like those they had left in Europe, though changes in Europe's fashions were always several decades late taking hold in Virginia. For the first half-century, Englishmen in Tidewater built stolid medieval houses like those of rural England. Late in the century, they built larger houses with more windows in what has been called the Transitional style. Not until after 1710 — the beginning of Virginia's greatest prosperity — did plan-

tation building achieve its golden age. This was the age of Georgian architecture.

Few medieval buildings survive in Virginia: time and war have destroyed all but a few in the first eight counties. All are characterized by massive walls of multilayered brick, steep roofs, and narrow casement windows. Usually they show Dutch, Flemish, or German influence. Adam Thoroughgood built such a house about 1634 in Princess Anne County. Arthur Allen built Bacon's Castle in the medieval criss-cross style across the James from Jamestown in 1655, and Parke Poindexter erected the similar Christ's Cross in New Kent about 1685. The brick church at Jamestown in 1639 was medieval, as was St. Luke's Church in Isle of Wight, reared after 1632.

Of the same style was Governor Berkeley's huge Green Spring manor, near Jamestown, begun about 1645 and demolished 150 years later. Lady Berkeley called it "the only tolerable place for a governor in all America."

One of the few medieval houses remaining in Virginia is Bacon's Castle, built in Surry County across the James River from Jamestown about 1655. *Virginia Chamber of Commerce*

Stratford Hall in Westmoreland County is unique in form in America. It was built in Transitional style by Thomas Lee in 1725-30. *Virginia Chamber of Commerce*

Transitional structures had similar vertical lines, but they were graced by larger windows, more concern for comfort, and better proportions. From about 1680 onward, houses were often of brick and two rooms deep. The typical arrangement was a wide central staircase hall with two rooms on either side. The "knock-head" gabled or gambrel roof was punctured by dormer windows to cross-ventilate the bedrooms — one for husband and wife and the other for the children. Privacy was a rare luxury in those simple times.

One feature of Transitional buildings was the sash window or guillotine window, which began to replace the casement window in Virginia about 1680. The College of William and Mary, built 1695-97, had them. So did the Capitol, for which sash windows were specified in 1699, and the Governor's Palace, built in 1707-10. The largest house in this period was Stratford Hall, built by Thomas Lee in Westmoreland County in 1725-30. Brick for these were made in Virginia, while stone and glass had to be brought from England, with endless delay and expense.

Plantation life produced its handsomest building in the Georgian age, named for the four Georges whose reigns began in 1714. It was a time of rapid changes. The Capitol at Williamsburg set a new tone. Virginia "may be said to be altered and improved in wealth" since 1710 "more than in all the scores of years before that," observed Hugh Jones. The Negro population trebled between 1700 and 1730. Taking the Governor's Palace as their model, planters surrounded their mansions with servants' quarters, shops, storehouses, stables, and barns. On a small scale, they resembled medieval manor houses, surrounded by serfs.

The improved style of living excited Robert Beverley's admiration. "The private buildings are also in [Governor Spotswood's] time very much improved, several gentlemen there having built themselves large brick houses of many rooms on a floor;" Beverley wrote, "but they don't covet to make them lofty, having extent of ground to build upon. They love to have large rooms, that they may be cool in summer. Of late they have made their stories much higher than formerly, and their windows

Houses, Roads, Ferries, and Inns [81]

The Governor's Palace, built in Williamsburg in 1707-10, set the taste for Georgian plantation houses in Virginia. *Photo by Stephen Toth for Colonial Williamsburg*

larger, and sashed with crystal glass, adorning their apartments with rich furniture. All their drudgeries of cookery, washing, dairies, etc., are performed in offices apart from the dwelling houses, which by this means are kept more cool and sweet."

Large plantations made their own nails, hogshead, cloth, candles, soap, brick, and ironwork. Slaves cut trees, dressed lumber, and from it made shingles, clapboard, wagons, farm implements, and even furniture. Meat was salted and hung in smokehouses, and foods were stored in icehouses and subterranean cold cellars. Many houses, like Captain Samuel Wentworth's Smithfield townhouse, built in 1752, had an English basement below ground where food was prepared and eaten. Main and bedroom floors were above it.

How did early Virginians achieve such beauty and durability in their houses? The most obvious answer is that they had abundant slave labor to make bricks, cut lumber, and set them in place. For guidance, they had the houses of England's rich merchants and gentry, built with profits of empire.

English house plans were published in manuals and were followed by colonists, who looked to the Mother Country for artistic and intellectual leadership.

Early Virginia had a few "undertakers," as contractors were called, and they were in demand. Such was Henry Cary, who built Williamsburg's Capitol and Palace, and David Minitree, who built Carter's Grove. However, many planters were self-taught builders. Thomas Jefferson was one, popularizing at Monticello the Palladian style of the Italian Renaissance.

Brick was used in Tidewater because it resisted fire; tidal area settlers did not have the Valley's limestone and fieldstone. However, Tidewater's clay could be burned to produce brick of handsome color and durability. By firing with hickory, brick was produced whose butt-ends had a purplish hue. By alternating dark headers with light stringers, Old World patterns known as English and Flemish bond were reproduced. Flemish bond and white clapboard were the trademark of Tidewater buildings.

The charm of Georgian buildings lay in generous proportions, interesting finish, and

Log cabins were built by settlers along Virginia's northern frontier about 1700. This reconstructed servant's house is at Stratford Hall. *Photo by LeRoy Anderson*

handsome details. Typical of English architecture of that day, their beauty was one of refined simplicity. Ceilings were high, doors wide, and windows full. Brickwork was carefully patterned and of rich texture. Cornices were sumptuous, and large central halls and rooms afforded space and ventilation. The chief drawback of these houses was that dormered bedrooms were insufferably hot when summer's sun beat down upon their gable roofs. Another shortcoming was their paucity of porches. Summer houses, called gazebos or belvederes, were a poor substitute.

Such were the homes of the well-to-do, stoutly contrived to perpetuate Virginia dynasties. But there were many simpler structures which were built much as the first Jamestown houses had been. Often the outbuildings of a plantation were made of rough-sawn clapboard or vertical siding. Building methods changed little, and almost any man could follow them. The wattle-and-daub and cruck buildings of early Jamestown were slowly superseded by the timber-framed house, which became the usual building technique. Buildings were reared of timbers which had been de-barked with an adz and joined with tongue-and-groove and with wooden pegs, called trunnels, or tree rails. Roofs were covered with thatch or bark or with Dutch-type pantiles. By 1640 split cedar "shake" shingles were becoming the most popular roofing.

Log cabins were unknown in early Virginia, as in England. However, they were introduced in the northern colonies by early Swedish and German settlers and by 1700 were familiar on the Virginia frontier.

Most of Virginia's early crafts have disappeared, taking with them picturesque buildings that seem more European than American: windmills, water mills, taverns, coffee houses, glebes, brewhouses, iron furnaces, tanneries, guard houses, blockhouses, and silk factories.

But the spacious nature of eighteenth-century life is still visible in such plantations as Mount Vernon, Monticello and Gunston Hall. Each shows that century's admiration for classic balance. A jealous French official wrote in the seventeenth century "that most rich Englishmen have residences" in Virginia and that "1,000 English ships go there yearly." In a family-centered society, planters strove to create beautiful homes where their scions could live in comfort.

The cost of paint caused most buildings to be left unpainted, or simply to be whitewashed. White, gray, and tan were favorite house colors. Interiors were decorated by 18th-century builders in hues which picked up the colors of damask curtains and Turkey carpets. Besides exalting beauty of form, the 18th century also appreciated beauty of color.

What was true of houses was true of their furnishings. In 169 brief years, pioneer Virginia had become a settled society which enjoyed many luxuries. Crude homemade benches made way for heavy Jacobean and then for graceful Chippendale chairs. Rough trestles were succeeded by gate-leg and banquet-end tables of mahogany. Brick or rush-covered floors were replaced by pine and then covered by Turkey carpets. The fitful light of oil-soaked rushes was superseded by candle chandeliers and sconces.

Although they lacked London's amusements, Virginia planters by the time of the Revolution lived the most luxurious lives of any of His Majesty's subjects outside the British Isles.

The westward movement of the Chesapeake Society began in the late seventeenth century as venturesome people passed beyond the fall line onto the Piedmont plateau, year by year clearing lands for tobacco culture, merging the new with the old, and organizing local governments authorized by the assemblies. Between 1732 and the outbreak of the Revolution, Virginia established twenty-one new counties east of the Blue Ridge, of which fifteen, together with five new Valley counties, comprised the Old Dominion's portion of the Back Country.

Carl Bridenbaugh, in *Myths and Realities,
Societies of the Colonial South*, 1952

The Western Frontier

In August, 1716, Governor Alexander Spotswood and a cavalcade of 63 horsemen rode from Williamsburg to admire the colony's new ironworks at Germanna, near Fredericksburg. Then, pushing west over plunging hills, they scaled the Blue Ridge Mountains and gazed lustfully at the Valley of Virginia below. So rich and verdant were the Shenandoah River shores that they called it "the Euphrates." Thus, 109 years after England entered Virginia, she prepared to move against the Indians who held the three mountain ranges — Blue Ridge, Shenandoah, and Alleghany — which cut lowland Virginia from its inland empire.

Spotswood's horsemen, dubbed "Knights of the Golden Horseshoe," were pioneers of a procession which swept into the Valley from the 1720s and until after the Revolution. Though not the first Europeans to see the Shenandoah, their journey kindled an Arthurian legend which added to the Old Dominion's romance. A century and a half later, "the Virginians of the Valley" were hymned as

*The knightliest of the knightly race
    Who, since the days of old,
Have kept the lamp of chivalry
    Alight in hearts of gold;
The kindliest of the kindly band,
    Who, rarely hating ease,
Yet rode with Spotswood round the land,
    And Raleigh round the seas.*

Virginians pressed westward to settle the Northwest Territory which the Virginia Company of London claimed in its 1609 charter from King James I. Seven states and parts of others were carved from this after 1789. *From teachers' map chart, Indians of Virginia, published by Hearne Brothers, Detroit, Mich.*

But Spotswood's was no empty gesture. In asserting Virginia's claim to the west, he was heading off French colonization of Virginia from the Ohio River.

The beautiful but savage Valley challenged easterners just as the Wild West did in the nineteenth century. Although Virginia shared the Back Country with other colonies, she claimed the lion's share because Virginia's 1609 charter defined her boundaries as "from sea to sea." For this reason, the Old Dominion fought off all claimants to the Northwest Territory until she reluctantly ceded it to the Union in 1784, to form Ohio, Illinois, Indiana, Michigan, Wisconsin, and part of Minnesota.

Western Virginia was as different from eastern as a log cabin from a plantation. Its hills were pocked with limestone. Its first settlers were rugged homesteaders who cared nothing for the niceties of Tidewater Englishmen. Even its Indians were more savage. Unlike the lowland Powhatans, the Shawnees and Cherokees roamed the highlands and burnt thousands of acres each fall to attract buffalo herds. Time and again they swooped down on mountain cabins to scalp and burn, leaving survivors crazed with grief.

Germans and Swiss followed Spotswood into the Valley. They came first in 1726, spurred by the Governor's grant of large tracts to promoters like William Beverley of Essex County, who guaranteed to fill them with settlers. The first were led by Jacob Stover in 1726 to the Shenandoah River — Spotswood's "Euphrates." A second colony in 1730 settled near Luray, led by Adam Miller, or Muller. The trickle became a stream in 1732 when Joist Hite led Alsatian settlers south from Pennsylvania to settle on the 40,000 acres granted by the Governor to John and Isaac Van Meter of Pennsylvania. Soon Northern Virginia was dotted with their clearings.

It was a long trek south from Philadelphia, but land at 10 or 20 shillings an acre was worth the journey. Farming was the Germans' passion — farming and the Bible. They had farmed along the Rhine in Alsace-Lorraine until their Protestantism offended Louis XIV's Catholic Majesty in 1688-93, and his troops laid waste their farms. Then, lured by Penn's toleration, they had braved the Atlantic and settled in Pennsylvania's York and Lancaster Counties. When more Germans came, they learned of Virginia's cheap lands and started south.

The emigrants followed The Great Philadelphia Wagon Road, or Wilderness Road. From Philadelphia, it ran westward to Lancaster County, across the Susquehanna River to York and Gettysburg, and thence to Maryland and across the Potomac into Shenandoah Valley. Once in Virginia, it followed the Indian warrior's trail that traversed the Valley southward. By the treaty of Lancaster in 1744, the Indians agreed to move westward and relinquish the Valley route. The villages of Martinsburg, Winchester, Stephensburg, Strasburg, Woodstock, and Staunton soon grew along the road.

On their *Map of the Most settled Parts of Virginia*, Peter Jefferson and Joshua Fry labelled this route "The Great Wagon Road from the Yadkin River through Virginia to Philadelphia distant 435 miles." By means of

Many eastern Virginia explorers and traders blazed trails into the Appalachian region. From *Virginia: History, Government, Geography*, by Francis Butler Simkins and Spotswood Hunnicutt, published by Charles Scribner's Sons.

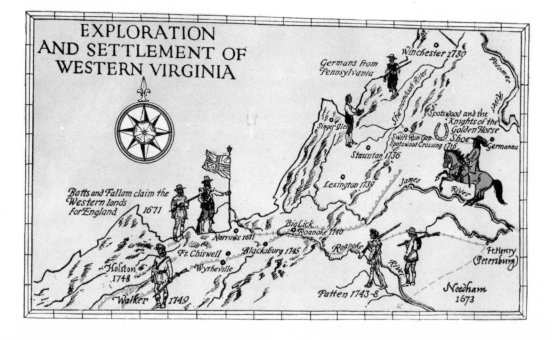

Most of the settlers of western Virginia followed the trail developed after 1700 over the Indian Warriors Path. Called first the Wilderness Road and then the Great Philadelphia Wagon Road, it linked upland Virginia and the Carolinas with Maryland and Pennsylvania. *Diorama by Virginia Department of Highways*

this artery the Scotch-Irish spread through the back-country from Pennsylvania southward to Georgia, from 1717 to 1775.

The Germanic pioneers were plain-spoken peasants of the same stock as the Pennsylvania Dutch. They were chiefly Lutherans, but some were communicants of the Reformed Church, and others were Dunkers (Church of the Brethren), Mennonites, and Amish. They chose good limestone lands and laid out farms around their churches, for God was the center of their lives. Their oldest surviving chapel is Hebron Evangelical Lutheran in Madison County, built in 1740 by descendants of the Germanna vintners and iron miners.

The Germans and Swiss spread over a dozen counties, beginning in Clarke, Frederick, and Jefferson, the latter now in West Virginia. They were self-sufficient peasants,

trading and marrying within their own communities. The Lutherans, worldliest of the lot, played a hesitant part in county government, after they learned English. They were the first to accept acquisitive American habits and to sell wheat, corn, hemp, and cattle. Their first cabins were hewn of logs, which were then adzed and pegged to fit tightly. As they prospered, they built Pennsylvania-type houses of fieldstone, limestone, or brick. Houses and barns were painted dark red, often with hex signs to ward off evil. For refuge against Indians, they dug vaulted cellars arched with stone. Even so, many were cruelly murdered.

The Germans were businesslike even in church. At Upper Peaked Mountain church in Rockingham County in 1767, Lutheran members paid fees to support their parson and schoolmaster: 2 shillings 6 pence for baptism, 5 shillings for confirmation, and a like amount for each holy communion and burial in the churchyard.

Plainness was a principle of the Brethren and Mennonites. Men shaved their heads and substituted wigs or white caps. Breeches were short, fastened at the knee, and worn with long stockings. Their low and broad-brimmed hats were characteristics of pietistic Protestants. Women wore simple shifts and tight calico caps. They joined men in gathering harvests and in driving ox-drawn plows or mowers.

The thrift of the hausfrau was proverbial. She kept a spotless house and cooked good food: yeastbread, sauerkraut, sausage, scrapple, pig's knuckles, apple butter, and other German specialties. Houses were provided with homemade furniture, often painted with Bible verses, flowers, and birds. Dancing and other revels were discouraged.

The Germans brought to the valley a knowledge of fertilizers and crop rotation. Their cooperative habits of building houses and barns, planting, and harvesting, pro-

This fort house was built in 1785 in Wise County, on the Kentucky border, and is still standing. Occupants could defend themselves against Indians by using gun ports on each side. An attic is reached by trap door. *Photo by L. F. Addington*

duced early results. They were also tanners, tinsmiths, wagonmakers, and cabinetmakers. A few were gunsmiths and introduced from Pennsylvania the Jaeger (hunter) rifle, or squirrel gun, which became the standby of

From Pennsylvania, many Scotch-Irish and German emigrants came into Virginia beginning about 1730 by this wagon road from Philadelphia. *The Mariners Museum*

Valley pioneers. Henry Spitzer in New Market, Adam Haymaker in Winchester, the Sheetz family near Luray, and other German gunsmiths made these long weapons, later called Kentucky rifles.

Said Great Britain's General William H. Howe after the Revolution: "The terrible guns of the rebels, perfected with little knowledge of ballistics, made the American rifle the greatest factor in the Revolution when wielded by the sharpshooting, keen-eyed men of the colonies."

Other Germanic skills were choral singing and printing. Lutherans rejoiced in the great hymns of Martin Luther; "A Mighty Fortress" typifies their faith:

A mighty fortress is our God, a bulwark
*   Never failing,*
Our helper He amid the flood of mortal
*   Ills prevailing:*
For still our ancient foe doth seek
*   To work us woe;*
His craft and power are great, and armed
*   With cruel hate,*
On earth is not his equal.

A school of Germanic music grew up at Singer's Glen, near Harrisonburg, run by Joseph Funk. A few years later, Solomon Henkel set up the first Valley press at New Market, printing Lutheran tracts and "shaped note" hymnals. The Henkels, it has been said, "issued more truly Lutheran theological works in an English dress than any similar institution in the world."

The Germanic settlers kept touch with their northern kinsmen; Philadelphia was their cultural capital. In 1722, Peter Muhlenberg, a Pennsylvanian, was ordained by the Anglican church and later became the Lutheran pastor at Woodstock, in Shenandoah County. At the end of one sermon in 1776, he cast off his clerical gown to reveal his uniform. "I am a clergyman, it is true," he said, "but I am a member of society as well as the poorest layman and my liberty is as dear to me as to any man. Shall I then sit still and enjoy myself at home when the best blood of the continent is spilling? Heaven forbid it!" The towering German rose to the rank of general by the time of the battle of Yorktown. Few Germans, however, figured so largely in Virginia history.

One of the earliest Germanic pioneers was John Peter Salling, who settled in the 1730s in present Rockbridge County. He and Thomas Morlin, an itinerant peddler, penetrated Shenandoah Valley to the Roanoke River, where Salling was captured by the Cherokees. He gave a hair-raising account on his return: he had been taken by

The Reverend Peter Muhlenberg was pastor of a Lutheran congregation at Woodstock in 1776, when the Revolution came. He became a general in the colonial army. *Virginia State Library*

Isaac Hollingsworth replaced his log house with Abram's Delight, oldest house in Winchester. His father, Abraham Hollingsworth, was an early settler here. *Winchester-Frederick County Chamber of Commerce*

his captors to the Tennessee territory and then to the salt licks of Kentucky, where he was captured anew by Illinois Indians and adopted by a tribe at Kaskaskia. He then had accompanied the Illinois south to the Gulf of Mexico, where he was purchased by Spanish explorers for three strands of beads and a calumet. According to his account, he made his way to Quebec and back again to Virginia.

Close upon the Germans came the Scotch-Irish. Emboldened by union with England in 1707 and Virginia's Toleration Act of 1699, they entered Virginia in force. Driven from their Ulster homeland by drought in 1717, they found the opportunity in America which England had denied them at home. Their Great Migration continued until the American Revolution. By 1729, both England's Parliament and Americans were worried by their vast influx. "The common fear is that if they thus continue to come," protested the colonial secretary of Pennsylvania, "they will make

themselves proprietors of the Province. It is strange that they thus crowd where they are not wanted."

From Pennsylvania they came south in hordes. Whole families bumped over the Philadelphia road in big-wheeled Conestoga wagons, trailing cattle and dogs. Nearly all were Presbyterians, once employed in the Irish linen and wool trades. Half were so poor that they indentured themselves to obtain passage.

By-passing the Germans, the Scotch-Irish settled in numbers in Augusta, Rockbridge, Highland, Bath, and southward. Unversed in farming, they frequently chose rocky, hardscrabble land and later moved; the Scotch-Irish seldom retained the first site they chose. Apple and peach trees were planted early, for cider and brandy were household necessities. By 1730 they established Winchester, and six years later Staunton. Then came Lexington, Fincastle, Big Lick (Roanoke), and Draper's Meadows (Blacksburg). Augusta and Rockbridge became the most Scotch-Irish counties in America. Other Ulstermen continued on to the Carolinas and the western territories.

The Scots farmed against heavy odds. One song had it:

> Tazewell County and Tazewell Town
> Lord have mercy and do look down
> Poor and rocky and hilly, too
> Lord have mercy, what will these
>   poor people do?

Bold and feisty, the Scotch-Irish were a good match for the murderous Shawnees. Unlike the Germans, they made no effort to placate them. Instead, a young Augusta County Scotsman, named Andrew Lewis raised a company of militia in 1756 and went to war against them.

Virginia's border ran with blood for the next eighteen years. This French and Indian War was part of a larger European conflagration, the Seven Years War, by which England won Canada and France lost all her American colonies. Lewis' Virginians and Cherokee scouts first forced the Shawnees westward from the Ohio River. When the Indians rose up again in 1774, Lewis led two regiments of militia to defeat them at Point Pleasant, at the mouth of the Kanawha River in the present West Virginia.

Lewis' younger brother, Charles, served with him in the Indian wars and was killed in the battle of Point Pleasant. He was celebrated by this dirge, reminiscent of a Highland eulogy:

> Farewell, Colonel Lewis, till pity's
>   Sweet fountains
> Are dried in the hearts of the fair
>   And the brave.
> Virginia shall weep for her chief
>   Of the mountains
> And mourn for the heroes who sleep
>   By his grave.

Andrew Lewis of Augusta County led Scotch-Irish militiamen in the French and Indian War and the Revolution. *Kegley's Virginia Frontier*

The Lewises were typical of the Scotch-Irishmen. Long resistance to England had hardened them. Disdaining suave English manners, they were quick-tempered, reckless, and impetuous. Though puritanical in dress and religion, they liked liquor and argument. "A Scotch-Irishman" it was said, "keeps the commandments of God — and everything else he gets his hands on." A typical Presbyterian elder prayed to be guided aright, for, he conceded, "Thou knowest, Lord, that I am unco' hard to turn."

Scotch-Irishmen resembled New England Puritans in the austerity of their faith. In their bitter fight with Roman Catholicism in the old country, these followers of John Knox had discarded all "Popery." They rejected liturgy not sanctioned by the New Testament. Their early Valley churches had no pulpit, and even John Knox's Book of Common Order was thought too formalistic. Prayers lasted forty-five minutes, the congregation standing. Then the preacher held forth two hours while his flock squirmed. No musical instruments were permitted, and even hymn- and psalm-singing were too "Romish" for a few congregations. After recess for dinner on the grounds, another three-hour service began.

Like the Germans, the Scotch-Irish were centered in their church. The Session stood in judgment of moral offenses: desecration of the sabbath, "promiscuous dancing," swearing, fighting, and the like. The guilty could be ousted from church unless he confessed or repented, sometimes before the whole flock. Diversions were simple and vigorous: wrestling or racing or markmanship for men, quilting parties for the women. It was a man's world — or a saint's.

The first influential Scotch-Irishman in Virginia was James Patton, an early land promoter. Born in Ulster and "bred to the sea," he became a shipowner and crossed the Atlantic a dozen times to bring Scotch-Irish emigrants to Rappahannock River ports. Before he was killed by the Shawnees in 1755 in the Massacre of Draper's Meadows, his daughter Margaret had married John Buchanan. Patton and Buchanan promoted Scotch-Irish settlement in a huge area which became Botetourt County, including the territory of Kentucky. Buchanan explored the Southwest as far west as Dunker's Bottom, the present site of Radford.

Another Scotch-Irish family were the Prestons, who stemmed from John Preston of Ulster and his wife, Elizabeth, sister of James Patton. Settling in Augusta, they founded a dynasty rivalling Tidewater's. Their daughter married the Rev. John Brown, who taught at Augusta Academy at Timber Ridge, near Lexington, and fathered an early Kentucky governor. Their son, William Preston, an Indian fighter with Andrew Lewis, wrote Brown in 1763: "I have built a little fort in which are 87 per-

Belle Grove was built in Frederick County about 1787 by Major Isaac Hite, Jr., grandson of a pioneer German settler. His limestone blocks were quarried nearby. *Photo by Jack Boucher, Library of Congress*

Along upland streams in western Virginia, Scotch-Irish settlers built mills to grind wheat and corn. This was the McDonald Mill near Lexington. Sketch by Elizabeth Waller Wilkins in *Kegley's Virginia Frontier*.

sons, 20 of whom bear arms. We are in a pretty good position for defense, and, with the aid of God, are determined to make a stand."

Contentious by nature, the Scotch-Irish plunged into politics and Indian fighting. They fought well and willingly, cursing Tidewater all the while for using them as mercenaries to protect planters' interests. Anti-monarchists to the core, they never wavered in loyalty to Virginia, from generals like Winchester's Daniel Morgan — hero of Saratoga — and Augusta's William Campbell — victor in the battle of King's Mountain — down to buckskinned privates. King George III sneered that the Revolution was "a Presbyterian war."

But the full impact of Virginia's "Macocracy," as Charles Lee derided it, was felt only after the Revolution. It showed itself in simple dress, the decline of "aristocratic" manners, (the broad "a," the periwig, and the tricorn hat), disestablishment of the English church, an increase in evangelistic sects, and the Jeffersonian simplicity which came to prevail. It still makes itself heard in Scottish proverbs and the flat Scottish speech of the Appalachians. The Scotch-Irish said "gude" for good, "kirk" for church, "verra" for very, and "oot" for out; some descendants still do.

These embattled Covenanters first built fortress-houses against the Indians. Squared logs chinked with clay nogging were their first materials. Their earliest surviving churches at Fort Defiance, built in 1747-49, and Timber Ridge, built in 1755, were of limestone. After the Revolution they reared handsome brick buildings in such towns as Fincastle and Staunton. However, Valley settlers seldom built as beautifully as the lowland English, who were closer to the Greek and Roman influence of the Renaissance.

This house, built about 1770 at the Valley cross-road which became Lexington, was reportedly the house of Andrew Reid, first clerk of Rockbridge County. *Courtesy of Royster Lyle and Rockbridge Historical Society*

A large mill was built at Waterford in Northern Virginia in 1755 by Amos Janney, a Quaker from Pennsylvania. It ground wheat and corn until 1938. *Waterford Foundation, Inc.*

A lowland Virginian, John Sergeant Wise, was struck with the Scotch-Irishmen's severe architecture when he came to Lexington:

The blue limestone streets look hard. The red brick houses, with severe stone trimmings and plain white pillars and finishings, were stiff and formal. The grim portals of the Presbyterian church looked cold as a dog's nose . . .

Dotting the Virginia mountains are still a few early Scotch-Irish cabins and grist mills of squared logs, their crevices crammed with clay, their stone chimneys askew. Some even keep their shingle roofs of white oak or chestnut, rived with mallet and froe. Along a few rapid mountain streams are mill races — now trout streams — dug to deflect a watercourse and turn a mill for

Malcolm Allen built this limestone house in Botetourt County after moving upland from Prince Edward County about 1756. *Kegley's Western Frontier*

Log houses were built by Daniel Boone and other early settlers in western Virginia and the Kentucky territory. *Voyage dans L'Amerique, by Collot (Paris, 1826)*

grinding wheat and corn. Against the mountains' blue haze, these gnarled ruins stagger under cascades of trumpet vine and Virginia creeper.

Andrew Lewis' victory at Point Pleasant in 1774 drove the Shawnees west of the Ohio River and opened up Virginia's territory across the Appalachians. Pioneers now pushed through the mountains to build forts at Harrodsburg, Boonesborough, and Louisville. But this vast region beyond the mountains — called "The Dark and Bloody Ground" — could be reached by horse only after Daniel Boone in 1774 cut a trail through the Cumberland mountains near the North Carolina border, following the route which Dr. Thomas Walker had found in 1750.

Cumberland Gap opened the gates to the west. A spur was hastily built from the Great Philadelphia Wagon Road into eastern

Kentucky, and in 1776 Kentucky became Virginia's westernmost county, with a log courthouse at Fincastle for a county seat. The 12,000 pioneers in Kentucky in 1783 had risen to nearly 80,000 in 1792 when that territory entered the union.

Though the Scotch-Irish led the western thrust, eastern Virginians were also part of it. Thomas Walker, the Fredericksburg physician who became a pioneer in Albemarle, led five explorers into Kentucky to stake out the claim of the Loyal Land Company in 1750. Walker built the first cabin west of the Alleghanies. Christopher Gist explored northwest Virginia from the Potomac the same year, penetrating the Ohio territory to the shores of Lake Erie. In 1756 Colonel John Chiswell of Hanover discovered lead deposits near the present Wytheville and established a mine with a fort to protect it from Indians. Fort Chiswell attracted settlers to Southwest Virginia, and its mines provided bullets for Continental troops in the Revolution.

Joshua Fry and Peter Jefferson mapped the frontier in 1750 and established the Virginia-Carolina boundary. Thus Colonel Jefferson passed to his son Tom his love for the frontier and its people.

Land promoters also advanced the movement. The Fairfax family, heirs to the huge Northern Neck Proprietary, peopled ten mountainous counties through sales of land. From his Greenway Court, near Winchester, the sixth Lord Fairfax sent 17-year-old George Washington in 1749 to survey this tract. As a result of this experience, Washington could lead Virginia militiamen to Fort Duquesne, on the present site of Pitts-

burgh, to warn the French against encroaching on Virginia. After Great Britain defeated France in 1763 and took over French possessions in the New World, Britain forbade colonists to move west of the Alleghanies to avert war with the Indians. But Virginians felt the land was theirs. Many settled there anyway.

The frontiersman lived a dangerous life. Indians called him "Long Knife" and feared his coming. Living beyond the Covenanters' reach, he devoted himself to "fighting, fiddling, and fun." Sometimes he holed up for months in a forest cabin, trapping and buying pelts from the Indians. More often he went in company with other hunters and an Indian guide, with packhorses to carry booty. Like Canadian *coureurs de bois*, trappers came to know the red man's trails. In

An early settler in western Virginia and its Kentucky territory was Daniel Boone, shown protecting his family against Indian attack. *Russell County Public Library*

A promoter of western settlement was the sixth Lord Fairfax, who built his fortress-home, Greenway Court, near Winchester. *Howe's Historical Collections of Virginia*

trade for colored baubles, they received beaver and sable for export to Europe.

The hunter traveled light. Hitting the trail in autumn, when bare trees made movement easier, he wore a wool or deer-skin shirt, breeches, leggings, moccasins, and cap of beaver or otter. He slung his hatchet in his belt and his knife in a sheath from his shot-pouch. For warmth he carried an extra shirt, a blanket, and flints to light camp-fires. Brandy served as medicine, disinfectant, and good cheer. Salt — highly prized — was needed to cure animal skins. For his meat, he kept his rifle with him. The mountains abounded in bear, deer, and wildcats, while buffalo roamed the valleys. Fed, whiskeyed, and settled by his campfire, the frontiersman thought himself the luckiest man in the world. "Wa-a-l-l now," he would exclaim to the stars, as he wiped the brandy from his lips, "Ef I just had the ol' woman and babbies here, I should be fixed!"

The renegade mountaineer, in rebellion against Society, became a familiar frontier type. Near Winchester, a wealthy trader named Isaac Zane, formerly a Quaker, openly kept a mistress. A visitor to western Augusta snorted, "nothing but whores and rogues in this country."

When the government at Williamsburg called up the militia in 1754-60 and in 1775 to defend the frontier against the French and Indians, the western citizen-soldiers rushed to arms looking like the trappers they were.

Compared to the gaudy militia of other colonies, buckskinned Virginians cut a sorry figure, but they could shoot like wizards. Those who lived were rewarded with land grants of fifty to 3,000 acres. Who could ask for more?

Nearly every westerner seemed to hold military rank. Noted a visiting journalist: "There is not a tavern-keeper or stage-owner in all western Virginia, or a great wood chopper, who has not some military title. And anyone who kills a rattlesnake is made a major on the spot."

Virginia's frontier was a preview of the bustling commercial America which the Revolution brought. It had little in common with polite eastern Virginia, which now seemed hopelessly old-fashioned. Eastern Virginians talked and looked alike; but western Virginia pitted settler against land promoter, Tuckahoe against Cohee, German against Ulsterman, Indian against Long Knife, and life itself against sudden death.

However cruel and deadly it proved, the opportunity which the Virginia frontier gave these Europeans was worth fighting for. By the time the Revolution came, they were Americans.

We know, O Lord, we have the Devil and all the gates of hell against us, but if thou, O Lord, be on our side we care not who be against us . . . And seeing by thy motion and work in our hearts we have left our warm nests at home and put our lives into thy hands principally to honor thy name and advance the kingdom of thy Son, Lord, gives us leave to commit our lives into Thy hands . . .

From a prayer by The Rev. William Crashaw, brought to Jamestown as a part of *Laws Divine, Moral, and Martial,* 1611.

Therefore we ask no ecclesiastical establishments for ourselves, neither can we approve of them when granted to others . . . we are induced earnestly to entreat that all laws now in force in this commonwealth which countenance religious domination may be speedily repealed — that all, of every religious sect, may be protected in the full exercise of their several modes of worship and exempted from all taxes for the support of any church whatsoever. . . . This being done, all partial and invidious distinctions will be abolished, to the great honour and interest of the State. . . .

From a memorial by the Presbytery of Hanover to the General Assembly of Virginia, 1776.

The Church and Dissenters

When Virginia was settled, Europe's monarchs believed that the religion of a king should be the religion of his people. The colony established at Jamestown accordingly brought with it a Church of England clergyman and accepted the jurisdiction of the Anglican hierarchy over the faith and morals of their new land.

In authorizing Virginia's settlement, King James I directed that the "word and service of God be preached, planted, and used as well in the said colonies and also as much as might be among the savages bordering them."

For nearly a century, Virginians, living in the purple afterglow of medieval autocracy, obeyed the King's command that only those who accepted the tenets of his church were loyal to His Majesty. Then, as the Enlightenment began to infuse England's colonies, many of her subjects demanded the right to dissent from the established faith. By the year 1740, the Great Awakening began to move Great Britain and her colonies. Driven by resentment against other institutions, this wave at last shattered the establishment of religion in Virginia. In 1779 the Church of England was disestablished by the Virginia Assembly, and official support of it ended.

Jamestown's settlers built a wattle-and-daub church at the center of their triangular fort. The Anglican Church was the established church through the colonial period. This reconstruction is at Jamestown Festival Park. *The Jamestown Foundation*

Men lived and died for their faith in Virginia's first century. Churchgoing played a large part in life. But the secular forces of science began to encourage independence of mind as the Enlightenment spread. By the time of the Revolution, Virginia was a battleground of sects, most of them bent on destroying the monolith of the Established Church.

Three sects chiefly fought for religious freedom in Virginia: Quakers, Presbyterians, and Baptists. (The Methodist Church did not come into being until 1784.) More causative than any of these, however, was the untenable position in which Britain's

oppression placed her colonists reared in the fold of Established Church. By the time of the Revolution, many members found it difficult to accept a faith whose clergy were Loyalists and whose head was King George III.

That church, which Chaplain Robert Hunt first planted at Jamestown, had been born after endless pain. It had evolved as Protestant in spirit but Catholic in form — a compromise between the Romanism and Puritanism which had split Elizabeth's kingdom. Its theology was the accretion of centuries, while its liturgy was the creation of poets and hymnists of the highest order. Its

The Anglican practices of infant baptism and of holy communion were depicted in a broadside titled "The Christian's Jewell," published in England in 1624. *The Guildhall Library, London*

clergy were polished products of Oxford and Cambridge, usually well-born, and forbidden to demean themselves by physical work. They ranked in England's caste system as gentlemen; in Virginia they became part of the planter class.

Anglicanism permitted wide variations in the form of its services. Its clergy were divided by one satirist into "The High-and-Crazy, the Broad-and-Hazy, and the Low-and-Lazy."

Typical of the Anglicans' spirit was the epitaph of William Sherwood, attorney-general of Virginia, who died at Jamestown after 1676. It described him as:

A Great Sinner
Waiting for
A Joyful Resurrection

Unlike Puritans and Presbyterians, Anglicans joyously accepted worldly pleasures. The theme of their worship was the triumph of God over death. They exuded confidence in Christ's power to redeem man's sins and save him from darkness. In liturgy and music, their services exalted the spirit with the vision of an orderly universe, presided over by a merciful God. But their formalism required that worshippers be literate. Only the instructed could offer the prayers and responses or understand the long metaphysical sermons. In eighteenth-century Virginia, many people were unprepared to join in such worship.

Visiting Englishmen complained that the church in Virginia seemed more Presbyterian than Anglican. This was indeed true of its simple, low-church service, but not of its blithe anti-Puritanism. Tidewater Virginians felt no guilt in wearing rich clothes, singing, dancing, horse-racing, cock-fighting, or in the pleasures of the bottle. Their Sunday was not a day of penance but of praise of their Creator, followed by an hour of sociability in the churchyard before a huge plantation dinner.

But the Anglican Church had many members of deep piety. One such was the Reverend Anthony Gavin, who wrote to the Bishop of London in 1738 from Goochland County:

I have three churches, 23 and 24 miles from the Glebe [the parsonage lands], in which I officiate every Sunday; and besides these three I have seven places of service up in the mountains, where the clerks read prayers, four clerks in the seven places. I go twice a year to preach at twelve places which I reckon better than 400 miles backwards and forwards, and ford 19 times the North and South Rivers. In my first journey I baptized, white people, 229; blacks, 172; Quakers, 15; and Baptists, 2.

For almost a century, Church of England bishops largely ignored Virginia's problems. It made little effort to win converts, and it had no machinery for missions. Not until William and Mary came to the throne in 1688 did the Anglican hierarchy awake to Virginia's need for clergymen and schools, which were then a churchly function. To this task, the Bishop of London in 1689 named the Reverend James Blair as his commissary, or deputy, to organize the clergy and strengthen the church in Virginia.

Blair arrived at a crucial moment. Virginia's tobacco growers were becoming a plutocracy based on slaves and vast acreage of land. Small farmers, unable to compete, were going west or going wanting. Yeomen and Negro slaves got little help from the church. Their children grew up with no formal education.

The Orthodox true Minister,

the Seducer and false Prophet.

Dissent against the Established Church was common in seventeenth century England. An illustration from *A Glasse for the Times* in 1648 contrasted the teachings of "The Orthodox true Minister" with those of "the Seducer and false Prophet." *The British Museum*

Vestries refused to guarantee tenure to ministers, who were accordingly reluctant to move to Virginia. Local vestries exercised church controls and placed preachers at their mercy. The church which evolved was lax and irregular in its governance. Weddings and funerals were often held at planters' homes for the family's convenience rather than in church. Often the rite of confirmation, normally administered in adolescence, was overlooked.

While Blair did little to stop the planters' autocracy, in his fifty-four-year reign, he attempted to soften it. He realized that the clergymen sent over were often misfits, whose university ways were unsuited to rural Virginia. He often sympathized with vestries' complaints that English rectors failed to serve all classes as they should: many thought of it as "England's church" instead of "our church."

All this made Blair realize that Virginia's ministry should be rooted in her soil. He proposed in 1691 that a grammar school and college be built in Virginia to train preachers and teachers. As a result of his diligence, the King and Queen in 1693 granted a charter for the College of William and Mary. Blair, named president for life, guided it through turbulent years until he died.

A typical service at Bruton Parish

Church during Blair's rectorship there from 1710 to 1743 is thus described by the Reverend W. A. R. Goodwin:

We notice that the men sit on the north side of the aisle, and the women on the south; we know that in accordance with custom, this is the ruling of the vestry. Mr. Peter Pelham enters, ascends the organ loft, and begins to play the new organ lately purchased in England. The students from the College of William and Mary take their places in the galleries . . .
The door at the west end of the church opens. The minister enters, passing down the aisle into the chancel at the east end . . . The clerk takes his place at the desk below the pulpit, which stands in the southeast corner of the crossing.
Again the west door opens, and now the Court procession enters, and the Governor passes down the aisle to his pew . . . The Council of State, members of the House [of Burgesses], and the Surveyor General take the pews officially assigned them. The service begins; the minister reads, the responses are led by the clerk, the congregation saying them just a word or two behind, for prayer books were not as easily had then as now . . . The beadle keeps his eyes upon the college youth in particular . . .

Thus church and state were interwoven in Anglican Virginia; he who pledged himself to support England's King pledged also to worship England's God.

Almost from the beginning, this church-state relationship was attacked. A few hapless Puritan dissidents ventured to the colony in the first years. Most of them settled obscurely in Isle of Wight, Surry, Nansemond, and Norfolk counties, which thereafter retained a puritanical cast. However, when they lured three Puritan clergymen from Massachusetts, in 1642, the General Assembly passed a law requiring ministers to conform to the Church of England or depart. Puritans thereafter were quiet.

The first important dissent in Virginia came from the Quakers. These peace-loving people, originating in 17th-century England, were considered a threat because they refused to bear arms. They first came into Virginia during England's Civil War, in 1642. To deter them, the Assembly in March, 1660, passed this "Act for the Suppressing the Quakers:"

Whereas there is an unreasonable and turbulent sort of people, commonly called Quakers, who contrary to the law do daily gather together unto them unlawfull assemblies and congregations of people, teaching and publishing lies, miracles, false visions, prophecies and doctrines . . .
It is enacted, that no master or commander of any ship or other vessel do bring into this colony any person or persons called Quakers, under the penalty of one hundred pounds sterling, . . . that all such Quakers as have been questioned, or shall hereafter arrive shall be apprehended, wheresoever they shall be found, and they be imprisoned without bail or mainprize till they do adjure this country . . . And that no person do presume on their peril to dispose or publish their books, pamphlets, or libels, bearing the title of their tenets and opinions.

But other Quakers came. The Assembly in 1663 expelled John Porter, a burgess, from membership because he "was too loving to Quakers and stood well affected towards them, and had been at their meetings, and was so far an Anabaptist as to be against the baptizing of children." Other Quakers came into the Valley of Virginia from Pennsylvania in the 1730s. Hopewell Meeting, the first, was established in Frederick County in 1734. However, Quaker pacifism and enmity to slavery converted few Virginians.

Presbyterians were a lesser thorn in the Church of England's side, but a thorn they nevertheless were. Ever since James VI of Scotland had been enthroned in 1603 as James I of England, the two churches which he headed had been in contact. A half-dozen

The first serious dissent in Virginia came from Quakers, whose members "testified" at clandestine meetings. The colony passed laws in 1660 to suppress them. *Colonial Williamsburg*

The first meeting house built by Quakers in Virginia was Hopewell, built in Frederick County in 1734 and still in use. *Winchester-Frederick County Historical Society*

Church of Scotland ministers in the seventeenth century were licensed to serve as rectors of Anglican parishes in Virginia. However, the Governor and Assembly regarded the parish as basic to government, and they required the loyalty and taxes of non-Anglicans for its support. Presbyterians and other denominations were permitted to worship only after certification of time and place by the appropriate county court, though such approval was usually given freely.

The hold of the Established Church was first loosened in 1689, when the liberal Whig Parliament of King William and Queen Mary enacted the toleration act. Titled "An Act for exempting their Majesties' Protestant subjects dissenting from the Church of England from the penalties of certain laws," it permitted dissenters to worship without limit to place or numbers. However, the General Assembly did not extend the act to Virginia until 1699. Even then, the act did not apply to Catholics or Unitarians, who accordingly avoided the colony.

More toleration became necessary in Britain as new lands came under her sway. In Virginia, the process was hastened by the influx of nationalities and faiths. The Presbyterians' numbers gave them the greatest force. Their infiltration began in 1683, when the Reverend Francis Makemie came from Ireland to the Eastern Shore. This founder of Presbyterianism in America soon crossed Chesapeake Bay to the Norfolk area, where he was licensed to minister to Lynnhaven and Elizabeth River's Anglican parishes and their Scottish merchant families. He later organized a congregation in Accomack County, where he married and lived between missions. A remarkable man, he was described by the Governor of New York as a "preacher, a doctor of physics, a merchant, an attorney, and what is worst of all, a disturber of government."

Christ Church was built about 1732 in Lancaster County with funds given by Robert "King" Carter. It is typical of early Anglican parish churches. *Virginia State Library*

The English Wesleyan evangelist George Whitefield launched The Great Awakening in Virginia with a sermon in 1739 at Bruton Parish Church. *Illustration by Erle Prior for Virginia Methodism — A History, by William Warren Sweet*

The full impact of Presbyterianism was felt thirty years later, when that church was stirred by the Great Awakening. This fervid movement had started at Oxford University and spread first through the fiery preachings of John and Charles Wesley, George Whitefield, and Francis Asbury, all Anglican clergy who led the reform movement known as Methodism. In the Awakening, for the first time, the church's message reached Virginia's common people — small farmers, artisans, and slaves.

Whitefield fired the first blast in 1739 at Bruton Parish Church, with the consent of its rector, James Blair, then 85 and three years short of death. His text was "What think ye of Christ?" The *Virginia Gazette* reported "a numerous congregation," adding evasively, "His [Whitefield's] extraordinary manner of preaching gains him the admiration and approval of most of his hearers."

From this time until after the Revolution, Virginia was in ferment. The Great Awakening and the spirit of independence were felt at every level.

The dissenting churches puritanically objected to the Anglicans' social pleasures. One presbytery pronounced that "A man who drives his team on the Sabbath day either going to or returning from market, he who sets out on a journey on this day or spends his time in talking about secular concerns — his crops, his gold mines, his lands, or the news of the day — is guilty of a dreadful profanation." A Presbyterian session declared Sunday was not "for visiting and for idle and worldly conversation."

In place of the Anglicans' decorous faith, the Awakeners noisily threatened hell to the unrepentant. Speaking the language of the people, they pled and shouted their appeal for salvation. They thumped pulpits and pointed accusingly at sinners. In pathetic

Anglican evangelists who influenced Virginians to become Wesleyans were George Whitefield, left; John Wesley, upper right, and Francis Asbury, lower right. Their adherents in 1784 formed the Methodist Church. *Asbury print from the Rev. Melvin Lee Steadman, Jr.*

tones they invoked visions of families separated on Judgment day. The effect was electric. Ignorant and emotional listeners shouted "hallelujah!" or writhed on the ground in convulsions. Cries of "Amen" came from the congregation.

The Awakeners' emotionalism was far different from the sober homily of the old style Anglican divine. The new revivalists preached primarily to the poor and humble for whom the church had shown little concern. Lacking their own churches, they usually gathered outdoors, welcoming workingmen and slaves. Often they met in county courthouses.

Soon after the first Wesleyan preachers came to Virginia, a new type of Presbyterian evangelism appeared. Its source was the Synod of Philadelphia, where the Reverend Gilbert Tennent had founded a "Log College" in Bucks County, in 1727 to train Presbyterian clergy without dependence on Scotland. Soon Tennent's "New Side" Presbyterians were preaching rousing sermons through the middle colonies, following the lead of the eloquent Jonathan Edwards. From this group to Hanover County in 1748 came the Reverend Samuel Davies, the first "New Side" cleric in Virginia.

Davies and his fellow circuit-riders soon stirred up the Piedmont counties. Anglicans and "Old Side" Presbyterians objected that they were "preaching the terrors of the law in such a manner and dialect as had no precedent in the Word of God . . . and so industriously working on the passions and affections of weak minds as to cause them to cry out in a hideous manner, and fall down in convulsion-like fits, to the marring of the profiting both of themselves and others . . ." that they cannot attend to or hear what the preacher says . . ." Nevertheless, the Great Awakening continued to gather converts.

Samuel Davies brought the "New Side" Presbyterian evangelism to Virginia from Pennsylvania in 1748, at the age of 25. *Princeton University*

Davies was soon the most celebrated preacher in Virginia. He was the center of its Awakening and the source of much Revolutionary feeling. Young, vigorous, and eloquent, he preached at seven meeting houses in Hanover, Henrico, Louisa, Goochland, and Caroline counties, supported by 180 families. So many Anglicans thronged to hear him that the Reverend William Dawson, Blair's successor as commissary, warned his bishop in London that since Davies "has been allowed to officiate in so many places, there has been a great defection from our religious assemblies."

Davies stirred other opposition. Attorney-general Peyton Randolph, a leading Anglican, advocated that dissenters' meetings be limited; it would weaken the Established Church, he cautioned "if they [New Side Presbyterians] are permitted to range and raise contributions over the whole country, when our clergy are confined to a single parish." Governor Sir William Gooch attacked New Sides as "False teachers . . . professing themselves ministers under the pretended influence of new light, extraordinary impulse, and such like fanatical and enthusiastical knowledge . . ."

Yet Davies continued to preach, though saddened to note that Anglican churches "ring with exclamatory harangues, accusations, arguments, railings, warnings, etc., etc., etc., against New Lights, Methodists, Enthusiasts, Deceivers, Itinerants, Pretenders, etc." All, like the Presbyterians, objected to paying taxes to support the English church.

Davies' success as herald of the Awakening resulted from tact as well as zeal. Anglicans were few but potent in Davies' section of Virginia, and he was careful not to attack the status quo too directly. He never advocated abolition of slavery. Like the Anglican clergy, he argued that slavery did not destroy spiritual freedom and that conversion did not warrant emancipation.

Cast in the role of David against the Anglican Goliath, Davies helped solidify Revolutionary feeling. In England, Horace Walpole told Parliament, "There is no use crying about it. Cousin America has run off with a Presbyterian parson, and that is the end of it." Young Patrick Henry was among those whom Davies influenced, declaring the evangelist the greatest orator he ever heard. The echo of his sermons lingered long after he left Virginia to succeed Jonathan Edwards as president of Princeton in 1759. He died two years later, only 38.

What the Wesleyan and New Sides revivalists started was taken up about 1750 by the New Light Baptists, whose gospel was even simpler. Its main priciples were the literal interpretation of the Bible and the baptism of adults by immersion in an out-door stream, as Christ baptized his disciples in the waters of the River Jordan. New Light preachers were humble men who felt themselves "called" by God to save their fellow men. They were not required to have a liberal education, as Anglicans and Presbyterians were. If they "preached the word of the Lord," that was good enough.

Regular Baptists, who had lived peaceably in Virginia for many years, opposed the New Lights just as Old Side Presbyterians had opposed New Sides. The Reverend Robert Semple, a Baptist himself, wrote of them:

Their manner of preaching was, if possible, much more novel than their doctrines . . . [they] had acquired a very warm and pathetic address, accompanied by strong gestures and a singular tone of voice. Being often deeply affected themselves while preaching, correspondent affections were felt by their pious hearers, which were frequently expressed by tears, trembling, screams, shouts, and acclamations.

Such outbursts offended some, but they pleased more. The New Lights spread rapidly.

The Wesleyans grew similarly. They remained unhappily within the Established Church until 1784. They then separated and formed the Methodist Episcopal Church. By that time they were second only to the Baptists in number. Their strongest Virginia preacher was Devereux Jarratt, who served the Southside counties which Whitefield had first cultivated. Jarratt remained an Anglican, but the Reverend Jesse Lee, born in Prince George County, left that church to plant Methodism through New England.

Both Baptists and Methodists converted many Negroes. By 1790, one Negro in 23 had been Christianized, 80 per cent as Baptists and Methodists.

Baptist minister John Leland urged Jefferson and Madison to achieve religious freedom in Virginia. *Virginia Baptist Historical Society*

The evangelical preachers went westward with the pioneers, but the Anglicans and Presbyterians moved more deliberately. It was said of the western mission movement later, with a little truth:

> The Baptists and Methodists went on foot
> The Presbyterians went by horseback
> The Episcopalians waited for the railroad.

The dilemma of the Established Church worsened as Virginians became inflamed with Revolutionary ideas. The church was inseparable from Tory rule, and many Loyalist clergymen lost the support of parishioners as these ideas spread. Yet obviously Anglicanism had much to gain by preserving the existing order. Like Voltaire's Dr. Pangloss, the American colonies' dependence on England seemed to it "the best of all possible worlds."

Lack of evangelical fervor added further to the Anglican problem. Most planters opposed slaves' baptism because slaves mistook it to mean freedom. Only if a planter would accept a godfather's responsibility for his servant was baptism permitted. This discouraged slave baptism.

The Church of England finally expressed concern for "lesser breeds" in 1701, creating The Society for the Propagation of the Gospel in Foreign Parts under the Reverend Thomas Bray, who became James Blair's counterpart as Commissary of Maryland. It also created "Dr. Bray's Associates," a missionary body which conducted Negro schools from 1760 to 1774 in Williamsburg, and from 1765 to 1770 in Fredericksburg. Only a fraction of Virginia's slaves were thus taught, however.

Besides the loss of members in the Great Awakening, the Anglicans were weakened by the Enlightenment. Many Anglicans like Jefferson and Madison were influenced by deism, which denied the divinity of Christ and advocated a universal faith. The theory of the "natural rights of men," which was the Revolution's creed, also opposed an established church or a pro-English God.

Although a nominal Anglican, Jefferson expressed approval of some of the beliefs of Unitarians and endorsed the self-government of Presbyterians and Baptists. Many other men of influence in eastern Virginia were deistic. The faculty and students of William and Mary were full of "French deists"; old-fashioned Anglicans sent their sons instead to Princeton or to Presbyterian schools in Virginia. Half the founding trustees of the Presbyterian Hampden-Sydney College in 1776 were Anglicans.

The Anglican establishment in Virginia was thus beleaguered by opposing forces. On

James Ireland was imprisoned in Culpeper County jail in 1769 for preaching at Baptist meetings in violation of Virginia law. He was freed under the Toleration Act in 1770. *Painting by Erwin M. Hearne, Jr., for the Southern Baptist Convention*

Lacking churches, Baptists and Methodists gathered at camp meetings to hear sermons and sing hymns. They slept in tents and frame dormitories.

the left were liberal deists. On the right were dogmatic evangelists. To compound its problem, the establishment was miserably run. Even after the Bishop of London made Blair his deputy, control of Virginia's church remained split between Commissary and Governor, who warred constantly. Blair usually won; three governors were recalled after crossing him. Unfortunately for the church, however, his successors lacked his steel. To govern it, Virginia's Mother Church desperately needed her own authoritative bishop, empowered to recruit native clergy and to fight off politicians. But low-church Virginians would not have it. "The people hate the very name of the bishop's court," wrote Hugh Jones in 1724, and his judgment was correct.

The spiritless state of the Established Church — inherent in any establishment — was criticized by the evangelicals. A Lutheran pastor wrote:

The English Church . . . has adequate means and materials for building the Kingdom of God. It lacks only fruitful laborers, which is the complaint everywhere. It seems that its sons contend more for the empty shell or cicatrix of ordination in apostolic succession than they do for the kernel, the spirit of the great Shepherd and Bishop of souls . . .

Thus, as Virginia approached the Revolution, its once-monolithic church was split. It had been a civilizing institution, whose urbane standards had uplifted the planter class. Espousing the old ideal that the wise and virtuous should govern, it had helped

The Church and Dissenters [113]

produce gifted statesmen. It had planted the first college south of Massachusetts, bringing clergymen and scholars to a savage land.

Yet England's classic orthodoxy was not enough for heterodox America. The ethnic ferment of the Revolution did not fit an Elizabethan mold. The settlers' diverse backgrounds, class differences, and explosive aspirations were bound to assert themselves in sects and schisms. It was the Baptists and Methodists who embodied the equalitarianism of a new century.

When the Revolution had been won and the Mother Church was disestablished, even Anglicans — renamed Episcopalians — recognized at last that God meant for Americans to be free to choose their individual roads to salvation.

And though you suppose them born to the greatest fortunes, yet the pru-
dent management of a large Virginia estate requires so frequent and close
an inspection, in order, not only to improve but preserve it, that the pos-
sessor, when once he comes to be charged with the care of it, can expect
but little of that leisure and repose which are requisite for a pleasurable
or successful engagement in such parts of literature as the languages,
criticism, and curious and deep researches into antiquity.

8

The Reverend James Maury, 1762

The Plantations

The character of Virginians was shaped by their outdoor life. Having few roads or towns, most colonists spent their lives at home. Lacking stores, they grew most of their food and made most of their clothes. Unable to travel easily, they took their pleasure at home. Neighbors and visitors were few.

The Virginia homestead was a world of its own. Whether a Tidewater plantation or an upcountry farm, its occupants seldom ventured farther than to church on Sunday and to the county courthouse on Court Day each month. In this age of mass transport, it is difficult to realize what stay-at-homes the colonists were.

While "plantation" has a lordly ring, the earliest clearings along the James were no more than farms. It did not take Virginians long to enlarge them. To their first fifty or one hundred acres, they added more by purchase or occasionally by gift from the King or Governor. Early planters could annex fifty acres apiece for each passenger whose way they paid to Virginia. By 1700, one family in four owned from 500 to 20,-000 acres.

Unless a grantee was fortunate enough to get land made up of Indian "old fields," he had to clear his own, for Tidewater was almost solidly forested. However, he soon learned the Indian method of cutting away a girdle of bark, leaving the tree to die, and then burning it. Stumps were then dragged up by oxen; horses were not strong nor patient enough for such work.

Deeds to land described boundaries in terms of natural features such as creeks and ravines. Boundaries in each parish were "processioned" every three years by the parish vestry on Rogation days; on foot or on horseback, vestrymen followed property lines and renewed the markers. Unlike closely-settled England, early Virginians seldom built fences. They branded hogs, goats, and cattle, turned them loose, and counted on their neighbors not to claim stray animals. "Vast numbers of swine or hogs" ran wild in the woods. Many lawsuits resulted.

The first Tidewater plantations usually fronted the water, as at Chippokes or Berke-ley. However, a flowing stream as at Green Spring or rich farmlands, as at Stratford Hall, were inducements to build a manor house. Remoteness was no problem. As Philip Alexander Bruce has observed, "Love of isolation in the situation of his dwelling house has always been a characteristic of the Englishman."

The development of plantations was a gradual process, reaching its zenith during the spread of slavery after 1710. Such a plantation as Mount Vernon represented the accumulated effort of four generations, beginning with the settlement of George Washington's great-grandfather in Virginia about 1660. His rise began in 1674 when Lord Culpeper, who then owned the Northern Neck Proprietary, granted 5,000 acres jointly to him and to Nicholas Spencer.

Typical of the elaborate scale reached in the eighteenth century was the George Washington plantation, Mount Vernon. *Mount Vernon Ladies' Association of the Union*

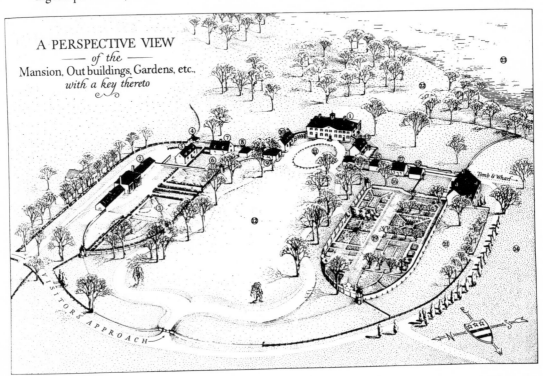

A PERSPECTIVE VIEW
— of the —
Mansion, Out buildings, Gardens, etc.,
with a key thereto

Oxen were used to pull stumps and draw carts on early plantations. They had greater strength and patience than horses. Sketch by Sidney E. King. *The Jamestown Foundation*

The Washington half passed through two more generations before George Washington acquired it in 1752.

Like all successful Virginia planters, Washington added to his buildings and acreage, for Virginians had the Englishman's concept of land as the basis for family power and prestige. In his 45 years as owner, he bought four adjoining farms and raised his acreage from 2,126 to 8,000. Each farm was an entity, with its own buildings, slaves, equipment, and livestock. Unlike his hard-working emigrant great-grandfather, George hired overseers to run his farms. Having moved into the great planter class, he could afford to absent himself when public affairs needed him. Even so, he enjoyed

farming most. "I think with you that the life of a husbandman, of all others, is the most delectable," he wrote Alexander Spotswood. "It is honorable. It is amusing, and with judicious management, it is profitable."

Virginia farming differed from England's. In the old country, seed was sown broadcast in small fields, and crops were cultivated by hand with hoes and mattocks. Plows were made of wood, with iron points and shares. For harvesting, scythes and a two-wheeled cart were used. It did not take Virginia's settlers long to see the advantage of planting seeds in hills between treestumps in newly-cleared fields, as the Indians did. Often a hill was planted simultaneously in corn, beans, and squash to save space.

The Plantations [117]

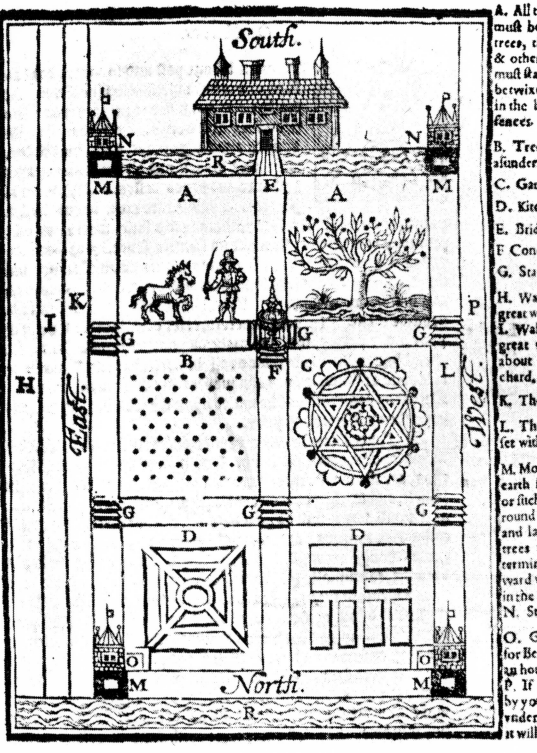

South.

North.

East.

West.

A. All these squares must bee set with trees, the Gardens & other ornaments must stand in spare betwixt the trees, & in the borders and fences.

B. Trees 10. yards asunder.

C. Garden knot.

D. Kitchen garden.

E. Bridge.

F. Conduit.

G. Staires.

H. Walkes set with great wood thicke.

I. Walkes set with great wood round about your Orchard.

K. The out fence.

L. The out fence set with stone fruit.

M. Mount. To force earth for a mount, or such like, set it round with quickes and lay boughs of trees strangely intermingled, tops inward with the earth in the middle.

N. Still-house.

O. Good standing for Bees, if you have an house.

P. If the River run by your doore, and under your mount it will be pleasant.

Virginia gardens followed formal geometric patterns popular in Europe since the Renaissance. Gervais Markham suggested this form in his *New Orchard and Garden*, published in 1638. *The Guildhall Library, London*

Planters learned to sing as they planted the seed in each hillock:

One for the blackbird
One for the crow
One for the cutworm
And one to grow.

Later, as larger plots were cleared, Virginians cultivated fields by ox-drawn plows and harrows. The scale of American farming led to better equipment and more time-saving methods than England had.

By far the most laborious crop was tobacco. From the time the seed was planted in March until the cured leaf was packed in October, it required constant attention. But the oversupply of tobacco and exhaustion of the soil brought a diversity of crops in the mid-eighteenth century, especially wheat and corn. After Eli Whitney invented the cotton gin in 1793, this fibre was widely grown.

Early attempts were made to produce supplies needed by the British navy. Chief among these were pitch and tar, used to caulk ships, and hemp to make rope. Dismal Swamp and Norfolk produced large amounts of pitch and tar, but its quality was poor, and little was exported. However, English rope-makers were pleased with Virginia hemp and pronounced it superior to Russia's.

Attempts were also made to produce flax, which was needed for sails, indigo for dye, and ginseng, a medicinal root. Some indigo was raised, but the English market was soon glutted and the crop abandoned. Sassafras continued to be dug and shipped for medicinal use. More successful was the production of wooden clapboards, shingles, and barrel staves from Virginia's abundant pine. Much of this went to the West Indies in exchange for sugar, molasses and rum.

On Tidewater plantations, slaves were early taught net-fishing to supply household needs. Crabs and oysters were not highly regarded at first, but later generations learned to relish them; the oyster roast then became a popular event. Settlers learned to rake up oysters with hinged tongs. Fish were caught in stationary weirs copied from the Indians, and in seines and purse nets pulled by boats or teams of horses on shore. Millions of shad and herring, schooling upstream each spring to spawn in tidal rivers and creeks, were netted and salted down.

A few English coaches were brought to early Virginia, but most roads were passable only on horseback. This late seventeenth-century coach was portrayed in Loggan's *Oxonia Illustrata. The Guildhall Library, London*

The Plantations [119]

William Beverly in 1740 ordered for his Blandfield plantation a 20-fathom seine, eelpots, and perch lines. George Washington in 1760 bought a 40-fathom seine, specifying that it be "well rigged — not to be above eight feet deep."

Export of Virginia's fish was not practical so long as English trawlers continued to find an abundant catch off the Grand Banks of Newfoundland. Furthermore, the Navigation Laws made salt expensive and difficult to obtain in Virginia. However, Virginia planters developed a few domestic fisheries. From Potomac waters, George Washington sold up to 500 barrels of herring and shad each year to Alexandria merchants. At Westover, William Byrd III rented to the highest bidder several large fisheries on the James River. Large quantities of the Virginia catch were cured and shipped to the West Indies. Washington boasted to a Norfolk merchant that Mount Vernon's smoked herring was "equal, if not superior, to any that is transported from this country."

The profusion of fish delighted the settlers. Shad were often three feet long, while drum reached six feet and sturgeon 12. Swiss visitor Francis Louis Michel in 1702 described the landing of a 100-pound fish by the crew of the Indian King while the ship awaited a sea-going wind at the Virginia Capes. It caused "great joy and rejoicing."

One of the earliest descriptions of a Tidewater plantation was published in London in 1649 as "A Perfect Description of Virginia." Its account of Denbigh, the estate of Captain Samuel Mathews near Newport News, aptly sums up the wide range of the self-sustaining planter:

Planters netted fish in tidal rivers to feed their family and slaves. Here shad are caught in the James River near Richmond. *Virginia State Library*

He hath a fine house, and all things answerable to it; he sows yearly store of hemp and flax, and causes it to be spun; he keeps weavers, and hath a tan house, causes leather to be dressed, hath eight shoemakers employed in their trade, hath forty Negro servants, brings them up to trades in his house; he yearly sows abundance of wheat, barley, &c, the wheat he selleth at four shillings the bushel, kills store of beeves, and sells them to victual the ships when they come thither; hath abundance of kine, a brave dairy, swine great store, and poultry; he married the daughter of Sir Thomas Hinton, and, in a word, keeps a good house, lives bravely, and a true lover of Virginia; he is worthy of much honor.

By 1750 many Tidewater plantations had grown by purchase of land to 5,000 acres or more. So large an operation required the supervision not only of the planter and his wife but also of an overseer and white servants. Such a ménage was described by John Fiske in *Old Virginia and Her Neighbors:*

... The space is in great part cleared for the planting of vast fields of tobacco, but here and there are extensive stretches of woodland and coppice, with noble forest trees and luxuriant undergrowth, much rougher and wilder than an English park. The cabins for slaves present the appearance of a hamlet. These are wooden structures of the humblest sort, built of logs or undressed planks, and afflicted with chronic dilapidation. An inventory of 1696 shows us that the cabin might contain a bed and a few chairs, two or three pots and kettles, "a pear of pot-racks, a pot-hook, a frying-pan, and a beer barrel:" and advertisements for runaways describe Cuffy and Pompey as clad in red cotton, with canvas drawers, waistcoat, and wide-brimmed black hat. Their victuals, of "hog and hominy" with potatoes and green vegetables, were wholesome and palatable. If there were white servants on the estate, they were commonly but not necessarily somewhat better housed and clothed.

Leaving the Negro quarters, with their grinning mammies and swarms of wooly pickaninnies, one would presently come upon other outbuildings; the ample barns for tobacco and granaries for corn, the stable, the cattle-pens, a hen-coop and a dove-cot, a dairy, and in some cases a malt-house, or perhaps, as we have seen, a country store. There were brick ovens for curing hams and bacon; and the kitchen likewise stood apart from the mansion, which was thus free from kitchen odors and from undue heating in summer time. There was a vegetable garden, with "all the culinary plants that grow in England, and in far greater perfection," besides "roots, herbs, vine-fruits, and salad-flowers peculiar to themselves," and excellent for a relish with meat. Nearer to the house, among redolent flower-beds gay with varied colors, some vine-clad arbour afforded shelter from the sun.

A short walk across the mown space shaded by large trees, called, as in New England, the yard, would bring us to the mansion, very commonly known as the Great House. From this epithet no sure inference can be drawn as to the size of the building, for it simply served to contrast it with its dependent cabins and outhouses. It was often called the Home House. It was apt to stand upon a rising ground, and from its porch you might look down at the blue river and the little wharf, known as "the landing," with pinnaces moored hard by and canoes lying lazily on the bank or suddenly darting out upon the water. Turning away from the river, the eye would rest upon an orchard bearing fruits in great variety, and a pasture devoted to horses or some special breed ...

To supervise his estate, the planter spent his morning on horseback, conferring with his overseer and observing his slaves. Returning home, he would devote the afternoon to his accounts, kept in his office. Here he computed expenses and profits, ordered supplies, and wrote to merchants in English or Virginia ports to get the highest prices for his produce. If he were a vestryman, a justice of the peace, or a burgess, he kept up with official duties. Here also he read the *Virginia Gazette* and books and periodicals from London.

An insight in the daily life of George Mason, builder of Gunston Hall in Fairfax County, is given in this recollection of his son, John Mason:

It was very much the practice with gentlemen of landed and slave estates . . . so to organize them as to have considerable resources within themselves; to employ and pay but few tradesmen, and to buy little or none of the coarse stuffs and materials used by them . . . Thus my father had among his slaves carpenters, coopers, sawyers, blacksmiths, tanners, curriers, shoemakers, spinners, weavers, and knitters, and even a distiller.

His woods furnished timber and plank for the carpenters and coopers, and charcoal for the blacksmith; his cattle killed for his own consumption and for sale supplied skins for the tanners, curriers, and shoemakers; and his sheep gave wool and his fields produced cotton and flax for the weavers and spinners, and his orchards fruit for the distiller. His carpenters and sawyers built and kept in repair all the dwelling-houses, barns, stables, ploughs, harrows, gates, etc., on the plantations, and the outhouses at the house.

His coopers made the hogsheads the tobacco was prized in, and the tight casks to hold the cider and other liquors. The tanners and curriers, with the proper vats, etc., tanned and dressed the skins as well for upper as for lower leather to the full amount of the consumption of the estate, and the shoemakers made them into shoes for the Negroes. A professed shoemaker was hired for three or four months in the year to come and make up the shoes for the white part of the family. The blacksmiths did all the ironwork required by the establishment, as making and repairing ploughs, harrows, teeth, chains, bolts, etc. The spinners, weavers, and knitters made all the coarse cloths and stockings used by the Negroes, and some of the finer texture worn by the white family, nearly all worn by the children of it. The distiller made every fall a good deal of apple, peach, and persimmon brandy . . .

All these operations were carried on at the home house, and their results distributed as occasion required to the different plantations. Moreover, all the beeves and hogs for consumption or sale were driven up and slaughtered there at the proper seasons, and whatever was to be preserved was salted and packed away for after distribution.

My father kept no steward or clerk about

him. He kept his own books and superintended, with the assistance of a trusty slave or two, and occasionally of some of his sons, all the operations at or about the home house. . . . To carry on these operations to the extent required, it will be seen that a considerable force was necessary, besides the house servants, who for such a household, a large family and entertaining a great deal of company, must be numerous. . . .

The planter's wife was equally busy. Such a housewife was Helen Skipwith Coles, wife of Tucker Coles of Smallwood plantation in Albemarle county. A niece wrote of her:

I would recall to you the picture which I have often attempted to describe . . . of Aunt Helen, who was up by sunrise every day, making the rounds of the kitchen, the smokehouse, the dairy, the weaving room, and the garden, with a basket of keys on one arm, and of knitting on the other; whose busy fingers never stopped; and who, as the needles flew, would attend to every one of the domestic duties and give all the orders for the day, only returning to the house in time to preside at a bountiful breakfast table, then resuming her rounds to visit the sick, to give out work to the spinners and weavers, and those engaged in making clothes for the hands; prescribing for all usual ailments of the young and old in the absence of the doctor, caring for her flowers, and then sitting down to her books and her music . . .

On wash-day seventeenth century women soaked clothes in water heated over an outdoor fire, beat out the grime with paddles, and rinsed the garments before hanging them. Sketch by Sydney R. Jones from *Old English Household Life*.

Prospering planters admired English fashions. Virginia builders after 1700 were influenced by such details as these in an English house about 1690. *Radio-Times Hulton, London*

In this case, the planter's wife had learned her role well from her parents, Sir Peyton and Lady Skipwith, whose seat was Prestwould plantation on the Roanoke River in Mecklenburg County. Lady Skipwith left a legend of industry and frugality. Far from idling, she was busy from sun-up till long after sunset; she even took time to mend Prestwould's hundreds of grain sacks. Sir Peyton relied on her to direct the slaves in his absence: "Pray, my Rib, order Bub, Miller Sam, and Hez. I say to you, look and talk them into industry, and possibly the little Gentleman at the mill into honesty, as I must, and more, suspect him of injustice in his management. Pray my love,

attend to Peyton's flu case with sassafras tea."

No matter how affluent a planter was, his wife directed the household. Mrs. Edward Carrington thus describes her visit to Mrs. Washington at Mount Vernon:

Let us repair to the old lady's room, which is precisely in the style of our good old aunt's — that is to say, nicely fixed for all sorts of work. On one side sits the chambermaid, with her knitting; on the other, a little colored pet, learning to sew. An old, decent woman is there, with her table and shears, cutting out the Negroes' winter clothes, while the good old lady directs them all, incessantly knitting herself. She points out to me several pairs of nice colored stockings and gloves she had just finished, and presents me with a pair half done, which she begs I will finish and wear for her sake.

The Plantations [123]

A tutor taught the children of well-to-do planters, as was done in England. An illustration from *The Elizabethan Home* shows this seventeenth century scene. *The British Museum*

An ill-assorted member of planter households was the tutor, usually an unmarried clergyman. He prepared sons to enter college and daughters to read, write, "do sums," and acquire "ladylike accomplishments."

Tutors were first obtained as indentured servants from England and Scotland; later they were hired on graduation from American colleges. In 1767 Councillor Robert Carter of Nomini Hall paid Philip Fithian £40 sterling a year to come from Princeton and teach seven of his children. Similarly, David Meade Randolph thirty years later brought young William Ellery Channing from Harvard to his Ampthill estate in Chesterfield County.

To the detriment of Virginia, the English concept of education for an elite delayed the growth of grammar schools which were greatly needed. For the few at the top, however, a plantation upbringing developed breadth and leadership. Henry Adams wrote of young John Randolph, of Roanoke, that he "lived in a boy's paradise of indulgence, fished and shot, rode like a young monkey, and had his memory stuffed with the genealogy of every well-bred horse in the state."

From such a background came Washington, Jefferson, and most of Virginia's other Revolutionary generation. From the example of their fathers, these men learned to deal with others. Management of plantation industries and slaves taught them the value of labor. Drought and flood enabled them to develop resourcefulness. Trained to ride, to shoot, and withstand pain, they were later able to survive sore hardship and win victories.

Plantation hospitality was fabled. A visitor bringing news and gossip was welcomed. Half starved for companionship all winter, Virginians made up for it when spring came. After the ballroom was added in 1751 to Williamsburg's Governor's Mansion, it became the style for planters to add one.

The scale of living in eastern Virginia rose each decade in the eighteenth century. The simple gabled houses built at early Jamestown, with one ground-level room and a loft above, were by 1730 thought fit only for slaves; they were still prevalent, however, along the western frontier, which lived as Tidewater had a hundred years earlier. Now, confident of continued wealth, planters expanded their houses or built new ones. Philip Ludwell Lee tore down the 150-year-old Green Spring mansion after 1798 and replaced it in newer style. Mann Page at Rosewell on the York reared the largest and handsomest private house in all America.

Gardens grew apace with houses. Virginians had the English love of nature and framed their estates with boxwood gardens and avenues of trees. Like English country gentlemen, Tidewater dwellers in the eighteenth century planted elaborate allees and parterres, variously inspired by Italian Renaissance and Dutch designs.

The planter's life was an odd contrast: on the one hand elegance, on the other crudity. In a sense, he had one foot in England and the other in Virginia. For intellectual stimulation he looked abroad; from London he received books and periodicals like the *Spectator*, the *Tatler*, and the *Gentleman's Magazine*. But Virginia was his living: his land, his slaves, his livestock, his food, his home.

Wealthy scions of hard-working Tidewater pioneers often became dissipated idlers. A British soldier, John Ferdinand Smyth, wrote of one such planter:

The gentleman of fortune rises about nine o'clock; he may perhaps make an excursion to walk as far as his stable to see his horses, which is seldom more than fifty yards from his house; he returns to breakfast between nine and ten, which is generally tea or coffee, bread-and-butter, and very thin slices of venison, ham, or hung beef. He then lies down on a pallet, in the coolest room in the house, in his shirt and

Dancing of reels and minuets was popular in the plantation age. From the title page of John Playford's *The Dancing Master*, published about 1725. *The Folger Shakespeare Library*

trousers only, with a Negro at his head and another at his feet, to fan him and keep off the flies; between twelve and one he takes a draught of bombo, or toddy, a liquor composed of water, sugar, rum, and nutmeg, which is made weak and kept cool; he dines between two and three, and at every table, whatever else there may be, a ham and greens, or cabbage, is always a standing dish.

At dinner he drinks cider, toddy, punch, port, claret, and madeira, which is generally excellent here; having drunk some few glasses of wine after dinner, he returns to his pallet, with his two blacks to fan him, and continues to drink toddy, or sangaree, all the afternoon; he does not always drink tea. Between nine and ten in the evening he eats a light supper of milk and fruit, or wine, sugar, and fruit, etc., and almost immediately retires to bed for the night. This is his general way of living in his family, when he has no company. . . .

Despite the steady growth of Virginia's exports, some Tidewater planters went deeper into debt to support the high style of eighteenth century living. The value of Virginia exports was usually greater than its imports, but shipping and brokerage charges kept tobacco planters in the red. With justification, planters accused merchants of excessive profits.

When the government of George III deepened the debt with new taxes in 1765, Virginians' tempers rose. Jefferson said planters' debts were "hereditary from father to son for many generations, so that the planters were a species of property annexed to certain mercantile houses in London." Virginians were £2,000,000 in debt to British creditors when the Revolution came, he estimated.

When Virginia abolished primogeniture in 1785, the gradual division of the great estates was already under way. Soil exhaustion and wartime losses contributed, as well as high living. The heyday of plantation-building was past.

George Washington enjoyed farming above all other pursuits. In this painting by Junius Brutus Stearns he is shown supervising the wheat harvest. *Virginia Museum of Fine Arts*

Virginia's 100 Wealthiest Planters

The wealthiest and most influential of Virginia's planters were concentrated along the James, Rappahannock, and Potomac Rivers and on the Northern Neck. Based on tax returns in 1782 and subsequent years, here are the 100 wealthiest as listed by Professor Jackson T. Main in the July, 1954, issue of *The William and Mary Quarterly:*

Richard Adams of Richmond city, William Alexander of Princess Anne, William Allen of Surry, John Ambler of James City, John Armistead of Caroline, Roger Atkerson of Dinwiddie, Henry Banks of Richmond city, Burwell Bassett of New Kent, Edmund Berkeley of Middlesex, Robert Beverly of Essex, Theodorick Bland of Prince George, William Blunt of Sussex, William Brent of Stafford, Cuthbert Bullitt of Prince William, Lewis Burwell of Mecklenburg, Nathaniel Burwell of James City.

Joseph Cabell of Buckingham, William Cabell of Amherst, Charles Carter of Charles City, Edward Carter of Albemarle, George Carter of Lancaster, John Carter of Loudoun, Landon Carter of King George, Robert Carter of Westmoreland, Robert W. Carter of Richmond county, Archibald Cary of Chesterfield, Wilson Miles Cary of Elizabeth City, William Churchill of Middlesex, Allen Cocke of Surry, Chastain Cocke of Powhatan, John Cocke of Surry, John Hartwell Cocke of Surry.

Francis Corbin of Middlesex, Gawin Corbin of Caroline, Richard Corbin of King and Queen, John Parke Custis of New Kent, Nicholas Davis of Bedford, Francis Eppes of Chesterfield, Francis Eppes of Amelia, Moore Fauntleroy of Richmond county, George Washington Fairfax of Fairfax, Henry Fitzhugh of King George, Thomas Fitzhugh of Stafford, William Fitzhugh of King George, William Fitzhugh of Stafford, Muscoe Garnett of Essex, Philip L. Grymes of Middlesex, Benjamin Harrison of Charles City, Carter H. Harrison of Cumberland, Nathaniel Harrison of Prince George.

James Henry of King and Queen, Patrick Henry of Prince Edward, Adam Hunter of Stafford, Thomas Jefferson of Albemarle, Joseph Jones of Dinwiddie, Peter Jones of Amelia, Robert Lawson of Prince William, Henry Lee of Westmoreland, Richard Lee of Westmoreland, William Lee of James City, Warner Lewis of Gloucester, William Lightfoot of Charles City, George Mason of Fairfax, Stevens Thomson Mason of Loudoun, Joseph Mayo of Powhatan, Daniel McCarty of Westmoreland, Thomas Nelson of York, Thomas Nelson of York (another of the same name).

Wilson Cary Nicholas of Albemarle, John Page of Gloucester, Mann Page of Spotsylvania, John Paradise of James City, David Patterson of Buckingham, Edmund Pendleton of Caroline, John Perrin of Gloucester, Edmund Randolph of Richmond city, Peyton Randolph of Powhatan, Thomas Randolph of Henrico, Thomas Mann Randolph of Chesterfield, William Randolph of Charles City, Thomas Roane of King and Queen, Willian Ronald of Powhatan, David Ross of Richmond city, Edmund Ruffin of Prince George.

Henry Skipwith of Buckingham, Sir Peyton Skipwith of Mecklenburg, Alexander Spotswood of Spotsylvania, James Southall of Williamsburg, John Tabb of Amelia, Richard Taliaferro of James City, John Taylor of Richmond county, John Taylor of Caroline, Alexander Trent of Cumberland, George Turberville of Westmoreland, John Turberville of Westmoreland, Robert P. Waring of Essex, George Washington of Fairfax, and Ralph Wormeley of Middlesex.

The first Negroes were brought to English America in 1619, when a Dutch frigate docked at Point Comfort and traded 20 Africans in return for food. Painting by Sidney King. *Colonial Williamsburg*

For the true and faithful service of one of my Negroes, known as "Virginia Will," I leave him his freedom, and also fifteen bushels of clean shelled corn, and fifty pounds of dried beef annually so long as he lives; also one kersey coat and breeches, a hat and two pair of shoes, two pair of yarn stockings; two white and blue shirts, one pair of blue drawers, one axe and one hoe; the same to be delivered annually.

Will of Daniel Parke, 1689

There is not a man living who wishes more sincerely than I to see a plan adopted for the abolition of it [slavery].

George Washington

Nothing is more certainly written in the book of fate than that these people are to be free.

Thomas Jefferson

The Negroes

In 1619 a Dutch frigate docked at Point Comfort and traded 20 Negroes to Virginia settlers in return for food. Thus Negro servitude began in Virginia, to spread through the colonies until arrested 200 years later by public opinion and civil war.

The first Virginia Negroes had been captured on the Guinea coast of Africa, where warring Negro tribes for centuries had sold captives into slavery. While a novelty in English America, nearly 900,000 of them already had been brought to Spanish and Portuguese colonies and mines in South America, herded in dark squalor aboard slave ships. Nearly 3,000,000 were brought to the Americas in the seventeenth century, the influx rising to 7,000,000 in the eighteenth.

Slave traders had visited Africa since the Middle Ages, and bartered mirrors, beads, cloth, and rum for Negroes. From west Africa, in the Sudan, they took tall blue-black Wolof and Hausa tribesmen. From the equatorial forests to the south they led away thousands of other "bush" Negroes, who were shorter of stature and lighter of color than the regal Sudanese. To obtain European goods, African chieftains sold even their kinsmen to Europeans. Whole villages were burned and their fleeing Negroes seized and herded into corrals to await sale and shipment to the New World or Europe.

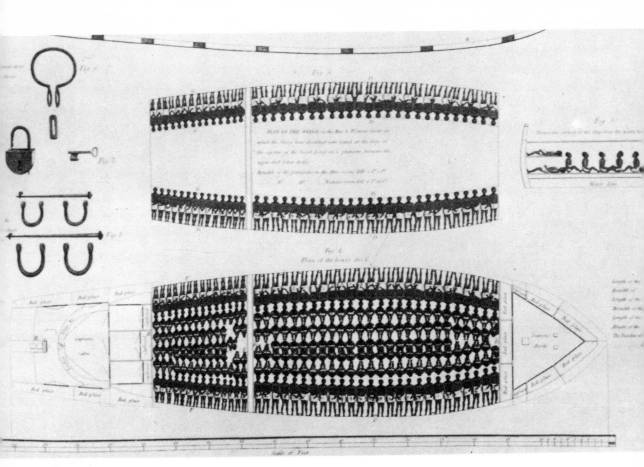

Slaves were crowded aboard ship and manacled to the deck to prevent mutiny or escape overboard. Many died of the heat and illness. *National Maritime Museum, Greenwich*

In 1619 England's sea captain John Hawkins entered the fetid trade in competition with the Dutch and Portuguese. Before the century had ended, these three maritime powers operated nearly forty so-called factories on Africa's coasts to buy and sell slaves. In 1663, after the Navigation Acts had restricted colonists' trade to the mother country, England gave to its Royal African Company a monopoly on slave trade to the English colonies. The booming business was opened up to all English subjects 35 years later.

Traders bought only able-bodied Negroes, leaving the old and sick to die in factory corrals. Once aboard ship, the captives were chained to the deck to prevent escape or insurrection. Equatorial heat and shipboard diseases killed many, about 15 per cent dying in transit: one vessel reaching Virginia in 1702 had lost 100 of its original 330 Negroes at sea.

The first Negroes in Virginia were treated as indentured servants, but in 1670 slavery was recognized by Virginia law. "All servants not being Christians imported into this colony by shipping" were declared to be "slaves for their lives." Their descendants inherited this status.

Few early settlers could afford to own

many servants. By 1670, the Negro population was less than 1,000, and by 1700 it made up only 16,390 of Virginia's people. But a rise in tobacco prices after 1670 spurred slavery's growth. William Byrd II complained in 1736 that Virginia "will some time or other be confirmed by the name of New Guinea," but importation was not forbidden by Virginia until 1774. By the time of the Revolution, nearly half of Virginia's people were Negroes.

Slaves became a major source of England's riches. Bought at African factories for £4 to £6 apiece, they were sold in the colonies at prices ranging from £16 in the seventeenth century to £40 by 1750 and £100 by 1775. Top prices were paid for carpenters and craftsmen. Slaves sold fastest in the growing season, when planters were "abundantly more fond of them." In Virginia's barter economy, many were bought on consignment by merchants or planters with good credit.

Shippers in Bristol and later in Liverpool sent more than 100,000 Guineamen and women each year from slave factories on Africa's Gold Coast to the West Indies and North America. The Virginia colony tried to halt the flood, but the Crown forbade it. England's Board of Trade also annulled im-

At slave markets on the African coast, tribal chiefs sold their war captives to European traders. They were kept in corrals until sold as slaves. Reprinted by permission from *Virginia: History, Government, Geography,* by Francis B. Simkins, Spotswood Hunicutt, and Sidman P. Poole. *Copyright 1957 by Charles Scribner's Sons*

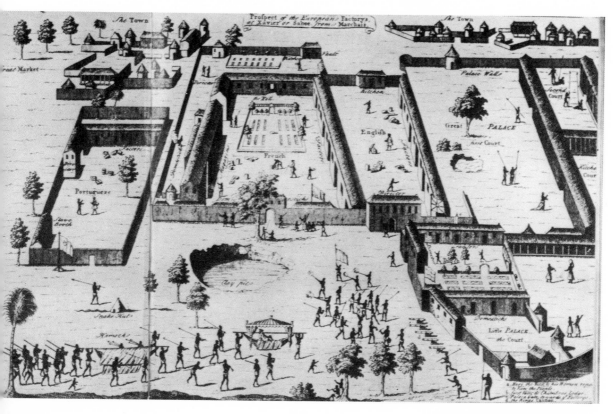

port taxes which Virginia's General Assembly had imposed in an effort to control the flow. The Crown's encouragement of the trade confirmed Virginia's opposition to British trade policy; in the recital of Britain's offenses which he included in his first draft of the Declaration of Independence, Thomas Jefferson cited Britain's slave trading.

The colonists themselves finally entered the profitable trade. After the Royal African Company's monopoly was ended in 1678, Virginia vessels brought slaves from the West Indies. New England merchants began slave-trading on a larger scale after 1737, building ships with hundreds of slave cells. Returning from Africa with a full cargo, the merchants traded them in the West Indies or southern colonies for products needed in New England. Boston and Newport were centers of this trade, which enriched many shipmasters and merchants.

Virginians at first feared the newcomers and their black magic. In 1705 the Assembly prohibited Negroes from any "office, civil, ecclesiastical, or military, or any place of public trust or power." Tidewater was repeatedly swept by rumors of slave uprisings, and Negroes who fomented trouble were hanged. Colonial slave-holders developed a severe code: slaves were forbidden to leave their owner's premises without a written pass; they were not permitted to make contracts or to testify in litigation involving whites; they could not own property or be taught to read and write; and they could not assemble in a group unless white persons were present.

A slave away from his plantation without a permit was subject to twenty lashes, or worse. Burning the palm of a slave's hand was an early punishment for theft, while castration was the penalty for rape of a white woman. Advertisements for runaway slaves frequently appeared in the columns of the *Virginia Gazette* after its founding in 1736.

Severe action was taken to recover fugitives who might lead slave uprisings. In 1701 the General Assembly called for the arrest of "one Negro man named Billy," who "has several years unlawfully absented himself from his master's services, lying out and lurking in obscure places, ... devouring and destroying stocks and crops, robbing the houses of and committing and threatening other injuries to several of His Majesty's good and liege people." It offered Billy's finder a reward of 1,000 pounds of tobacco. Anyone who aided or harbored the fugitive was declared guilty of a felony.

The punishment for a slave's false testimony against another was to stand for an hour with his ear nailed to the pillory, after which it was sliced off. After the slave turned the other ear, he received 39 lashes. Theft from one's master could be a capital offense.

Virginia law provided no penalty to the killing of a slave by his master, but it permitted a master to recover his slave's value if he were killed by a third party. Slaves were forbidden to possess weapons or medicine, the latter out of fear of attempted poisoning. The slave who robbed a house or store could be given 60 lashes by the sheriff and placed in the pillory. In practice, however, slaves were seldom punished to the limit of the law. The planter instead regarded them as valuable property, to be treated with care. Whipping was the usual extent of punishment.

Problems arising from intercourse between slaves and whites proved more diffi-

Slaves worked Virginia tobacco fields and served as artisans in plantation shops. Their varied labors are shown in this engraving of a tobacco plantation in the West Indies. *Arents Collection, New York Public Library*

cult. Such relations were usually initiated by the white partner, and because of the Negro's defenselessness, they were not easily stopped. Colonial Virginia policy from 1607 had opposed settlers' cohabitation with Indians, and in 1660 similar laws were passed applying to Negroes. Any minister performing a mixed marriage could be fined 10,000 pounds of tobacco. The degraded status of the children of such unions was felt to be society's most effective deterrent.

Despite all penalties, miscegenation was common, if we may judge from newspaper notices of missing mulatto slaves. Frequently, mulattoes were the offspring of white male servants and slave women, or of Negro fathers and indentured white women, since male Negroes greatly outnumbered females during colonial times. Any white who married a Negro or mulatto was banished by law after 1691.

The caste-consciousness of the age was nowhere more evident than in Virginians' attitude toward Christianizing the Negro. Baptism of slaves was first forbidden as irreconcilable with slavery. However, the General Assembly relaxed this in 1667 and clarified the status of "Christian servants:"

The Negroes [133]

Whereas some doubts have risen whether children that are slaves by birth, and by the charity and piety of their owners made partakers of the blessed sacrament of baptism, should by virtue of their baptism be made free; It is enacted and declared by this grand Assembly and the authority thereof, that the conferring of baptism doth not alter the condition of the person as to his bondage or freedom; that diverse masters, freed from this doubt, may more carefully endeavor the propagation of Christianity by permitting children, though slaves, or those of greater growth, if capable, to be admitted to that sacrament.

Peter Kalm, a Swiss botanist who visited the colonies in 1748, commented on the general indifference to the slaves' Christianization. He wrote that the masters "are poorly led by the conceit of its being shameful to have a spiritual brother or sister among so despicable a people, partly by thinking that they should not be able to keep their Negroes so meanly afterwards; and partly through fear of the Negroes growing too proud, on seeing themselves upon a level with their masters in religious matters."

The severity of slave-masters relaxed in the eighteenth century as Negroes gained literacy and wider utility. The paternalism which survived from feudal days induced a fatherly responsibility in most planters. With third-generation familiarity came confidence. Colonists' letters increasingly alluded to elderly Negro "uncles" and "aunts." With the birth of the Society for the Propagation of the Gospel in Foreign Parts in 1701, the Anglican Church began to exert pressure on its clergy for the Christian upbringing for slaves, but few of the blacks received it.

The spread of the Enlightenment slowly began to undermine slavery's foundations. The age of science questioned autocracy, exploitation, and the injustice inherent in European imperialism. As early as 1692, John Page of York County had provided in his will for the care in their old age of his Negroes and their descendants. Robert Beverley wrote in 1705 that "no people more abhor the thoughts of such usage [cruelty] than the Virginians." House servants reared their master's children, worshipped with his family, shared his joys and sorrows, and were often buried in the family cemetery.

A few slaves were freed, but they found difficulty earning a living. Small farmers were at the mercy of both planters and merchants in Virginia, and few towns existed to offer work to craftsmen, whether white or black. Obviously, freedmen were an anomaly, fitting neither in the slave or white worlds. Virginia law after 1699 required freedmen to leave the colony in six months. Some intermarried with Indians. Others migrated westward or into North Carolina.

Emancipation of individual slaves was discouraged for fear of their insurrection. A slave-owner might obtain such permission only from the governor and council. If set free without license, a slave could be arrested by parish wardens and sold for public benefit. Not until the end of the eighteenth century were these restraints removed. Then such men as Mason, Washington, and Jefferson by will freed their slaves, though few other planters followed their example.

Slaves were usually lodged in wooden barracks or cabin rows close to the plantation house and the overseer's quarters. Furnishings were few: homemade chairs, beds, and washstands. The slave spent most of his day working in the growing fields, until he was too old to work. An English traveller, John Ferdinand Smyth, described a typical slave workday:

He is called up in the morning at daybreak, and is seldom allowed time enough to swallow three mouthfuls of hominy, or hoecake, but is driven out immediately to the field to hard labor, at which he continues, without intermission, until noon . . . About noon is the time he eats his dinner, and he is seldom allowed an hour for that purpose . . .

They then return to severe labor, which continues in the field until dusk in the evening, when they repair to the tobacco houses, where each has his task in stripping allotted him. That employs him for some hours.

These conditions did not seem overly severe in an age when people worked from sun-up to sundown, with no holidays except Christmas and Whitsuntide. Wrote an English observer, Harry Toulmin, in 1793 after visiting Virginia and Kentucky: ". . . I am of the opinion that a large proportion of the slaves are better off than the poor of England."

An affirmative view was also expressed by Phillis Wheatley, a slave, born in Africa and brought to Massachusetts. She wrote:

Twas mercy brought me from my pagan land,
Taught my benighted soul to understand
That there's a God, there's a heaven, too.

House servants often had no cabins of their own, sleeping on pallets in the hall or children's room of the master's house. Slave clothing was of a native cotton "Virginia cloth" or "Negro cotton," cut and sewn by a plantation seamstress. Winter clothes were of English osnaburg or Russian drab. Except for coachmen, butlers, and "serving wenches," few servants wore any but the coarsest clothing. Ebenezer Hazard noted in 1777:

The Virginians, even in the city [Williamsburg] do not pay proper attention to decency

When the year's tobacco had been harvested and cured, it was packed in hogsheads and rolled by slaves and draft animals to the plantation dock. *Virginia State Department of Highways*

in the appearance of their Negroes; I have seen boys of 10 and 12 years of age going through the streets quite naked, and others with only part of a shirt hanging part of the way down their backs. This is so common a sight that even the ladies do not appear to be shocked at it.

The slaves' work ended Saturday afternoon. "Every face (especially the Negroes') looks festive and cheerful," noted Philip Fithian at Nomini Hall, as Saturday night approached. After supper the slaves gathered in their quarters for juba dancing, to the clapping of hands and the rhythmic wail of tribal chants. From these slave hoe-downs emerged the popular "jubilee" songs and jazz rhythms of later decades. Early reli-gious services gave rise to the deeply-felt spirituals. Sundays were for sleep and tending garden plots.

Marriage between slaves was solemnized by "jumping the broomstick." After obtaining their master's permission, the couple presented themselves to the matriarch of the Negro quarters, who often served as midwife. She called the Negroes together and recited verses from the Bible. Then the couple linked arms and jumped over a broomstick laid on the floor to signalize their union. They were then considered man and wife.

Slaves performed a variety of tasks. In his study of *The Negro in Eighteenth Cen-*

Plantation house servants became loved and respected members of the household. In the Governor's Palace kitchen at Williamsburg, a chicken is cooked in the fireplace. *Colonial Williamsburg*

After work, slaves often amused themselves with dancing and singing in the plantation servants' quarter. This picture was probably painted about 1800 in South Carolina. *Abby Aldrich Rockefeller Folk Art Collection*

tury Williamsburg, Thad W. Tate, Jr., found advertisements in eighteenth century Williamsburg which referred to slaves trained variously as nurse, laundress, cook, seamstress, spinner, butcher, gardner, coachman, hostler, personal man-servant, and waiter. Records have been found of others who served as barber, blacksmith, cabinetmaker, carpenter and joiner, carter, cooper, harnessmaker, shoemaker, tanner, and tailor.

A traveller in Williamsburg in 1783 was impressed with the servants:

In our hotel we had a very good though dear entertainment. Negro cooks, women waiters, and chambermaids made their courtesies with a great deal of native grace and simple elegance and were dressed neatly and cleanly ...

Even more accomplished was a slave advertised for sale in Williamsburg in Purdie and Dixon's *Virginia Gazette* in 1767:

A valuable young handsome Negro fellow, about 18 or 20 years of age, has every qualification of a genteel and sensible servant, and has been in many different parts of the world. He shaves, dresses hair, and plays on the French horn. He lately came from London, and has with him two suits of new clothes, and his French horn, which the purchaser may have with him.

Not all slaves worked on large plantations. In Tidewater and Piedmont Virginia, three-fourths of all families held slaves, including small farmers, shopkeepers, tavern keepers, and shipmasters. Nearly half of the slave-owners held fewer than five Negroes — often a Negro husband and wife and their children to help with farm chores. Contrary to the chivalric fiction of the 1800s, no Virginia planter owned as many as 1,000 slaves at a time.

The average owned by Virginia's 100 leading planter families in the 1780s was

Great Britain's Chief Justice, Lord Mansfield, in 1772 ruled that slavery violated Magna Carta. The decision freed all slaves in the British Isles but did not affect Britain's colonies. *Central Office of Information, London*

Lord Mansfield, ruled slavery in violation of Magna Carta and set free thousands of Negroes brought into the British Isles from American and West Indian colonies.

Unfortunately, the immediate effect of this decision was all but lost on Revolutionary Americans. However, in Pennsylvania, where the influence of William Penn was strong, the Society of Friends the same year excommunicated all members who would not free their slaves. Virginia's Quakers and a few Baptists followed.

To a thoughtful few Virginians who realized slavery's inconsistency with their own fight for freedom, some plan for emancipation seemed necessary. In the 1776 Virginia Convention, which called on the Continental Congress to declare independence, this inconsistency disturbed George Mason, Thomas Jefferson, and George Wythe. Though slavery was an ironic denial of Mason's Declaration of Rights' premise that "all men are by nature equally free," these men supported its adoption as an argument in itself for emancipation. But to Virginia's loss, these hopes were never realized.

Appointed by the Convention to propose a revision, with Edmund Pendleton, of Virginia's laws, Jefferson and Wythe prepared a plan for gradual emancipation to be considered by the Assembly in 1779, but it was untimely. "It was found that the public mind would not yet bear the proposition," Jefferson wrote later, "nor will it bear it even at this day. Yet the day is not distant when it must bear and adopt it, or worse will follow. Nothing is more certainly written in the book of fate than that these people are to be free. . . ."

Had more men shared Jefferson's and Mason's radical view, the United States

about 180, according to a study by Professor Jackson T. Main. The largest slaveholder at that time was Charles Carter of Cleve, who owned 785. Other large holders were William Allen of Claremont, who had 700; Robert Beverley of Blandfield, with 592; Robert Carter of Nomini Hall, with 445; and David Ross, a Richmond merchant and planter, who owned 400. Besides these men, only 18 others in the colony owned more than 200 slaves.

The tide of opinion began to turn against slavery in mid-eighteenth century England and to spread to the colonies. John Wesley and George Whitefield denounced it from the pulpit, while poet William Cowper, novelist Laurence Sterne, and even the Tory essayist Samuel Johnson took up their pens against it. In 1772 Britain's Chief Justice, might have been spared civil war. Jefferson was especially vehement. In "A Summary View of the Rights of British America," in 1774, he accused Britain of blocking the colonies' desire for abolition. He proposed a similar indictment in the Declaration of Independence, but it was stricken. In the same spirit, he asked the 1784 Continental Congress to forbid slavery after 1800 in states formed from Virginia's Northwest, but the step was not taken until the Constitutional Convention met.

The Tidewater oligarchy was unwilling to emancipate its slaves, no matter how strongly the Piedmont and Valley might have felt about it, and Tidewater had the votes. Even more violently against emancipation were South Carolina and Georgia planters, who accused Jefferson of wanting to quit the game after winning the marbles.

For a few months in the beginning of the Revolution, slavery was under pressure. Virginia's royal governor, Lord Dunmore, proclaimed freedom to all slaves who fought with the British. Many plantations were soon denuded. In 1778, an estimated 30,000 slaves left Virginia masters and fled to British lines. Similar losses occurred in Maryland and South Carolina. The colonies opposed arming slaves to be soldiers, but Virginia enlisted Negro freedmen as drummers, fifers and sailors. Negroes who had sailed in the West Indies trade joined the crew of James Barron's *Liberty* and other sloops of Virginia's "mosquito fleet" and fought bravely.

The Revolution did not end slavery, but it halted it. No slaves were permitted to enter the colony after 1774 except those whose masters moved in. The process of freeing a slave was simplified, and residence of freed Negroes in Virginia was at last permitted.

James Lafayette was a freed slave who won Lafayette's praise for his Revolutionary services. "He perfectly acquitted himself with some important commissions I gave him," the French commander wrote after the war, "and appears to me entitled to every reward his situation can admit of." *Virginia Historical Society*

Evidence of anti-slavery spirit increased after the Great Awakening and the Revolution. In the American Museum Magazine, which circulated through the states, this song appeared in 1790:

> The time is at hand — nay,
> Already appears —
> When the empire of reason
> Shall govern the world,
> And error, though sanctioned
> By thousands of years,
> With contempt, as it ought,
> From our bosoms be hurled.
> That in feature or color no
> Difference can be,
> In the eye of that mind
> Which called forth mankind,
> To make them one family,
> Happy and free

A popular sentiment was *The Negro's Complaint*:

Fleecy locks and black complexion
  Cannot forfeit Nature's claim.
Skins may differ, but affection
  Dwells in white and black the same.

Widely read also was a narrative poem, "The Sorrows of Yamba," which blamed slavery and the slave's lot on the avarice of English ship captains.

But Jefferson, himself the owner of 230 slaves, stated the case best. He wrote in his *Notes on Virginia* in 1782:

The whole commerce between master and slave is a perpetual exercise of the most boisterous passions, the most unremitting despotism on the one part, and degrading submissions on the other. Our children see this, and learn to imitate it . . . The man must be a prodigy who can retain his manners and morals undepraved by such circumstances . . . With the morals of the people, their industry also is destroyed. For in a warm climate no man will labor for himself who can make another labor for him. This is so true that of the proprietors of slaves a very small proportion, indeed, are ever seen to labor. And can the liberties of the nation be thought secure when we have removed their only firm basis, a conviction in the minds of the people that these liberties are the gift of God? That they are not to be violated but with his wrath? Indeed, I tremble for my country when I reflect that God is just.

Despite such warnings, Virginia could not bring herself to end the human servitude which had once made her rich. In the exciting infancy of the new republic, she tried to ignore the direful warnings of the seer of Monticello. For a few more years her leadership was unquestioned, but it was not to be for long.

Virginia wants not good victuals, wants not good dispositions, and as God has freely bestowed it, they as freely impart with it.

John Hammond, *Leah and Rachel*, 1656

10

Deer were shot in such extraordinary numbers that it was said the people had grown tired of eating venison. There were few counties in which there were not large flocks of sheep; and mutton was much relished. So abundant were chickens that they were not included in the inventories of personal estates; no planter was so badly off that he could not have a fowl on his table at dinner. The wild turkeys frequenting the woods were of remarkable weight and afforded a popular repast. The clouds of wild pigeons arriving at certain seasons in incredible numbers were killed by the tens of thousands, and for many weeks furnished an additional dish for the planter's table. So vast were the flocks of wild ducks and geese in the rivers and bays during the greater part of the year that they were looked on as the least expensive portion of the food which the Virginians had to procure for the support of their families. Fish of the most delicate and nourishing varieties were caught with hook, or net, or speared at the very door. . . . Oysters and shellfish, without previous planting, could be scraped up by the bushel from the bottom of the nearest inlet or tidal stream.

Philip Alexander Bruce,
Social Life of Virginia in the Seventeenth Century, 1927

Food, Drink, and Merriment

The joyous hedonism of Elizabethan England survived a full century in Virginia. It was a land of good living. "Eat, drink, and be merry," it seemed to say, "for to-morrow we die." Believing that their faith would save them on "the dreadful day of Judgment," Anglicans enjoyed worldly pleasures without the sense of guilt which afflicted the followers of John Calvin, John Knox, and the other Protestant reformers.

The English Church preached a faith suited to men's needs in the first cruel years in Virginia. Victory over Spain convinced Englishmen they enjoyed God's favor. Through their patron saint, they besought God's special protection, confidently flying as their banner the red Cross of Saint George. In Virginia, as in England, they celebrated Saint George's Day each April 23 with prayers and feasting. Scotsmen celebrated St. Andrew's Day.

This cavalier spirit went almost unchallenged until puritanism entered Virginia in full force with the Germans and Scotch-

Fairs were held each year at Public Times, when the Virginia Assembly met at Jamestown and later at Williamsburg. County court days also were social occasions. The scene shown is in England. *The Bodleian Library, Oxford University*

Irish in the 1730s. Soon the Great Awakening, spreading south from New England, gradually altered the tone of Virginia life. With the Revolutionary triumph of the equalitarian spirit, the debonair Renaissance tone of early Virginia was subdued — subdued but not subjugated.

Early Virginians observed the seasons of the ecclesiastical year. In December came Advent, presaging the birth of Christ. This was the season of harvests and weddings, leading to the twelve joyous days of Christmas. On January 6 came Epiphany, celebrating the arrival of the Magi at the manger in Bethlehem. Forty days before Easter, Anglicans began the observance of Lent, commemorating Jesus' fast in the wilderness before his crucifixion — this was a period of fasting and penitence when social pleasures were foregone. Seven Sundays after Easter came Pentecost, commemorating the descent of the Holy Spirit on the apostles.

These festivals divided the years for religious, social, and some governmental purposes. Festival seasons were favored for weddings, which were announced on three successive Sundays in the parish church. "I publish the banns of marriage between .... and ....," the rector read. "If any of ye know cause or just impediment, why these two persons should not be joined together in Holy Matrimony, ye are to declare it . . ."

Other occasions for sociability were Court Days, held monthly at county seats, and Public Times, held each fall when the General Assembly met. Both were occasions for trading or for buying and selling, mixed with simple, rural conviviality. After the capital was moved to Williamsburg in 1699, the annual gatherings of the Burgesses were the signal for a more elaborate fair on the green, sometimes offering games of skill and strength, auctions, horse-races, and night-time balls and dramatics. Cudgelling, wrestling matches, and contests to catch a greased pig and climb a greased pole drew delighted crowds.

But the real social center of early Virginia was the hearth. The amusements of those days were the amusements of the home: family meals, small talk around the fire, spinning thread and weaving cloth, laying-in food for winter, and teaching the youngsters to read and write and do sums. "Many hands make light labor," parents told their children as they shelled peas for the winter ahead. After the "starving time" of early Jamestown, Virginians learned to put aside summer's produce for winter use in cold cellars and ice-houses.

The fare of Virginians was a combination of English and Indian. Its mainstay was Indian maize, which the settlers called corn. They ate it boiled or roasted on the ear, cut and mixed with other vegetables in stews, hulled and boiled as hominy, or ground and baked with other ingredients as cornpone, cornbread, eggbread, and a dozen other breads. Virginians, however, could not claim spoonbread, hush puppies, or hominy grits, which developed further south.

Wrote Robert Beverley in 1705:

The bread in gentlemen's houses is generally made of wheat, but some rather choose the pone, which is the bread made of Indian meal. Many of the poorer sort of people so little regard the English grain that though they might have it with the least trouble in the world, yet they don't mind to sow the ground, because they won't be at the trouble of making a fence particularly for it. And therefore their constant bread is pone, not so called from the Latin panis, but from the Indian name *oppone*.

Soups and stews were daily fare in early years, for the fork had not made its way from Italy, and knives and spoons were the only table silver. Into the ever-present fire-

Early colonists were home-loving people whose lives centered around the hearth. This seventeenth century woodcut shows an English family at dinner. *The Roxburghe Collection, British Museum*

Jamestown had several public houses which dispensed food and drink. Assemblymen gathered there during Public Times, as their successors enjoyed Williamsburg's inns. *The Roxburghe Collection, British Museum*

side stewpot went domestic meats as well as game, depending on what was available. Favorite stews were succotash, made of corn and butterbeans, and Brunswick stew, which developed in Brunswick County. Originally made with squirrels and vegetables, it came to include almost anything which the housekeeper had on hand. Like the Indians, the Virginia housewife threw into the pot whatever the season brought.

Pork long remained the favorite meat, for hogs were easier to raise than cattle or sheep. Settlers at Jamestown turned them loose to grub for roots and acorns in the woods. The wiry razorbacks trebled in weight in eight months. When the first freeze came in February, the largest was ready for slaughter. Its throat quickly cut, the porker was thrown into a vat of boiling water, scalded, skinned, and neatly butchered. While the housewife ground some parts into sausage and boiled fat with lye into soap, her husband salted the hams, shoulders, and side meat and hung it over a hickory fire to cure in the smokehouse. Other parts were salted down as fatback, salt pork, or sowbelly. Even chitterlings, jowls, and pig's feet were eaten.

Food, Drink, and Merriment [143]

The seventeenth century housewife needed many skills. She was her own butcher, baker, and brewer. In Virginia, she adopted Indian ways of cooking. *The Roxburghe Collection, British Museum*

Meat curing with sugar, molasses, and smoke, was developed to an art. Captain Mallory Todd, a former Bermuda ship captain, began to open up a wide market for Virginia meat when he exported hams from Smithfield to Bermuda in 1770. By this time planters had learned to grow pork by letting the porkers root peanuts left in the fields after the crop was dug up. The housewife's dependence on this staple was expressed by a frontier woman in James Fenimore Cooper's *The Chainbearer:*

I hold a family to be in a desperate way when the mother can see the bottom of the pork barrel. Give me the children that's raised on good sound pork afore all the game in the country. Game's good as a relish and so's bread; but pork is the staff of life.

The Swiss observer Francis Louis Michel agreed. He called Virginia pork "the best and the most delicate." Governor Sir William Gooch proudly sent hams to his brother, the Bishop of Norwich, and to the Bishops of London, Salisbury, and Bangor.

Common fare on the frontier was milk and mush. Mush was also eaten with molasses, boar's oil, or gravy.

Early fireplaces were kept busy cooking food and boiling water. They were large enough to hold long logs and a host of kettles and three-legged griddles called "spiders." Pans and pots were suspended from cranes built into the fireplace. Meats were speared on a spit, which was suspended over live coals and ashes. Occasionally, an oven was built into the fireplace for baking or roasting. A favorite bread, called ashcake, was made of cornmeal, wrapped in green cornhusks or cabbage leaves, and slowly cooked in wood ash.

As planters grew richer and houses grew larger, many kitchens were built separate from the main house. This prevented unwanted heat and food odors. On the Eastern Shore, the separate kitchen was often linked to the house by a breezeway. Writing in 1705, Robert Beverley reported that Virginians:

. . . have a great plenty and variety of provisions for their table, and as for spicery and other things that the country don't produce, they have constant supplies of 'em from England. The gentry pretend to have their victuals dressed and served up as nicely as at the best tables in London. Their richer sort generally brew their small-beer with malt, which they have from England, though they have as good barley of their own as any in the world. . . . Their strong drink is Madeira wine, which is a noble strong wine; and punch, made either of rum from the Caribee Islands, or brandy distilled from their apples and peaches; besides French brandy, wine, and strong beer, which they have constantly from England.

A noticeable growth in luxuries occurred in these years. An English cookbook, republished in Williamsburg in 1742 under the title *The Compleat Housewife, or accomplish'd gentlewoman's companion*, gives receipts (as the English and Virginians called them) for such luxuries as almond pudding, apple tansy, blanc mange, and syllabub (meaning "silly stomach"), the frothy ancestor of eggnog and tipsy squire. Ceremonial dinners ran to eight courses, punctuated by patriotic toasts. Such a feast began with soup, which was succeeded by ragouts, fricassees, and hors d'oeuvres. Next came roasts, then fish. Approaching the dinner's end — and perhaps his own — the guest was tantalized with sweets, then fruit in season, and finally conserves, marzipan, jams, and ices.

Seafood played an increasing part in the cuisine. Early settlers delighted in sturgeon and the panfish which abound in the Chesa-

Taverns and ordinaries slowly increased as Virginia grew in the eighteenth century. Men gathered in them to drink, talk, and hear the news read from England and American papers. This engraving, "The Coffee Mob," is from *The British Museum.*

peake: before long, they learned to plank shad on pine boards and broil it, as the Indians did, and to salt and smoke roe herring. In the eighteenth century, the evil-looking Chesapeake Bay crab and oyster were belatedly recognized for the delicacies they are. Receipts — or recipes — for pickled, smoked, stewed, fried, and stuffed oysters were exchanged by plantation mistresses. York River and Lynnhaven Bay, near Cape Henry, were celebrated for their oysters, but the Eastern Shore produced the greatest abundance of seafoods, including the cherished bluepoint oyster and cherrystone clam, which John Smith called "clamp."

Virginia wine cellars grew in proportion to their owners' prosperity. Ale and rum —

the first from England and the second from the West Indies or New England — were favored in earlier years, but homemade peach and apple brandy caught on as time passed. Wine was pressed from scuppernong and fox grapes which grew wild. Bourbon whiskey was first distilled in 1794 in Bourbon County, Kentucky, but Virginians long before that time made corn whiskey. When Governor Spotswood led his Knights of the Golden Horseshoe to the Valley of Virginia, a variety of drink was carried. Arriving at the Blue Ridge's peak, reported the official diarist:

We drank the King's health in champagne, and fired a volley; the Prince's health in Burgundy, and fired a volley; and all the rest of the royal family in claret, and a volley; we drank the Governor's health and fired another volley. We had several sorts of liquor, viz.: Virginia red wine and white wine, Irish usquebaugh, brandy, shrub, two sorts of rum, champagne, canary cherry, punch, water, cider, etc.

Despite the efforts of Thomas Jefferson to induce Virginians to drink wine, colonials preferred more potent drinks. John Randolph, a handy man with the bottle, scolded Cousin Jefferson for his un-Virginian preference for French wines, but the master of Monticello persisted. "I have lived temperately," he said on his seventy-sixth birthday, "eating little animal food, and that not as an aliment so much as a condiment for the vegetables, which constitute my principle diet. I double, however, the doctor's glass and a half of wine, and even treble it with a friend . . . Malt liquors and cider are my table drinks . . ."

Strong drink was so widely drunk that county courts regulated its price along with rates charged by inns for food, lodging, and stableage. The Isle of Wight County court, at Smithfield, permitted "good Barbados rum" to be sold at 10 shillings and "New England and other bad rum" at five. Hostelries regularly sold "small drink" — table wines, beer, and ale — with meals, while they dispensed headier wines and liquors at the bar.

William Randolph of Tuckahoe plantation, in a moment of epic exhilaration at a Williamsburg tavern, deeded 200 acres to Peter Jefferson in 1738 for "Henry Wetherburn's biggest bowl of arrack punch." The sweetened toddy and the mint julep were highly regarded as digestants and as proper drinks for ladies and invalids. Like

the English, gentlemen lingered after dinner over port and sherry, followed by cigars or pipes, while the ladies retired to escape the fumes and to gossip.

Eighteenth-century Virginians elevated eating and drinking to high ceremony. Over the Apollo Room mantel in Williamsburg's Raleigh Tavern were the words *Hilaritas Sapientiae et Bonae Vitae Proles* — "Jollity, the offspring of wisdom and good living," which was the spirit of the times. Christenings, royal birthdays, Easter, and Christmas were marked by health-drinking, toasts, and the firing of ceremonial guns. Men provided by will for drinks for their mourners. Rum

The Apollo Room of Williamsburg's Raleigh Tavern was frequented by Virginia's burgesses and councilors. Its overmantel motto — *Hilaritas Sapientiae et Bonae Vitae Proles* — bespoke the spirit of the age. From the film, *Williamsburg, The Story of a Patriot*

and funeral wines were said to be "as necessary a part of the funeral as the corpse."

The Reverend Edmund Watts objected. In his will in York County in 1676, he declared that "having observed in the days of my pilgrimage the debauched drinking at burials, tending much to the dishonor of God and His true religion, my will is that no strong drink be provided or spent at my burial."

The twelve days of Christmas were the high days of the year. Beginning in Advent, they brought a succession of church services, feasts, and hunts until Twelfth Night. At William and Mary, scholars traditionally barred the doors to the president and masters until they suspended classes, in mock indignation, and joined in a feast.

"The people spend most of their time visiting each other," exclaimed Monsieur Durand, who spent the season in Virginia in 1686. Along with nineteen other horsemen, the Frenchman casually dropped in on Colonel William Fitzhugh in Stafford County as Christmas approached. "He had a store of good wine and other things to drink, and a frolic ensued," Durand wrote. "He called in three fiddlers, a clown, a tight rope dancer, and an acrobatic tumbler, and gave us all the divertissement one would wish. It was very cold, but no one thought of going near the fire because they never put less than the trunk of a tree upon it, and so the entire room was kept warm."

A hundred years later the celebration had grown. The tutor, Philip Fithian, wrote in his diary at "King" Carter's Nomini Hall on December 18, 1773:

. . . When the candles were lighted we all repaired, for the last time, into the dancing room; first each couple danced a minuet; then all joined as before in the country dances; these

Country dances like this were popular at Christmas and other holidays. *The Roxburghe Collection, British Museum*

continued till half after seven, when at the proposal of several, we played button, to get pawns for redemption; here I could join with them, and indeed it was carried on with sprightliness and decency. In the course of redeeming my pawns I had several kisses of the ladies!

Half after eight we were run in to supper. The room looked luminous and splendid; four very large candles burning on the table where we supped; three others in different parts of the room; a gay, sociable asembly, and four well-instructed waiters! So soon as we rose from supper, the company formed into a semicircle round the fire and Mr. Lee by the voice of the company was chosen Pope, and the rest of the company were appointed friars in the play called "Break the Pope's Neck." Here we had great diversion in the respective judgments upon offenders, but we were all dismissed by ten, and retired to our several rooms.

Holiday feasts meant months of labor. William Byrd described his wife as "up to the elbow in sausages and black puddings" as Christmas 1736 approached. Old recipes for fruitcake, plum pudding, and mincemeat were followed with ritualistic care. No wonder a Virginia almanac wished its year-end readers "health, and good fires; victuals, drink, and good stomachs." To do justice to the hams, turkey, suckling pig, and wild game; the puddings and pastries; and the round of toasts in every liquor, the Virginian needed an iron stomach.

Besides her knowledge of cookery, the colonial housewife must know how to sew and knit so she could clothe her household. Daughters and woman servants were instructed and supervised in these domestic arts. So accustomed were unmarried women to the job of spinning that "spinster" came to have special meaning. If a housewife had leisure, she undertook fancy work like petit point embroidery of designs on canvas, or colorful crewelwork in worsted on a cloth background. Quilts were cut and pieced together of contrasting cloth, with filling of homespun or "linsey-woolsey" or goose down to give warmth. Quilting bees entertained pioneer women while their men raised a house or a barn.

Weddings, originally performed during Sunday church service, were celebrated at planters' homes in Tidewater as houses became more lordly. A houseparty of two or three days ensued, the guests feasting and dancing, playing cards, and teasing the newlyweds. Dances like the Virginia reel, which derived from country dances of England, were performed to fiddles and gourd banjos, played by slaves. These vied in later years with stately minuets, to music of the

Along the western Virginia frontier, corn huskings and other work gatherings were enlivened with music and food. *Colonial Williamsburg*

Food, Drink, and Merriment   [149]

harpsichord. The bridal couple remained for several days at her parents' house, for honeymoon trips were not feasible. There was no place to go.

In simpler Tidewater houses and along the Presbyterian frontier, the bride and groom were unceremoniously treated to a shivaree — a pots-and-pans serenade outside their bedroom. In German households of Northern Virginia, the bride was subjected to the prankish theft of her shoe, despite the bridesmaids' frantic vigil.

How Virginians loved to dance! "Blow high, blow low, Virginians will dance or die," exclaimed a Northern visitor in 1774. Arriving in Williamsburg in 1727, Governor Gooch wrote to his brother in England, "The gentlemen and ladies here are perfectly well bred. Not an ill dancer in my government." When Governor Dunmore and his lady visited Norfolk just before the Revolution, a townsman glowingly described the ball at Masons' Hall:

> . . . by and by the fiddles struck up, and there went my Lady Dunmore in the minuet, sailing about the room in her great, fine hoop-petticoat (her new-fashioned air baloon, as I called it), and Colonel Mosley after her, wig and all. Bless her heart, how cleverly she managed her hoop — now this way, now that. Everybody was delighted.
>
> Then came the reels, and here the Norfolk lads and lassies turned in with all their hearts and heels. This was my cue, and I led out my sweetheart, Nancy Wimble, in my best style, resolved to show all the sprigs of nobility what we Buckskins could do. In fact, I believe I cut some wonderful capers, sure enough, for I heard the young British dogs tittering one side . . . As for Nancy, I am sure she might have danced before the Queen. It is true, she hadn't a hoop then; but she didn't want one to set her off.

Dancing was expected of well-brought-up people. The Reverend Hugh Jones advocated that William and Mary's scholars should master "the accomplishments of music, dancing, and fencing." It was taught by masters in Williamsburg, Norfolk, Richmond, and even on isolated plantations. Charles Stagg of Williamsburg made a circuit of the Northern Neck each month to teach children the intricate steps of the Allemande, the Bretagne, the Rigadoon, and others. Minuets and French dances were especially popular.

Simpler pleasures abounded. Fish fries, oyster roasts, and barbecues — the latter introduced from Haiti — were frequent. Gaming was popular at all levels. So was gambling. It reached its nadir in the Revolutionary years, when high-living William Byrd III wagered and lost part of his estate. Having acquired the vice in London, Byrd indulged it recklessly in Virginia. A visitor to a Williamsburg tavern in 1765 encountered "professed gamesters, especially Colonel Byrd, who is never happy but when he has the box and dices in hand." He added, "This gentleman, from the greatest property of any in America, has reduced himself to that degree of gaming that few or nobody will credit him for ever so small a sum . . ."

Laws in England and Virginia restricted gambling and such sport as cards, dice, and cock-fighting to gentlemen, but they permitted all comers to indulge in them at Christmas, provided they had their masters' permission. Card games were of great variety, ranging from local inventions to European imports. Whist, ancestor of bridge, was a favorite of "the better sort." It was played to rules laid down by Edmond Hoyle in 1742 and replaced favorites like ruff and honors, slam, and the Spanish inventions, ombre and quadrille.

Jousting was popular at county fairs. The horseman who speared the most rings on his lance crowned the queen. *The British Museum*

Piquet was a two-handed game resembling both whist and cribbage, quickly played. An ancestor of the later seven-up or setback was all-fours or pitch, also two-handed. Put was the predecessor of poker, while lanterloo or loo became almost an obsession with Virginia ladies. A gambler's favorite, faro, pitted the luck of several players against a dealer, who turned up cards as his opponents bet. Chess and checkers — the latter known as draughts — were too deliberate for Virginians, but backgammon and hazard, resembling modern craps, were widespread. Lotteries could be authorized by the General Assembly; William Byrd III disposed of his property on Richmond's Church Hill by lottery in 1767.

Taverns were centers of life in Virginia, just as public houses, or pubs, were in England. Men of all ages gathered there to drink, game, and bowl or play cricket, shut-tlecock, or hand tennis on the green, as they had done since Jamestown's day. A ruckus occurred at Thomas Cocke's tavern at Varina in 1681 when two ninepin players disagreed in a contest for 400 pounds of tobacco. Charles Cotton observed in his *Compleat Gamester*, in 1674, that bowling was a waste of "time, money, and curses, and the last ten for one."

At county fairs, jousting was a favorite. A relic of medieval combat between lance-carrying horsemen, it was a devil-may-care contest between riders travelling at break-neck speed to impale on a lance a series of rings, suspended from supports along a straight course. The sport required a well-trained mount and a steady arm. The "knight" who collected the most rings crowned his lady as "queen."

Another manly sport was quoits. Contestants attempted to toss disks onto an iron

Bowls.

Quoits.

Skittles.

Lawn sports were played at taverns and on courthouse greens. John Marshall excelled at quoits, which resembled horseshoe-pitching. *The Guildhall Library, London*

stake, usually on a court or tavern green. Richmond men after the Revolution met weekly at Buchanan's Springs, on the edge of town, to throw quoits and drink punch and toddy. John Marshall was one, as were the town's amiable Anglican and Presbyterian parsons, the Rev. John Buchanan and the Rev. John Blair. Marshall was an expert, "with his long arms hanging loosely by his side, a quoit in each hand . . ." His awkwardness was deceptive!

Young and old visited kin for months on nearby plantations, for eighteenth-century families had abundant cousins. The households of the Thomas Nelsons at Yorktown and the John Pages at Rosewell, across the York, were forever exchanging visits, for five Nelson children married five Pages.

The late eighteenth century popularized summer journeys to the springs, a Virginian diversion which still flourishes. Dozens of these streams — some warm, some hot —

were found gushing through the limestone of upland Virginia in the eighteenth century. That intrepid explorer, Dr. Thomas Walker of Albermarle, found six invalids bathing at Hot Springs in Bath County when he discovered it in 1750. An inn and bath-houses were built there about 1766. The crusty bachelor, the sixth Lord Fairfax, journeyed from Greenway Court near Winchester to his Berkeley "Health Springs," now in West Virginia, to drink and bathe. He deeded it to the colony of Virginia in 1756 "for the welfare of suffering humanity." By 1776, Philip Fithian found 400 people seeking health at Bath County's celebrated springs.

After the Revolution, a rash of Virginia springs lured lowlanders: Warm Springs, White Sulphur Springs, Orkney Springs, Frye's Springs, Old Sweet Springs, Chalybeate Springs, and others *ad infinitum*. Mountain summers attracted families from the Carolinas and Maryland to escape the dog days. The usual route was by boat to Fredericksburg and then by stage over the hills to Orange, Charlottesville, and upland.

At Warm Springs, which Jefferson visited, separate bath houses were the rule. An early visitor advised others: "You should have a large cotton morning gown of a cashmere shawl pattern lined with crimson, a fancy Greek cap, Turkish slippers, and a pair of loose pantaloons; a garb that will not consume much time in doffing and donning."

But Virginians' entertainment remained centered in the family. Their lives, largely homebound and uneventful, were enriched by warm mutual hospitality. In this exhuberant spirit they lived and died.

Thermal and mineral springs in upland Virginia attracted health-seekers from the 1760s onward. This was Bath Alum Springs at the end of the colonial era. *Virginia State Library*

I have long been sensible that while I was endeavoring to render my country the greatest of all services — that of regenerating the public education, and placing the rising generation on the level of our sister states (which they have proudly held heretofore) — I was discharging the odious function of a physician pouring medicine down the throat of a patient insensible of needing it.

Thomas Jefferson

Students at William and Mary founded Phi Beta Kappa in 1776. Shown with the charter are John Marshall, William Short, Archibald Stuart, and Bushrod Washington, seated in the Apollo Room of Raleigh Tavern. *From the mural by Johannes Waller in Levere Memorial Temple, Evanston, Illinois.*

11

Learned institutions ought to be favorite objects with every free people. They throw that light over the public mind which is the best security against crafty and dangerous encroachments on the public liberty. They are the nurseries of skillful teachers for the schools distributed throughout the community. They are themselves schools for the particular talents required for some of the public trusts, on the able execution of which the welfare of the people depends. They multiply the educated individuals, from among whom the people may elect a due portion of their public agents of every description. . . .

The rich man, when contributing to a permanent plan for the education of the poor, ought to reflect that he is providing for that of his own descendants; and the poor man, who concurs in a provision for those who are not poor, that at no too distant day it may be enjoyed by descendants from himself.

James Madison

The Quest for Knowledge

To Virginia's first settlers, learning was a polite acquisition which set gentlemen apart from the lower classes. Its emphasis was decorative rather than useful, signifying that he who received it had reached a station where he could enjoy the acquisition of knowledge for its own sake. This caste connotation of "polite learning" retarded Virginia for centuries. Not until the bookish Scotch-Irish flooded the colony and Thomas Jefferson called for a better-educated electorate did schools begin to grow.

In view of their background, the colonists' neglect of education is understandable. England had no system of free education in 1607 or even until the 1870's. At the time

Jamestown was settled, half of England could neither read nor write. Parents who could afford it had sons tutored or paid their tuition to a "public school," endowed by church, trade guild, or benefactor. Finally, Oxford and Cambridge educated sons of nobles and gentlemen plus a few boys of poor families preparing for the professions. The product of the English university was judged to be a scholar and a gentleman, however humble his start in life.

Almost from the beginning, a few Virginia families of wealth sent sons to England for schooling: Sewells, Wormeleys, Catletts, Warners, Lees, Byrds, Custises, and others. In the colony itself, however, little schooling was available. An appeal was made in England in 1617 for funds to build an Indian school in Virginia, and Governor Sir George Yeardley in 1618 was told by his over-optimistic employers to build a university at Henrico, a town laid out in embryo forty miles above Jamestown, on the James. In 1621 gifts were received from England for a public free school on the present site of Hopewell to prepare students for the university to rise at Henrico. However, all these plans died aborning when Indians rose up in 1622 and massacred 347 of Virginia's 1,250 settlers.

The scattering of tobacco planters' families after 1622 made centralized schooling

Children learned the alphabet and Lord's Prayer from the wooden Hornbook, so-called because transparent horn protected the vellum text. *Virginia State Library*

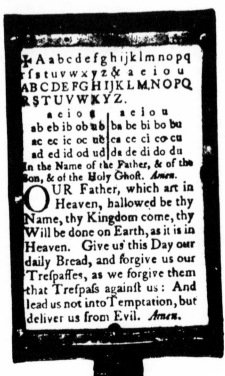

difficult. In a new country, whose settlers were young, the birthrate was high. Parents who could read and write usually taught their children between tobacco seasons, when severe weather kept them often indoors. They used primers and hornbooks containing the alphabet, a table of numbers, and the Lord's Prayer.

The first money for a free school was given by Benjamin Syms of Elizabeth City County in 1635. He gave two acres of land in the present city of Hampton, the proceeds from the sale of milk, and the calves produced by a herd of eight cows. Twenty-four years later, Thomas Eaton of the same county left land and cattle for a school adjoining Syms' and later combined with it. Here reading, writing, and "ciphering" were taught, together with the catechism and Anglican creeds and prayers. In 1675 a similar school was created by the will of Henry Peasley of Gloucester County. Mrs. Mary Whaley in 1706 created "Matty's School" in Williamsburg to honor her dead son, Matthew. Three other schools followed by 1721. However, only a few of Virginia's 175,000 people were within reach of these primary schools.

The situation at the secondary school level was no better. Nothing was done in Virginia's first seventy-five years to open a Latin grammar school to prepare boys of "good understanding" for a university. These were the schools Governor Sir William Berkeley dismissed with the observation, "I thank God there are no free schools nor printing, and I hope we shall not have these hundred years, for learning has brought disobedience and heresy and sects into the world."

(Berkeley disdained "free" Latin grammar schools because they opened the pro-

Rural Virginia had few schools despite the example of Benjamin Syms of Elizabeth City, who in 1635 gave land and goods for the first free school in the colony. Planters sent their sons to England or employed tutors. Woodcut illustration from *Orbis Sensualis*. *The British Museum*

fessions to poor scholars and because they had been fostered by the anti-monarchist Oliver Cromwell and his Puritan and Presbyterian followers. Royalists like Berkeley opposed their democratic effect. To its great gain, Puritan New England opened many such schools in these early years.)

Most young Virginians, in contrast with New Englanders, were home-trained, too often poorly. Thousands of indentured young people who came from England to Virginia under a contract to work in return for passage and keep were taught only by their masters. Under this apprentice system, poor or orphan girls were bound to mistresses until 18 and boys to masters until 21 to learn trades. In return for their work, they received food, clothing, lodging, and perhaps a few lessons. Indentured girls

learned household arts, while boys became shoemakers, weavers, tailors, blacksmiths, or other tradesmen.

The nearest seventeenth-century equivalent training to England's "public," or Latin, schools was given at plantation and parson's schools. A prosperous planter father engaged a schoolmaster to live as member of his family and instruct his children. Such was William Ellery Channing, who came from Harvard to Ampthill, the household of David Meade Randolph in Chesterfield County. Similar was a parson's school, or community school, usually conducted by the rector of a parish. The Reverend James Waddell, celebrated "blind preacher," had such a school in Louisa County. These were often built on worn-out land and known as "old field schools."

The Quest for Knowledge [157]

Most early schools had a brief life. Beside the free schools, we know that John Hicks opened a school in 1676 in Accomack and Nathaniel Capell in 1678 in Northampton. Soon afterward, Valentine Evans began to teach in York and Thomas Dalby in Henrico. The bookish Scotch-Irish started others after they arrived in the 1730s. Scottish parson Robert Alexander opened the first classical school in the Valley in 1749, and Samuel Davies' erstwhile adherents launched others from 1775 to 1795 in Prince Edward, Hanover, and Louisa. Still more were born in that turbulent era at Williamsburg, Fredericksburg, Alexandria, Winchester, Harrisonburg, and in other county seats. True to their faith, Scotsmen built many of these.

The long-awaited "university" did not emerge in Virginia until the last of the lackluster Stuart kings was deposed in the "Glorious Revolution" of 1688. And when it came, the "university" was partly Scottish in its beginnings. With the ascension of the Whig monarchs William and Mary in 1689, a new era began for the average Briton. The people gained Parliamentary power, and the long Catholic-Protestant vendetta ended. At this propitious moment, the victorious English Church moved to assert its belated concern for the souls of colonists.

The tough-minded, thirty-four-year-old cleric chosen for the job in Virginia was James Blair. Blair had been sent in 1685 as a missionary to Varina Parish, on the James River, and his common sense gospel was welcomed by the hard-working farmers. As a native of rural Scotland, educated at Marischal College and the University of Edinburgh, Blair understood the colonists' sense of exploitation by England. Serving briefly as a preacher in Scotland, he had found too few Anglicans to justify his tarrying there. Now, finding himself needed and welcome in this raw land, he shared its resentment of Colonial Office neglect. Blair spent the rest of his long life fighting for what he felt Virginia needed.

At Blair's first conference with his clergy, held soon thereafter at Jamestown, he found spirited support for a college to train preachers and scholars. Spotswood and his council were already enthusiastic, pledging £2000 and calling on wealthy planters for additional pledges. The Assembly followed by naming trustees and specifying that the "university" include grammar, philosophical, and divinity schools — that is, a liberal arts and divinity school with a preparatory Latin school. With inspired wisdom, the Assembly sent Blair to England as its agent to obtain the necessary charter and endowment.

It proved a happy choice. With the aid of Bishop Compton and the Archbishop of Canterbury, Blair obtained audience with William and Mary, who applauded "so good a design" and a year later granted a charter and sizeable money from taxes and lands. The adroit Blair also gathered other plums; among them were part of the "pirates' fund" which buccaneers paid for amnesty,

and a legacy from Robert Boyle for an Indian school, built in 1723. Blair was named president for life, with the Governor and others as trustees.

Despite the crown's backing, the college had to fight for its life. Virginia in 1690 was frankly materialistic. Planters lusted for land, servants, and mansions like English gentlemen's. Plantations were growing, and men willing to sweat were getting rich in the tobacco trade. Who could spare a son to conjugate Latin verbs when fortunes were to be made?

For the first few years, enrollment in the college grew slowly. Though the grammar school opened in 1694 and the college about 1698, it was 1729 before all six professors called for in the charter had been brought over from England and Scotland. At Blair's death in 1743, the college still had less than fifty students. Probably an equal number attended the grammar school.

Intellectual discipline was not easy for youths reared in Virginia's wide forests and fields. College rules forbade them to keep "any race horse at the college, in the town, or anywhere in the neighborhood." Betting on races was against rules. So were dawdling in ale-houses, cock-fighting, or leaving the college yard without permission. Students were not allowed to play billiards or to bring cards or dice to college. Like collegians at Oxford or Cambridge, they wore academic robes to show they were scholars.

To be sure, there were compensations. Williamsburg was the capital of England's largest colony and attracted observers from Europe and the colonies. The town buzzed with people during the Assembly's annual Public Times. Ships from abroad docked at the town landings. Collegians were awed to see the Governor in his carriage of state, with liveried coachmen, driving to the Capitol to represent the King at the opening of each session. Some planter scions brought their manservants, and food was ample. The housekeeper was required to provide "plenty of victuals; that breakfast, dinner, and supper be served up in the cleanest and neatest manner possible. There must be fresh meat

The opening of the College of William and Mary in 1694 raised the level of Virginia's intellectual life. The central structure contained classrooms and quarters for faculty and students. Built later were the Indian school, at left, and the President's House, right. From an eighteenth century engraving found in the Bodleian Library, Oxford University, now owned by *Colonial Williamsburg*.

as well as salt meat, and twice a week as well as Sundays, pies and puddings must show themselves on the table."

After its first hesitant years, the college began to exert the influence for which Blair and Nicholson had hoped. Its existence set a standard in the relatively refined eighteenth century, after the General Assembly in 1699 had transferred the capital from Jamestown to Middle Plantation. Here, in a century of greater leisure, a new generation grew up with more concern for God and man. When Wesleyan evangelist George Whitefield visited the college in 1739, he "rejoiced in seeing such a place in America."

Theological training never took deep root at William and Mary, for few early Virginians were notably pious or scholarly. The culture of Virginia was oral rather than literary. Learning was not at first widely esteemed. However, the college spread a luminous humanism in the generations of Thomas Jefferson, James Monroe, Benjamin Harrison, and its other sons who became statesmen of the early republic. Through James Blair and his Anglo-Scottish faculty, William and Mary transmitted to Virginia the Whiggish independence of mind of John Locke, who in old age wrote Blair from England, "I hope the college grows and flourishes under your care."

William and Mary was also responsible for much that was creative in the colony. The very structure itself, inspired by the architect Sir Christopher Wren, set a standard for Virginia buildings after 1698. Scholarship was advanced by the historical writing of the Reverend Hugh Jones, one-time master, and the Reverend William Stith, a graduate and early president; by the political pamphlets of Jefferson and James Bland, both alumni; and by the first Ameri-

The great English philosopher John Locke helped James Blair to found a college in Virginia. *From the life portrait by Godfrey Kneller in the Virginia Museum of Fine Arts.*

can textbook of the law by St. George Tucker, the college's second professor of law.

Joshua Fry, an early professor, mapped the western frontier, while Bishop James Madison, a graduate and a cousin of President Madison, who became William and Mary's president, made the survey for the Pennsylvania-Virginia boundary. Phi Beta Kappa was founded by fifty students of William and Mary at Raleigh Tavern in 1776. In the caliber of its men and its ideas, William and Mary profoundly influenced the growing self-confidence of America.

Great change overtook the college in the Revolution. To the new-style American, time spent on Latin and Greek seemed wasted in an age of science. The country needed lawyers, physicians, scientists; under Scottish influence, emphasis on practical knowledge was increasing. In the radical revision of the Virginia Constitution made by the Virginia Assembly in 1779, Governor Jefferson recognized the state's need for an educated electorate. He proposed that each county create public schools, with free schooling for poor children and the remainder paying tuition. The brightest graduates would go on to William and Mary, which Jefferson attempted to reform in his bill "for amending the constitution of the College of William and Mary, and substituting more certain revenues for its support."

Alas! Though Jefferson was right, he was as usual ahead of his time. As a result, the plan for public schools failed for lack of county support. His reorganization of the college was partially accomplished, however. This included abolition of its Anglican theological school, which, Jefferson concluded, was "not adapted to the life of a republican government;" in its stead, the teaching of law, medicine, and modern languages was begun. Also introduced was the elective system of studies, hitherto unknown in America.

The able lawyer George Wythe, who had taught John Marshall and other young men in his Williamsburg law office, was chosen professor of law, while Dr. James McClurg, a graduate of Edinburgh, came from Hampton Smallpox Hospital to be professor of medicine. To teach languages, the college installed Carlos Bellini, who had come to Virginia with his fellow Italian nationalist Philip Mazzei at Jefferson's encouragement.

With all its intellectual advances, however, Virginia in the Revolutionary era neglected science, whose discoveries were destined to transform nineteenth-century America from an agricultural to an industrial society. While medical schools, scientific laboratories, and factories like Eleuthere de Pont's were sprouting in the North, Virginians showed no zeal for clinical studies or experiments. Their scientific interest lay chiefly in the cataloguing of American flora and fauna, to satisfy the curiosity of Europeans concerning the unfamiliar birds and beasts of North America. (Everyone was especially fascinated by the opossum, which, it was said, carried its young in a pouch!)

John Clayton of Gloucester provided such information for *Flora Virginica*, published in Leyden in 1739, and corresponded with the famous scientists Carl von Linnaeus, John Bartram, and Benjamin Franklin. Mark Catesby of Williamsburg in the same period wrote the text and painted pictures of 220 birds and beasts for his *Natural History of Carolina, Florida, and the Bahama Islands*. Dr. John Mitchell, a physican by profession but a zoologist by choice, wrote *Nova Plantarum Genera* at his home in Urbanna. To European botanists, these men and others sent countless seeds, dried plants, and dead animals preserved in alcohol.

The aging Clayton and his enthusiastic disciple John Page founded The Virginia Society for Promoting Useful Knowledge in 1773. It enrolled a hundred members but died out in the Revolution.

The most influential advocate of the new science was Dr. William Small, Jefferson's favorite professor at William and Mary. Small's brilliance won the admiration of Governor Fauquier and all comers before his untimely return to Britain. "He fixed my destinies in life," Jefferson declared. No teacher in early Virginia won such praise.

When Richmond became Virginia's capital in 1780, the intellectual sheen of

Williamsburg slowly dimmed. The college lost Wythe, Dr. McClurg, and other luminaries, for Wythe was judge of Virginia's chancery court as well as teacher, and he chose to keep his role in Virginia's government. Lawyers and merchants followed the Assembly to the uncouth new capital, leaving houses and shops vacant. Williamsburg stopped growing. Its college was no longer at the crossroads of political life. Young scholars missed the exciting stimulus of fiery debate in the House of Burgesses.

Richmond tried to provide its new capital with an intellectual center, as Williamsburg had had. Led by a French scholar, the Chevalier Quesnay de Beaurepaire, Rich-

MÉMOIRE

STATUTS ET PROSPECTUS,

CONCERNANT

L'ACADÉMIE

DES SCIENCES ET BEAUX-ARTS

DES ÉTATS-UNIS DE L'AMÉRIQUE,

ÉTABLIE A RICHEMOND,

CAPITALE DE LA VIRGINIE;

PRÉSENTÉS A LEURS MAJESTÉS,
ET A LA FAMILLE ROYALE,

Par le Chevalier QUESNAY DE BEAUREPAIRE.

A PARIS,

De l'Imprimerie de CAILLEAU, Imprimeur
de l'Académie de RICHEMOND,
rue Gallande, No. 64.

1788.

The French scholar Quesnay de Beaurepaire issued this prospectus in 1788 for the Academy of Science and Fine Arts, which he opened in Richmond. *Virginia Museum of Fine Arts*

monders gave money for an "Academy of Arts and Sciences of the United States of America," which was built on the Broad Street site later occupied by the Medical College of Virginia. Young Quesnay proposed to offer medicine, astronomy, natural history, chemistry, mineralogy, painting, sculpture, architecture, and foreign languages. A lecture hall was built, and Virginia's Constitutional Ratification Convention met there in 1788. However, Quesnay's ambitious academy failed. Virginians lacked zeal for science and the arts.

In addition to its tax-supported "official" college, Virginia in these pulsating years developed two others — both through Presbyterian effort — before the Revolution. Liberty Hall Academy — later Washington and Lee University — and Hampden Sydney College were typical of the sectarian schools which predominated in America until Jefferson made higher education the responsibility of government. They also illustrate the contrast between Tidewater and frontier.

The Scotch-Irish who flowed into the Valley in the 1730s had the Scottish zeal for learning. One of them was Robert Alexander, a gaduate of Edinburgh, who opened a Latin school in Augusta County in 1749. His successor was the Rev. John Brown, an early graduate of Princeton. Their school, the first classical academy in the Valley, stood between Staunton and Lexington, close by the Great Pennsylvania Wagon Road. In its rustic simplicity and discipline, Augusta Academy was similar to Samuel Blair's academy at Flagg's Manor, in Pennsylvania, which had schooled Samuel Davies and other "New Side" preachers. It also had the same Scottish thoroughness. Most of Augusta's graduates entered Princeton to study for the ministry, or went on to read

The leading school west of the mountains was Liberty Hall at Lexington, which became Washington and Lee University. Walls of the early academy stand on a hill adjoining the present campus. *André Studio, Lexington*

law. Many entered the rugged politics and land trading of the frontier. Three or four founded colleges in Kentucky and Tennessee.

In 1780 the school, renamed Liberty Hall, moved to Lexington. There it flourished under the mastership of William Graham. A limestone schoolhouse was built on a Lexington hilltop. Through Graham's efforts, the General Assembly in 1782 empowered it to grant degrees. At the same time, the newly-incorporated academy passed from control of Presbyterians to independent trustees. Through the intervention of Graham's Princeton classmate, General "Lighthorse Harry" Lee, Washington was persuaded to give the academy $50,000 in canal stock which the General Assembly had awarded him. It was the largest gift to any American school at that time.

President William Graham, a Scottish Presbyterian minister, raised Liberty Hall Academy to collegiate status in 1782. George Washington gave it $50,000 in canal stock. *Lexington Presbyterian Church and Washington and Lee University*

The Quest for Knowledge [163]

An ACADEMY.

PRINCE EDWARD, *Sept.* 1, 1775.

BY the generous Exertions of several Gentlemen in this and some of the neighbouring Counties, very large Contributions have lately been made for erecting and supporting a public ACADEMY near the Courthouse in this County. Their Zeal for the Interests of Learning and Virtue has met with such Success, that they were enabled to let the Buildings in *March* last to several Undertakers, who are proceeding in their Work with the greatest Expedition. A very valuable Library of the best Writers, both ancient and modern, on most Parts of Science and polite Literature, is already procured; with Part of an Apparatus to facilitate the Studies of the Mathematicks and Natural Philosophy, which we expect in a short Time to render complete.—The Academy will certainly be opened on the 10th of next *November*: It is to be distinguished by the Name of HAMPDEN-SIDNEY, and will be subject to the Visitation of twelve Gentlemen of Character and Influence in their respective Counties; the immediate and acting Members being chiefly of the Church of *England*. The Number of Visitors and Trustees will probably be increased as soon as the Distractions of the Times shall so far cease as to enable its Patrons to enlarge its Foundations.——The Students will all board and study under the same Roof, provided for by a common Steward, except such as choose to take their Boarding in the Country. The Rates, at the utmost, will not exceed 10l. Currency *per Annum* to the Steward, and 4l. Tuition Money; 20s. of this being always paid at Entrance.

The System of Education will resemble that which is adopted in the College of *New Jersey*, save, that a more particular Attention shall be paid to the Cultivation of the *English* Language than is usually done in Places of public Education. Three Masters and Professors are ready to enter in *November*, and as many more may be easily procured as the increased Number of Students may at any Time hereafter require. And our Prospects at present are so extremely flattering that it is probable we shall be obliged to procure two Professors more before the Expiration of the Year. The Public may rest assured that the Whole shall be conducted on the most *catholic* Plan. Parents, of every Denomination, may be at full Liberty to require their Children to attend on any Mode of Worship which either Custom or Conscience has rendered most agreeable to them. For our Fidelity, in every Respect, we are cheerfully willing to pledge our Reputation to the Public; which may be the more relied on, because our whole Success depends upon their favourable Opinion. Our Character and Interest, therefore, being both at Stake, furnish a strong Security for our avoiding all Party Instigations; for our Care to form good men, and good Citizens, on the common and universal Principles of Morality, distinguished from the narrow Tenets which form the Complexion of any Sect; and for our Assiduity in the whole Circle of Education.

SAMUEL S. SMITH.

P. S. The principal Building of the Academy not being yet completed, those Gentlemen who desire their Children to enter immediately will be obliged to take Lodgings for them in the Neighbourhood, during the Winter Season; which may be done in Houses sufficiently convenient, on very reasonable Terms. 4

WAS left at the Subscriber's, in *Fredericksburg*, in 1773, a very large STILL-TUB and WORM, marked I H, N° 1. The Owner is desired to take it away, and pay all Charges. JACOB WHITLER.

SOUTH RIVER, *Augusta* County, *Sept.* 20, 1775.
STRAYED, or STOLEN, from *West*—

The Reverend Samuel Stanhope Smith, a Scottish Presbyterian graduate of Princeton, was the first president of Hampden-Sydney. *Hampden-Sydney College*

The first announcement of the creation of Hampden-Sydney College appeared in the *Virginia Gazette* in September, 1775. *Hampden-Sydney College*

The new Revolutionary accord between Tidewater and frontier is evident in Washington's letter to the trustees:

> To promote literature in this rising empire and to encourage the arts, have ever been among the warmest wishes of my heart, and if the donation . . . is likely to prove a means to accomplish these ends, it will contribute to the gratification of my desire.

Hampden-Sydney, which was similar in background to the college at Lexington, was an outgrowth of Samuel Davies' mission in Virginia from 1748 to 1759. Agitation for a college and seminary had arisen in Hanover Presbytery soon after Davies organized it in 1755, for the "French deism" of William and Mary disturbed upland families, and Princeton was far away. When Peter Johnston gave 98 acres in Prince Edward County in 1774, Davies' dream took shape in the tobacco farmland of Piedmont Virginia.

Announcement of "An Academy" at Prince Edward first appeared in the *Virginia Gazette* in 1775. When the institution opened next year it bore the name Hampden-Sydney College, though it included a preparatory school. The English patriots John Hampden and Sir Philip Sydney were heroes to the college's Revolutionary founders. But however anti-monarchist it might be, Hampden-Sydney was not to be anti-Anglican. It would have twelve trustees, it declared, "the immediate and acting members being chiefly of the Church of England." Madison and Patrick Henry, both Anglicans, were on the college's first board.

Experimental science appears to have been as neglected at early Hampden-Sydney as at William and Mary. However, the college shared Jefferson's enthusiasm for other useful knowledge. "The system of education," wrote President Samuel Stanhope Smith, "will resemble that which is adopted in the College of New Jersey [later Princeton]; save that a more particular attention shall be paid to the cultivation of the English language than is usually done . . ." Smith and most professors had attended Princeton, and relations between Presbyterian mother and her offspring remained close.

Hampden-Sydney was an instant success. It opened with 110 students, some in its academy and others in its college. Charges were £4 per session for tuition and £10 for board and room. These low rates were possible because clergymen-teachers were poorly paid and because food was cheap. Parents were advised:

> The Steward is appointed to furnish good and wholesome diet to the students, one half of the meat at least to be fresh, and one half of the bread to be made of the fine flour of wheat. And he obliges himself to furnish servants to keep their rooms clean and in good order, for which services he is to receive at the rate of eight pounds currency per annum; . . . The students will be obliged to provide their own beds, or to pay a moderate hire for them, and to buy their own candles and washing, which they may do at a final expense. For some years they will be permitted to take their wood off the land belonging to the Academy, gratis . . .

By modern standards, the scope of Virginia's three colonial colleges seems small. Their students at no time in this period totalled 400 men. Endowment was slight and professors' pay was poor. Nevertheless, they and their students lighted the lamp of knowledge in a vast section of America. As the oldest and largest of the colonies, Virginia saw hordes of her people migrate to Virginia territory which became West Virginia, Kentucky, and the Northwest Territory. Countless others went south. Wherever they went, the wise and godly teachings of Virginia's schoolmasters helped create a better land.

The First Virginia Collegians: Few but Famous

Virginia's first three colleges were small, but they produced great leaders of the Revolution. Moving westward and southward with the tide of settlement after 1781, many of them became statesmen, judges, or founders of colleges in new states that drew strength from Virginia. A sampling of early alumni:

The College of William and Mary, founded 1693

John Blair, Associate Justice of the Supreme Court
Richard Bland, member of the Continental Congress
Philip Pendleton Barbour, Associate Justice of the Supreme Court
Carter Braxton, signer of the Declaration of Independence
Benjamin Harrison, signer of the Declaration of Independence
Thomas Jefferson, President of the United States
John Marshall, Chief Justice of the United States
James Monroe, President of the United States
John Randolph of Roanoke, United States Minister to Russia
Edmund Randolph, Secretary of State of the United States
Peyton Randolph, first president of the Continental Congress
Spencer Roane, Chief Justice of the Virginia Supreme Court of Appeals
John Taylor of Caroline, author of "The Arator" papers, United States Senator
John Tyler Jr., President of the United States
Andrew Stevenson, Speaker of the House of Representatives, U.S. Minister to England
Bushrod Washington, Associate Justice of the Supreme Court
George Wythe, signer of the Declaration of Independence

Augusta Academy, founded 1749 (later Washington and Lee University)

The Rev. Archibald Alexander, president of Hampden-Sydney College
The Rev. George Addison Baxter, president of Washington College (later Washington and Lee University)
General James Breckenridge, Member of Congress from Virginia
John Breckenridge, author of the Kentucky Resolutions of 1798, Attorney General of the United States
James Brown, United States Senator from Kentucky
General William Campbell, hero of the Revolutionary battle of King's Mountain
The Rev. Samuel Doak, president of Washington College, Tennessee, and Tusculum College, Tennessee
The Rev. Moses Hoge, president of Hampden-Sydney College
Meriwether Lewis, Governor of Louisiana Territory
George Matthews, Governor of Georgia
Andrew Moore, United States Senator from Virginia
James Moore, president of Transylvania College, Kentucky
The Rev. James Priestley, president of Cumberland College, Tennessee (later George Peabody College for Teachers)
Th Rev. John Holt Rice, elected president of Princeton College
Thomas Todd, Associate Justice of the Supreme Court

Hampden-Sydney College, founded 1775

George Mortimer Bibb, Secretary of the Treasury of the United States
Nathaniel Francis Cabell, author of historical and religious works
William H. Cabell, a founder of the University of Virginia
William Branch Giles, United States Senator from Virginia
William Henry Harrison, President of the United States
Dr. John Peter Mettauer, leading physician and medical teacher
William Cabell Rives, U.S. Senator from Virginia, U.S. Minister to France
The Rev. Moses Waddel, president of Franklin College(later the University of Georgia)

They are such lovers of riding that almost every ordinary person keeps a horse; and I have known some spend the morning in ranging several miles in the woods to find and catch their horses, only to ride two or three miles to church, to the court house, or to a horse-race, where they generally appoint to meet upon business. . . .

The Rev. Hugh Jones,
The Present State of Virginia and the College, 1724

There are races at Williamsburg twice a year; that is, every spring and fall, or autumn. Adjoining the town is a very excellent course, for either two-, three-, or four-mile heats. Their purses are generally raised by subscription, and are gained by the horse that wins two four-mile heats out of three; they amount to an hundred pounds each for the first day's running, and fifty pounds each every day after; the races commonly continuing for a week. . . .

J. F. D. Smith,
Tour of the United States of America, 1787

12

Outdoor Life

Virginia was part of the frontier of European civilization through colonial times. The three-cornered palisade at Jamestown in 1607 was not far different from the blockhouse which Daniel Boone built against the Indians at Boonesborough in 1774. For 175 years, most Virginians grew up in an untamed land, fearing the insurrection of Indians and Negroes. Only the fit and fortunate lived out a normal life span.

The bantam, cocky John Smith was the classic Virginia outdoorsman. Scorning the safety of James Fort, he explored lowland Virginia for two years to map it and trade with its Indians before he returned to England. He was the first of many explorers, and

fighters to gain fame in Virginia: the Indian traders Abraham Wood and William Byrd I in the first century and later Alexander Spotswood, George Washington, Dr. Thomas Walker, Daniel Boone, and many others in the second century.

Like any frontier society, Virginia valued bravery as the highest virtue. Youths automatically served in the militia, which had to be ready on short notice to fight Indians or Spaniards. Up through its ranks came young Washington, who won a lieutenant-colonelcy at 21. It was this county militia which trained such Revolutionary leaders as Lighthorse Harry Lee of Westmoreland, Hugh Mercer of Fredericksburg,

The heavy matchlock musket protected Virginia's first settlers. This soldier of King James I wears a bandoleer over his shoulder containing charges of powder. He holds a spike to support the gun barrel when firing. *Woodcut from a broadside in the British Museum*

A halberdier or pike-bearer from the reign of James I illustrates use of the weapon in battle. He wears a breastplate and helmet with plumes like those worn by guardsmen in James Fort at early Jamestown. *Woodcut from 'A Schoole for Young Soldiers . . .' in the British Museum*

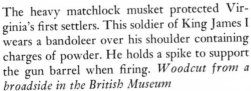

Cumbersome matchlock muskets are shown in this frontispiece decoration from a seventeenth century book, dedicated to the Earl of Oxford. *The British Museum*

and George Rogers Clark of Charlottesville. In the uplands, the Scotch-Irish produced Indian fighters like Daniel Morgan of Winchester, Andrew Lewis and William Campbell of Augusta, and James and Robert Breckenridge of Botetourt.

A Virginia father taught his sons at an early age to use a gun. An early law of the colony required the head of each family to keep one at hand, with two pounds of powder and eight pounds of shot for each dependent able to carry arms. Settlers were forbidden to trade them to Indians. Guns were listed in wills as items of importance.

The militia stood watch over the colony from the earliest years, springing into action in the French and Indian Wars and the Revolution. As each new county was created, the governor as commander-in-chief named its county lieutenant and subordinate officers. These in turn were expected to enlist and drill troops, though they were often lax.

The guns brought from England to Jamestown were matchlock muskets, which were so heavy that the barrel had to be rested on a support to be fired with any accuracy. These primitive weapons were loaded with loose powder from small vials, which the musketeer suspended from a bandoleer, worn from shoulder to waist, and fired by match. Such unwieldy weapons were slow to fire, and their loose powder was dangerous, as Captain John Smith learned when hurt by premature firing in 1610.

The matchlock was succeeded by the wheelock, whose powder was ignited by sparks from a built-in flint. About 1721 came the improved flintlock small-bore rifle, made by a Swiss emigrant to Pennsylvania. One early gunsmith was Henry Spitzer, who migrated from Pennsylvania to New Market, where he established a gun shop.

Deer abounded, and venison was a common meat. Settlers and an Indian are shown bringing a buck they have bagged into James Fort, reconstructed at Jamestown Festival Park. *The Jamestown Foundation*

He made a rifle each week, first for about $15 and later for more. "Old Spits" rifles were used in early Kentucky and Tennessee.

Hunting was widely enjoyed even by slaves. Great flights of wild ducks and geese passed over Virginia each fall. These and deer, wild turkey, partridge, sora, doves, and quail were considered proper sport for "the better sort," leaving rabbits, squirrels, and other small game for the "middling sort," and "the baser sort." Flights of pigeons darkened the sky until hunters totally destroyed them in the nineteenth century.

The most coveted quarry of early nimrods were buffalo, which were first described by Captain Samuel Argall in a voyage up the Potomac in 1613. The animals chiefly frequented the Valley of Virginia, where they were hunted mercilessly by Indians. In his exploration through Cumberland Gap in 1750, Dr. Thomas Walker stated: "We killed in the journey 13 buffaloes, 8 elks, 53 bears, 20 deer, 4 wild geese, about 150 turkeys, besides small game." The last buffalo in Virginia was seen in 1797 on New River.

Virginians hunted with few rules, disdaining the ritual which surrounded "shooting" in England. When he visited Robert Beverley at Blandfield in 1715, John Fontaine recorded in his Journal: "We killed some squirrels and partridges but did no hurt to the wild turkeys nor deer, though we saw several." Game was so abundant in colonial Virginia that dogs were not needed to find them.

Night hunting of possums and raccoons was familiar to every farm boy. The frantic baying of dogs as the possum or coon was treed echoed through the woods on spring and summer nights. Robert Beverley described it:

They have another sort of hunting, which is very diverting, and that they call vermin hunting; it is performed afoot, with small dogs in the night, by the light of the moon or stars. Thus in summer time they find abundance of raccoons, opossums, and foxes in the corn fields, and about their plantations; but at other times they must go into the woods for them.

Well-brought-up young men in colonial Virginia were also taught fencing. Popularized by King Henry VIII in England in the seventeenth century, it remained a "polite accomplishment" of Englishmen for 200 years. While it was useful in hand-to-hand combat with the Indians, its utility was

Daniel Boone, who led the exodus through Cumberland Gap into the Kentucky territory, carried a Kentucky rifle or "squirrel gun." *Cook Collection,* The Valentine Museum

Tidewater Virginia was pierced by hundreds of streams in which fish abounded. *Engraving from Civitatis Orbis Terrarum. The British Museum*

limited in musket warfare. It was taught in English schools and at the College of William and Mary. Virginians in their wills bequeathed silver-hilted swords, worn by gentlemen on formal occasions.

The ablest fencer in early Virginia was Colonel Daniel Parke, whom Commissary James Blair described as a "handsome young man of that country [Virginia], one . . . who, to all the other accomplishments that make a complete sparkish gentleman, has added one upon which he infinitely values himself; that is, a quick resentment of every the least thing that looks like an affront or injury. He has learned, they say, the art of fencing, and is as ready at giving a challenge, especially before company, as the greatest Hector in the town."

Hardly any sport was disdained by Virginians. Their variety was suggested by Robert Crowley in this seventeenth century doggerel:

To fish, to fowl, to hunt, to hawk,
Or on an instrument to play;
And some whiles to commune and talk,
No man is able to gainsay.
To shoot, to bowl, or cast the bar,
To play tennis, or toss the ball
Or to run base, like men of war,
Shall hurt thy study nought at all.
For all these things do recreate
The mind, if they canst hold the mean.

Fishing was popular as a sport, both in the Chesapeake's estuaries and in freshwater ponds. Washington caught blackfish and sea-bass, and Beverley listed other varieties:

Those which I know of myself, I remember by the names of herrings, sturgeons, shads, oldwives [alewives], sheep's-heads, black and red drums, trouts, taylors, greenfish, sun-fish, bass, chub, place, flounders, whitings, fatbacks, maids, wives, small-turtle, crabs, oysters, mussels, cockles, shrimps, needlefish, bream, carp, pike, jack, mullets, eels, conger-eels, perch, and cats, &c.

Beverley adds: "I have sat in the shade, at the heads of rivers, angling, and spent as much time in taking the fish off the hook as in waiting for their taking it." But the most prized saltwater catch were sturgeon, valued for flesh and caviar, which grew to 360 pounds. The Marquis de Chastellux described the methods which he found being used to catch these fish in 1780-82:

I saw two Negroes carrying an immense sturgeon, and on my asking them how they had taken it, they told me that at this season they were so common as to be taken easily in a seine

At millponds across Virginia, anglers trolled for freshwater fish using silk or horsehair line. This drawing by Francis Barlow illustrated *The Gentleman's Recreation. The Guildhall Library, London*

(a sort of fishing net), and that fifteen or twenty were found sometimes in the net; but that there was a much more simple method of taking them, which they had just been using. This species of monsters, which are so active in the evening as to be perpetually leaping to a great height above the surface of the water, usually sleep profoundly at mid-day. Two or three Negroes then proceed in a little boat, furnished with a long cord, at the end of which is a sharp iron crook, which they hold suspended like a log line. As soon as they find this line stopped by some obstacle, they draw it forcibly towards them, so as to strike the hook into the sturgeon, which they either drag out of the water, or which, after some struggling, and losing all its blood, floats at length upon the surface, and is easily taken.

Not all Virginians lived near salt water, but nearly everyone had access to a mill-pond stocked with bass, bream, crappie, and perhaps catfish. Such were Custis and Cohoke ponds in King William County or Bridgeforth's pond in Amelia. Light rods were rigged with horsehair or silk line, and baited with insects. Live flies, worms, grasshoppers, hornets, wasps, or snails were preferred, but dried wasps, clotted sheep's blood, corn, cheese, berries, or cherries would do in a pinch.

Fly-fishing was pursued by a few. In his seventeenth-century classic, *The Compleat Angler*, Izaak Walton promised the fly fisherman: "If he hit to make his fly right, and have the luck to hit also where there is store of trouts, a dark day, and a right wind, he will catch such store of them as will encourage him to grow more and more with the art of fly-making." A big "if," indeed.

Indians fished for sturgeon with arrow-tipped spears. This descendant of the Rappahannock tribe uses a log canoe hollowed by fire and stone hatchet. *Chiles T. Larson for The Jamestown Foundation*

Riding to hounds to catch foxes did not come in vogue until the eighteenth century. This sport was developed to rid the land of vermin which destroyed smaller game, and huntsmen found it exciting as they hurtled fence and thicket in pursuit of baying hounds. Unlike duck hunting, it was a gregarious pastime. George Washington, a devotee of fox hunting, kept it up until he injured his back at 63. Like many Virginians, he kept a pack of hunting dogs, affectionately named Mopsey, Truelove, Jupiter, Juno, Rover, Music, Sweetlips, Countess, and Lady.

THE
Commendation
of Cockes, and Cock-fighting.

Wherein is ſhewed, that Cocke-fighting *was before the com-ming of* Chriſt.

LONDON,
Printed for *Henrie Tomes,* and are to be ſold at his Shop ouer a-gainſt Graies Inne gate in Holburne,
1 6 o 7.

Heavy bets were made on cockfights. Tidewater Virginia meets sometimes had two dozen bouts and lasted several days. *The Folger Shakespeare Library*

Virginia fox hounds grew different from England's, for the nature of Virginia hunting was more expansive than England's. Virginians and Marylanders also developed the Chesapeake Bay retriever to bring back waterfowl shot in marshes.

Next to hunting and riding, cockfighting was the favorite diversion. An Englishman noted in 1781 that "the indolence and dissipation of the middling and lower classes of white inhabitants of Virginia are such as to give pain to every reflecting mind. Horse racing, cock fighting, and boxing matches are standing amusements for which they neglect all business." In Tidewater, teams of two dozen gamecocks were sometimes matched in a two-day series of battles to the death.

But of all outdoor diversions, horsemanship stood first. Over the entrance to Oaklands plantation in Chesterfield County was emblazoned: "There is nothing so good for the inside of a man as the outside of a horse." The first workhorses were brought to Jamestown in 1608, but oxen were found better suited for stump-pulling. Horses were chiefly used for riding and pulling carts. By the end of the first century, planters could go by horseback over the lengths of the Tidewater peninsulas. "The planter's pace" was a dead run.

Everybody had a horse. The Englishman J. F. D. Smyth noted that "Virginians, of all ranks and denominations, are excessively fond of horses . . . even the most indigent person has his saddle-horse, which he rides to every place, and when hunting; indeed, a man will frequently go five miles to catch a horse, to ride only one mile . . ." Hugh Jones termed them "such lovers of horses that almost every ordinary person keeps a horse; and I have known some [to] spend the

Riding to hounds in pursuit of a fox became a popular sport in eighteenth century Virginia. George Washington was an avid hunter. This early painting, "The End of the Hunt," is from the collection of the National Gallery of Art, gift of Edgar William and Bernice Chrysler Garbisch.

morning in ranging several miles in the woods to find and catch their horses only to ride two or three miles to church, to the court house, or to a horse-race."

"The saddle-horses, though not very large, are hardy, strong, and fleet," Hugh Jones wrote, "and will pace naturally and pleasantly at a prodigious rate." Their contrast with English horses was sharp, leading to the surmise that Spanish horses had been crossbred with English mounts in early years of the colony. (Fairfax Harrison, a Virginia historian, suggested that Edward Bland may have obtained the Spanish horses from the Occonneechee Indians in 1751.) Indeed, quarter horses resembled Chinco-

teague Island ponies, which descended from Spanish horses marooned on the Eastern Shore, lending credence to this theory.

Whatever the case, colonists had the English mania for racing. A race in 1674 at Yorktown between the entries of Matthew Slader and of James Bullock, a tailor, for 2,000 pounds of tobacco, ended in a fine for the presumptuous Bullock, "it being contrary to law for a laborer to make a race, [racing] being a sport only for gentlemen." Nearly every Tidewater county had its races. An entry in Henrico County in 1677 was Bonny, a mare owned by the grandfather of Thomas Jefferson. Citizens of Northumberland complained to the Burgesses in 1696 that Saturday races in that county led to re-matches on Sunday which profaned the sabbath, but the races went on unabated.

The compact saddle horses of Virginia were capable of great speed over short courses. They took off like lightning and held the pace to the end. Their racing impressed John Bernard as "the most animated" that he had ever seen. The finish met with a "tornado of applause from the winner's party, the niggers in particular hallooing, jumping, and clasping their hands in a frenzy of delight, more especially if the horses had happened to jostle and one of the riders been thrown off with a broken leg. . . ." No wonder migrating Virginians popularized the sport in Kentucky, Tennessee, and western North Carolina!

Such races were run over a narrow quarter-mile course known as a quarter-path. A pistol was fired or a trumpet blown to start the race. However, racing was improved in the eighteenth century by importation of thoroughbreds from England. These high-strung animals — descendants of the Byerley, Godolphin, and Darley stallions which had been imported from Turkey and Arabia and bred with English mares — instantly quickened the pace of American racing. Planters also followed Englishmen's lead by building oval tracks and lengthening races to three or four miles. Course-racing soon outdistanced quarter-racing in popularity nearly everywhere except on the frontier.

The new style racing was the main attraction at the Saint Andrew's Day celebration in Hanover County in 1737. "It is proposed that 20 horses or mares do run around a three miles course," the announcement said, "if permitted by the Hon. Wil-

liam Byrd, Esquire, proprietor of said land." William Parks' *Virginia Gazette*, in Williamsburg, reported a similar race over a one-mile oval course, won by Colonel John Chiswell's horse Edgecomb, of Hanover County. Washington and other members of the House of Burgesses attended Williamsburg races during Public Times each spring.

Virginians spent lavishly to import thoroughbred stallions. The first was the Scotch-Irish shipmaster James Patton, later of Rockbridge, who brought the celebrated English stallion Bulle Rock to the colony in 1730 for the Hanover merchant, Samuel Gist. During the following 70 years, at least 216 stallions were brought into Virginia from England. The colony became "the region of the racehorse" as planter families along the major rivers bred champion after champion. The late Fairfax Harrison in his *The Equine F.F.V.s* listed breeders thus in the order of seniority:

Carter of Shirley, Harrison of Brandon, Nelson of Yorktown, Wormeley of Rosegill, Booth of Gloucester County, Byrd of Westover, Tayloe of Mount Airy, Morton of Leedstown, Spotswood of Newport, Thornton of Stafford County, Brent of Richland, McCarty of Pope's Creek, Baylor of Newmarket, Burwell of Carter's Creek, Braxton of Elsing Green, Ambler of Jamestown, Ludwell of Green Spring, Cary of Ampthill, Harrison of Berkeley, Randolph of Tuckahoe, Lightfoot of Tedington, Bland of Cawsons, Baird of Hallsfield, Evans of Surry County, Lee of Stratford, Syme of Newcastle, and Fitzhugh of Chatham.

Among thoroughbreds brought from England, five are cited as outstanding by Jane Carson in *Colonial Virginians at Play*. The earliest was Monkey, bought by Nathaniel Harrison of Brandon in 1737 after having won major English races at Newmarket and York. Another was Traveller, which was imported by Joseph Morton of Leedstown plantation, in Westmoreland County, and which won fame as the sire of many champions. Imported in 1751 was Jolly Roger, bred by the Duke of Kingston and owned in Virginia by John Spotswood of Newpost and Bernard Moore of Chelsea. A fourth champion was Fearnought, purchased in 1764 by John Baylor, who named his Caroline County plantation "Newmarket" for England's favorite racecourse. Although soon disqualified for the track by injury, Fearnought sired 40 famous sons.

The top place in this galaxy of Virginia thoroughbreds was held by Janus, "the most perfect horse in colonial America." Like Fearnought, his racing days were cut short by injury, but he won fame as sire of sprinters and quarter horses. Brought to Glouces-

ter County from England in 1756 by the merchant and planter Mordecai Booth, he spent his last twenty years at stud in Southside Virginia and upper North Carolina, where quarter racing made a last stand after the Revolution. "The Januses became the first family of sprinters in turf history anywhere in the world," Miss Carson concludes.

After midcentury, English-style thoroughbreds raced frequently at Williamsburg, Yorktown, Gloucester, and Fredericksburg. Race meets were principal features of county fairs, held each fall. Such races were sponsored by local jockey clubs, with purses made up from members' and entry fees. The first horse to win two heats was the winner. Any horse which came in more than an eighth of a mile behind was eliminated.

Monkey was one of early Virginia's most famous racehorses. He was imported by Nathaniel Harrison of Brandon in 1737. This watercolor by James Seymour is one of the few pre-Revolutionary paintings of American-owned horses. *Collection of the late Willard S. Martin*

Describing the racetrack at Williamsburg in 1770, J. F. D. Smyth wrote:

Adjoining to the town is a very excellent course for either two, three or four mile heats. Their purses are generally raised by subscription ... they amount to an hundred pounds each for the first day's running, and fifty pounds every day after, the races commonly continuing for a week. There are also matches and sweepstakes very often for considerable sums. Besides ... there are races established annually almost at every town and considerable place in Virginia; and frequent matches, on which large sums of money depend ... Very capital horses are started here, such as would make no despicable figure at Newmarket; nor is their speed, bottom, or blood inferior to their appearance ... Indeed, nothing can be more elegant and beautiful than the horses here, either for the turf, the field, the road, or the coach; ...

Virginia's losses in the Revolution ended its reign as "the region of the racehorse." Plantations which had supported stud farms were impoverished by worn-out soil and loss of tobacco markets. Trade moved upland to Petersburg and Richmond, which briefly became citadels of postwar racing. The Richmond Jockey Club held its first subscription purse in 1785 at the Upper Richmond Course, and tracks were built about the same time at Tree Hill, Broad Rock, Fairfield, — all near Richmond — and at Petersburg.

But Virginia's most remarkable post-Revolutionary racing center was the little town of Bowling Green. In that Caroline County village Colonel John Hoomes in

One of the greatest racehorses of Virginia was Shark, bought in 1786 by Benjamin Hyde of Fredericksburg after a prizewinning career on English tracks. He was portrayed thus by George Stubbs, A.R.A. in the painting titled *Shark with his Trainer Price, 1775.* *Collection of Mr. and Mrs. Paul Mellon*

1788 organized the Virginia Jockey Club, laying out a course in his fields. There the high-living colonel rallied the remnants of Tidewater's planter-horsemen at annual meets for a decade, making the little town "the busiest breeding center on the continent." His track ceased when he died at 50.

The eclipse of the cavalier spirit in Virginia was evident soon after the Revolution in the decline in horse-breeding and racing. Many Tidewater plantations, impoverished by war and tobacco, were broken up. Baptists, Methodists, and Presbyterians, growing in numbers and political influence, were hostile to gaming and gambling. Virginia's exhuberance gave way to a subdued morality, and Maryland and Kentucky replaced Virginia as the home of thoroughbreds. The Virginia Asembly in 1792 virtually doomed racing by imposing a $7 maximum on all betting. Big stakes offered in Northern races soon lured the "sport of kings" away from Virginia.

Kentucky inherited much of early Virginia's style of life when it became a state in 1792. History was merely repeating itself when the *Kentucky Gazette* advertised in 1788 that Pilgarlick, son of the great sprinter Janus, was standing at stud in Mercer County. The puritanism of The Great Awakening had put an end to the lavish sportsmanship of eightenth-century Tidewater, but a better day would come. Virginians' love of the wholesome pleasures of field, track, and stream was too integral to life ever to die.

The thorough bred imported Horse, **Alderman,** Will stand the ensuing season, to cover mares at Mr. Isham Barrow's, in Halifax county. The terms of covering will be made known before the season commences.

THE NOTED HORSE **Dare-Devil,** Will stand the ensuing season, at my house in Chesterfield county. THOMAS GOODE.

RESTLESS,

IMPORTED from England last summer, will stand the next season at my plantation on Flat Creek, near Meade's Mill.

He is a dark bay, nearly sixteen hands high, of the best blood, and elegantly formed: a gentleman well acquainted with the blood and performance of the best horses in England has given me a full account of his performance taken from the Calendar, &c. He says "As to the blood of RESTLESS, it is not *merely unexceptionable, but could not be better,* being crossed with every thing valuable in England. He was got by Phenomenon, one of the best of Herod's sons, out of the famous Dutchess, decidedly the best Mare of her day.—Particulars will be given hereafter.
Wm. MURRAY.

Owners of thoroughbred stallions advertised their stud services in newspapers. These appeared in issues of the *Virginia Argus,* published by Samuel Pleasants, Jr., in Richmond at the end of the eighteenth century. *The College of William and Mary*

John Donne, dean of Saint Paul's Cathedral in London, preached annually to the Virginia Company. This is the title page of his *Eighty Sermons. The British Museum*

Methinks we see already that happy time when we shall surpass the Asi-atticians in civility, the Jews in religion, the Greeks in philosophy, the Egyptians in geometry, the Phoenicians in arithmetic, and the Chaldeans in astrology. O happy Virginia! . . .

> Student speaker at exercises of
> The College of William and Mary, 1699

The taste for reading is commoner [in Virginia] among men of the first class than in any other part of America.

> Duc de La Rochefoucald-Liancourt, *Travels through the United States of North America*, 1799

Arts and Entertainment

*The snail which everywhere doth roam
Carrying his own house still, still at home,
Follow (for he is easy paced) this snail.
Be thou thine own place, or the world's
    Thy jail.*

The loneliness of the pioneer Virginian was made bearable by his sense of adventure. In the communications of the Virginia Company, he was aptly termed "adventurer," for he risked life itself for gain. To the mystic poet John Donne, who as dean of St. Paul's Cathedral in London preached the annual sermon to Virginia's stockholders, enthusiasm for this life and faith in a life to come offered the only escape from the spirit's imprisonment. Life, for good or bad, was what one made it.

The colonial settler's ability to amuse himself was inexhaustible. Work occupied him from sunup to sundown in the years when Jamestown was capital of a rustic empire. Then, as successful planters bought slaves to work their fields, a class emerged which enjoyed more leisure. Tobacco profits produced a bountiful "golden age" which nurtured men of intellectual and artistic interests.

Except in architecture and politics, Virginians were not highly creative. They contributed little in the realms of music, painting, literature, or the drama. But they had a lively appreciation of the arts, growing out of the Englishman's stimulation by the wonders of the Renaissance. In matters of taste — the design of a town, an opera, a

Arts and Entertainment [181]

house, or a dress — even Englishmen admitted the preeminence of the Italians and the French.

Their libraries reveal the shape of Virginians' interests, for reading was the root of their culture, as it is in any society. Even a sword-wielding gallant like Daniel Parke conceded this. "Mind your writing and everything else you have learnt," he admonished his young daughter Frances, (who later married John Custis) "and do not learn to romp, but behave yourself soberly and like a gentlewoman. Mind reading . . ."

Books listed in wills indicate reading was chiefly for information rather than amusement. Although Jefferson advised that "the entertainments of fiction are useful as well as pleasant," he seldom indulged in novels. In this respect, he was typical of men of his day. Instead, such libraries as Ralph Wormeley's at Rosegill and Richard Henry Lee's at Stratford abounded in books of history, biography, and theology. Wormeley's 400 volumes, one of the largest in seventeenth-century Virginia, included 128 of religion and morals, eighty-six of biography and history, and many others of law, politics, the arts, and literature.

In an age which considered Greek and Latin to be essential, many copies of Ovid, Horace, Virgil, and Cicero were brought across the Atlantic. However, Jefferson, who demanded practical knowledge, scoffed at the classicist's notion that "nothing can be useful but the learned lumber of Greek and Roman reading." In a compilation of 300 books to guide a planter's reading, Jefferson included only 18 Greek and Roman titles.

Among books popular in seventeenth-century Virginia were *Purchas' Pilgrimes*, John Smith's *True Relation of Virginia*, Sir Francis Bacon's *Natural History*, and John Donne's *Sermons*. Toward the end of the century came John Locke's *Essay On Human Understanding* and other works setting forth the "natural rights of man" which influenced Richard Bland, George Mason, Jefferson, Madison, and others of their generations. The Bible, Shakespeare, Milton, Chaucer, Spenser, and manuals on law and medicine were also widely circulated.

Both planters and educated Scots settlers read with approval the works of the Enlightenment. Voltaire, Rousseau, and Montesquieu won Virginians' support for their opposition to kings. The Scottish economist Adam Smith, writing late in the century, won their approbation for his anti-mercantilist *Wealth of Nations*, which was used as a text at the College of William and Mary.

Such reading, of course, was confined to the small segment of society which could read well enough to enjoy it. As for the rest, the most they could expect was to hear the latest issue of the *Virginia Gazette* read aloud in the local tavern. Sneered the Reverend Charles Woodmason, a North Carolina Anglican who toured the back country, "Nor do they delight in historical books or wish to have them read to them, as do our vulgar in England, for here the people despise knowledge . . ."

The Scottish "common sense school" of political scientists was popular with literate Virginians, who liked their simplicity and economy. Among novelists, Daniel Defoe, Henry Fielding, Tobias Smollett, Oliver Goldsmith, and Laurence Sterne were widely read, while Alexander Pope's poetry was especially popular. Miss Lucinda Lee confided to her journal that she liked Pope's "Eloisa to Abelard" but found Eloisa's views "to amorous for a female."

SEPTEMBER 8, 1775.　　　THE　　　NUMBER 32.

VIRGINIA　GAZETTE.

ALWAYS FOR LIBERTY,　　AND THE PUBLICK GOOD.

ALEXANDER PURDIE, PRINTER.

A DECLARATION of the DELEGATES deputed by the several counties and corporations in the colony and dominion of Vir- emancipating our flaves; and reducing to ashes the principal city in this colony, added to the many alarming accounts received serious consideration the state of th colo y. Since our assembling, we have received authentick intelligence of the remorseless

A forum for Virginians' increasing political interest was provided by the two Virginia Gazettes published in Williamsburg. One was founded in 1736 by William Parks and the other in 1775 by Alexander Purdie. *Colonial Williamsburg*

Books were often read aloud. William Byrd II read part of John Gay's *Beggar's Opera* to others when a downpour kept them at the Randolph's Tuckahoe plantation in 1709. Thus, Byrd recorded, they "killed the time and triumphed over the bad weather." John Marshall courted Miss Mary Ambler at Yorktown in the same way, while her family listened enthralled. The earnest lawyer evinced "so much taste and feeling, and pathos too," wrote Mary's sister, "as to give me an idea of their sublimity which I should never have had an idea of . . ." Needless to say, John won Mary.

The favorite forum for Virginians' views was William Parks' *Virginia Gazette*, founded in 1736 in Williamsburg. In it and a rival *Virginia Gazette*, begun thirty-nine years later by Alexander Purdie, were printed tracts in the form of letters-to-the-editor, critiques of public policy, and poetry. Like Joseph Addison's essays in the English journal, *The Spectator*, the *Ga-*

zette's essayists remained hidden as Publius, Scipio, Freeman, or Horatius. Exposing oneself in print was not "genteel" in eighteenth-century Virginia.

The most skillful writer in colonial Virginia was William Byrd II, whose *History of the Dividing Line*, *A Progress to the Mines*, and *A Journey to the Land of Eden* were sprightly reading.

In an early issue, Parks set the tone for his *Gazette* in an "advertisement concerning Advertisements." He announced:

All persons who have occasion to buy or sell houses, lands, goods, or cattle; or have servants or slaves runaway; or have lost horses, cattle, &c, or want to give any public notice, may have it advertised in all these Gazettes printed in one week, for three shillings, and for two shillings per week for as many weeks afterwards as they shall order, by giving or sending their directions to the printer hereof.

And as these papers will circulate (as speedily as possible) not only over this but also the neighboring colonies and will probably be read

Arts and Entertainment　[183]

by some thousands of people, it is very likely they may have the desired effect; and it is certainly the cheapest and most effectual method that can be taken for publishing anything of this nature.

The classic examples of the political essay were the eighty-five Federalist papers, advocating adoption of the Constitution which appeared in a New York newspaper in 1787-88, signed Publius. The majority were written by Madison, with others by Alexander Hamilton and John Jay.

When the capital moved to Richmond in 1780, Dixon and Nicolson's *Virginia Gazette* moved with it, for John Dixon and Thomas Nicolson were the colony's Public Printers and depended on the colony's job printing. About the same time, Norfolk, Alexandria, Fredericksburg, Petersburg, and Lynchburg also had weeklies. In the Richmond *Argus*, founded by Samuel Pleasants in 1793, the essays by A British Spy appeared, later revealed as the lawyer William Wirt. In 1798 appeared the anti-federalist Richmond *Examiner* of Meriwether and Skelton Jones, and in 1799 the Richmond *Federalist* of William A. Rind.

A change clearly occurred in Virginia's political manners with the development of partisan spirit during the early days of the republic. Open political attacks began to appear in newspapers, where once references to political adversaries were veiled. While Virginians were once almost unanimously anti-monarchist, they now differed on domestic policy. The *Examiner* and *Federalist* traded sharp jabs with opponents. The old days of leisurely exposition in the *Virginia Gazette* were gone.

Along with the stimuli of reading and letter-writing went good talk. At two-hour dinners, conversation ranged from immor-tality to the price of tobacco. Talk flowed at fireside, alehouse, and dining table, especially when the ladies "retired" and the gentlemen were left to their port and madeira. "Good company and good discourse are the very sinews of virtue," Virginians said, echoing Izaak Walton. To provide for "assemblies" of guests, four Northern Neck planters built a "banqueting house" so that "each man or his heirs yearly" might use it to entertain family and friends. This primitive retreat abounded each spring in oysters, rum, and laughter.

Jefferson, probably the best talker in America, entertained at four-hour dinners where French wines were imbibed with politics, science, and art. Only the churlish John Quincy Adams complained that the Virginian invariably sought to top others' stories with his own.

Good music was rare, for professional musicians could not find a living in Virginia unless they worked primarily at another trade. Thus survived Peter Pelham, who came to Williamsburg from Massachusetts in 1752. Pelham played the organ in Bruton Parish Church on Sundays and kept the jail on other days. He helped install Bruton's first organ and played it for half a century. "There's the church fam'd for its noble organ of one hundred tones," exclaimed Alexander Macauley in 1783, "touch'd by the modern Orpheus—the inimitable Pelham." Behind the organ, sweating as he pumped the bellows, was a trusted prisoner.

Hymns and psalms set to music were familiar to colonists of all classes. The English church used a metrical psalm book authorized in 1562 and titled *The Whole Book of Psalms, collected with English meter, ... Faithfully perused and allowed according to the order appointed in the Queen's Majesty's* instructions: *very meet to be used by all sorts of people privately for their solace and comfort, laying apart all ungodly songs and ballads, which tend only to the nourishment of vice and corruption of youth . . .*

Because songbooks were scarce, the clerk in each parish church would "line out" psalms by singing each line so that the congregation could repeat it. Typical of metrical psalms was the 100th, sung to a tune known as "Old Hundredth":

All people that on earth do dwell
Sing to the Lord with cheerful voice
Him serve with mirth, His praise forth tell;
Come ye before Him and rejoice

The Forty-second Psalm was rendered thus:

Like as the hart doth pant and bray,
The well-spring to obtain,
So doth my soul desire alway
With Thee, Lord, to remain.

My soul doth thirst and would draw near
The living God of might;
Oh, when shall I come and appear
In presence of His sight?

Hymn singing was emphasized by the Methodists. Charles and John Wesley wrote many that became widely sung. "Hark! The Herald Angels Sing" and "Come, Thou

The first known performance of a play in America was on Virginia's Eastern Shore in 1665. Few early Virginians shared the Puritans' aversion to theatricals. From *Orbis Sensualis. The British Museum*

Most popular in pre-Revolutionary Virginia was John Gay's impudent *Beggar's Opera.*
This advertisement appeared in the *Virginia Gazette* in Williamsburg on May 26, 1768.
Virginia State Library

Long-Expected Jesus" are among the hundred hymns they introduced in Wesleyan services and camp meetings.

Early settlers played the virginal, hand lyre, lute, and recorder, but their descendants were apt to prefer the harpsichord, violin, flute, and hautboy (oboe). Jefferson performed on the violin with Governor Fauquier while a student at William and Mary, and Patrick Henry "fiddled" in country-music style. However, few Virginians knew the glorious music of their European contemporaries Bach, Mozart, Scarlatti, and Vivaldi unless they had been exposed to it in Europe or Williamsburg.

The *joie de vivre* of Virginia was evident in enthusiasm for theatricals. Governor Berkeley, among other accomplishments, wrote a play produced in London. The first known performance of a play in America took place at Pungoteague, on the Eastern Shore, in 1665. The event would have passed unnoted had not an Accomack County settler complained to the King's attorney that a play presented by three local men was offensive. Thereupon, the actors were required to appear before the county justices in costume and repeat the performance.

The play, *The Bear and the Cub*, was probably written by one of its actors on the relation of the new county of Accomack — the "cub" — to the capital of Jamestown — the "bear." The objector, Edward Martin, is thought to have been a Puritan who regarded play-acting as evil. In good Cavalier style, the justices exonerated the actors and required Martin to pay costs of the suit. Here was evidence of Virginia's early anti-Puritanism.

Fun-loving Virginians had another taste

of play-acting in 1704, when the English actor Anthony Aston performed on "both sides of the Chesapeake." Soon William Levingstone moved to Williamsburg from New Kent and engaged with Charles and Mary Stagg to teach acting and to present "comedies, drolls, or other kind of stage plays . . ." The playhouse which Levingstone completed about 1718 on the Palace Green was the first in America. After Levingstone failed in business, students of the college trod its boards until the building was dismantled.

A new playhouse was built by subscription near the Capitol in 1751, and actors came from New York for the first season. Opening night featured Shakespeare's *Richard III* and "a grand tragic dance, compos'd by Monsieur Denoier, call'd 'The Royal Captive,' after the Turkish manner . . ." From London the next year came a troupe headed by Lewis Hallam, which added to Williamsburg's pleasures almost until the Revolution.

Performing at Public Times, Hallam's plays drew many visiting Burgesses, including Washington and Jefferson. Nancy Hallam, niece of the producer, became the playgoers' darling. The Rev. Jonathan Boucher wrote a panegyric to her beauty and talent which was printed in the *Maryland Gazette*. Favorite playwrights were English writers who satirized their countrymen in comedies full of artifice and epigram, like Goldsmith, Sheridan, Farquhar, Congreve, and Colley Cibber.

Students occasionally performed plays to train them in declamation. Joseph Addison's tragedy, *Cato*, was a favorite because its long recitations required little acting. In a performance at the Rev. Thomas Warrington's school at Hampton in 1736, the min-

The star of Lewis Hallam's American Company of actors was Nancy Hallam. George Washington and other Williamsburg playgoers admired her in many roles, including Shakespeare's *Cymbeline*. Charles Willson Peale depicted her in the cave scene in 1771. *Colonial Williamsburg*

ister's daughter Camilla delivered a special epilogue which doubtless amused her hearers. Concluded Camilla:

For I, in exercising smiles and frowns,
To gain my prince, have scarce a thought
*   Of crowns;*
But hope to make a better wife, when I
Obtain my Princely Colonel by and by.

Princes and generals were unattainable in Virginia, but most counties had colonels, majors, and captains to spare.

Arts and Entertainment [187]

The first offering of the Hallam-Henry company in Richmond was *The School for Scandal*. It was performed in Quesnay's new Academy on Shockoe Hill in 1786. *Virginia Museum of Fine Arts*

With the outbreak of the Revolution, the Williamsburg theatre closed. However, touring companies began to visit the new capital in Richmond in 1780 and annually thereafter.

The Hallams' Old American Company after the Revolution was headed by Lewis Hallam the younger and by John Henry, who alternated as actors and managers. Their first season was launched in 1786 in Quesnay's new Richmond Academy on Shockoe Hill. Beginning with *The School for Scandal*, they offered *Hamlet*, *Richard III*, and contemporary hits. By 1790 Richmond seemed so promising that the English actor-manager Thomas Wade West brought his West-Bignall company to the town, which now had nearly 4,000 people.

Besides Mr. and Mrs. West, the troupe included their daughter, Anne West Bignall; Mrs. West's brother, Matthew Sully; and Sully's wife and children. Their circuit widened to encompass Norfolk, Charleston, S.C., Petersburg, Fredericksburg, and Alexandria before Thomas West died in 1799 in a fall. With him, unfortunately, died his ambitious plan to provide Richmond with a hotel-theater-assembly hall, designed by the gifted architect Benjamin H. Latrobe.

While comedy was preferred, tragedies and romances were also performed, most of them dealing with Greece, Rome, or kings and queens. A prologue or epilogue, spoken by one of the actors, set the scene or drew the moral. Dances were often interpolated. At the Williamsburg theater in 1768, three "gentlemen of the company" performed a dance called "The Cowkeepers" on the bill with the tragedy *The Gamester* and the farce *Polly Honeycomb*, all in an evening!

Magicians and puppet shows, like the company which played *Babes in the Wood* in

Lewis Hallam, the younger, who with John Henry headed the Old American Company which had earlier performed in Williamsburg. *Virginia Museum of Fine Arts*

This ticket admitted patrons to box seats at Hallam & Henry's Old American Company. *Virginia Museum of Fine Arts*

Williamsburg in 1769, made the circuit of towns. The producer promised "sea monsters sporting on the waves," and "a curious field of battle, containing the Dutch, French, Prussian, and English forces." A few nights later his puppets presented a comedy, *Whittington and His Cat*, followed by a sleight-of-hand act. Amusements were increasing in variety and sophistication.

A few Virginians tried playwriting, despite their reticence to write for publication. Colonel Robert Munford of Mecklenburg County satirized Virginia politics in *The Candidates*, written in 1770, and *The Patriots*, in 1775. Saint George Tucker of Williamsburg had his farce, *Up and Ride, or the Borough of Brooklyne*, produced by the Hallams' American Company about 1789. But in the realms of poetry and fiction, Virginians were less creative. As Timothy Flint wrote from Virginia's western lands in 1788, settlers were "too busy, too much occupied in making farms and speculations, to think of literature."

Early Virginians were no more creative in drawing, painting, or sculpting than in composing music or writing novels. True, Germanic settlers in the Valley decorated furniture with tulips and birds and drew stylized "fraktur" designs, reminiscent of medieval illuminated manuscripts. But most other painting in the colony was the work of itinerant artists. Probably the earliest Virginia portraits were those painted of Mr. and Mrs. Edward Jaquelin and their five children, limned by "an artist of the greatest merit" which the wealthy Jamestown planter could find on a visit to England. Thanks to eighteenth century artists like the Peticolas and Sully families, to John Trumbull, to Saint-Memin, and to John

German settlers in the Shenandoah Valley drew traditional Germanic *fraktur* pictures which resembled the illuminated manuscripts of medieval Europe. This is the birth certificate of the son of Henry and Elizabeth Manger. *Abby Aldrich Rockefeller Folk Art Collection*

Elizabeth Jaquelin was one of seven members of the Jaquelin family painted by an unknown artist in 1722. *Lent by the Ambler family to the Virginia Museum of Fine Arts.*

Wesley Jarvis, posterity could see — more or less — what the Revolutionary generation looked like.

Of all works of art in Virginia, the full-size figure of Washington commissioned by the Virginia Assembly in 1784 was the most ambitious. Jefferson and Franklin persuaded the French sculptor Jean-Antoine Houdon to come to America and undertake it. Modelled from life at Mount Vernon in 1785, the masterful marble was carved in 1791 and installed in the Virginia Capitol in 1796.

The end of the colonial years saw an outburst in building in Virginia. Continuing the classic revival which was sweeping England, Virginia built a new capitol in the style of the ancient Roman Maison Carrée in Nimes, France. The Greco-Roman style was further advanced by the arrival in Virginia in 1796 of English architect Benjamin Henry Latrobe, who designed buildings in Norfolk and Richmond. The classic style,

with columned portico and high ceilings, became the favored form for plantation houses, courthouses, and churches.

While colonial Virginians made few contributions to the arts, they enjoyed and enhanced the Renaissance heritage which came to them through England. Every gentleman knew something about architecture, books, and the stage. A few were acquainted with music, painting, and sculpture. However, most colonial energies were directed toward the attainment of life and liberty, leaving the pursuit of happiness to posterity.

To be fair to Virginia, none of the other colonies produced much creative literature, either. "There are few writers of books in the new world," wrote the American journalist Philip Freneau in 1788, "and amongst these very few that deal in works of imagination, and, I am sorry to say, fewer still that have any success attending their lucubrations."

Henry Adams exaggerated only a little when he wrote, "Law and politics were the only objects of Virginian thought," but he was eminently correct in concluding ". . . within these bounds the Virginians achieved triumphs."

Benjamin H. Latrobe designed a theatre and inn for Richmond, but his patron's death in 1799 prevented its erection. *From a sketch by Perry, Dean, Hepburn, and Stewart in the Valentine Museum.*

Arts and Entertainment [191]

A marble statue of Washington was modelled from life by Jean-Antoine Houdon in 1785. It stands in the Capitol at Richmond. *Virginia Chamber of Commerce*

Manners were not all their charm; for the Virginians at the close of the eighteenth century were inferior to no class of Americans in the sort of education then supposed to make refinement. . . . Those whom Liancourt called "men of the first class" were equal to any standard of excellence known to history. Their range was narrow, but within it they were supreme. . . . Social position was a birthright, not merely of the well-born, but of the highly gifted. . . . Law and politics were the only objects of Virginia thought; but within these bounds the Virginians achieved triumphs. . . .

Nowhere in America existed better human material than in the middle and lower classes of Virginia. As explorers, adventurers, fighters — wherever courage, activity, and force were wanted — they had no equals; but they had never known discipline, and were beyond measure jealous of restraint. . . .

Henry Adams, History of the United States

Epilogue

When George Washington took the oath as President on April 30, 1789, in New York, the colonial era of America came to its end. It had been 182 years since the three ships had brought the first Virginians to Jamestown. Now thirteen states stretched from Georgia to Massachusetts, and the tide of settlement was flooding through the Appalachians into the west.

Virginia was the colossus of this new nation. Her 79 counties stretched from the Atlantic to the Ohio River, 400 miles away, and enclosed 747,610 people. Another 73,677 Virginians lived in the territory which would become the state of Kentucky in 1792. No state approached Virginia in population except Pennsylvania, which had 434, 373 settlers.

Despite England's past efforts, Virginians still refused to cluster in cities. Only eight Virginia towns had as many as 1,400 people in the census of 1790. The largest was Richmond, at the falls of the James, which had grown to 3,500 in the ten years it had been the capital. (When the General Assembly met there each spring, its homes and taverns sheltered 500 more.) Virginia's

Busy Tidewater ports like Yorktown declined after 1750 as Chesapeake shipping centered on Norfolk, Richmond, Alexandria, and Baltimore. *Sidney King, National Park Service*

main port, Norfolk, had 3,000 souls, while the newly prosperous tobacco market of Petersburg had 2,800. The only other towns gaining in size were Alexandria with 2,700, Portsmouth with 1,700, Winchester with 1,650, and Fredericksburg with 1,500.

Many tiny Tidewater ports like Yorktown were dwindling, for population and trade were moving inland. Once-exuberant Williamsburg had shrunk to 1,344, while Jamestown had reverted to thickets and fields, its ruined statehouse and church overgrown with weeds.

And yet, while Virginia remained a state of farmers, the northern states were developing cities, whose manufacturers and shippers would ultimately change the shape of the American union. New York City in 1790 had reached 33,000 population, while Philadelphia had 28,000 and Boston 18,000. Antifederalist Virginians like Patrick Henry and Richard Henry Lee gloomily predicted that rural Virginia would soon be sacrificed to Northern industrial interests, just as it had once been to English mercantilist policy. But most Virginians took a more hopeful view.

Nearly all families still grew their food and made their clothes. Tobacco and wheat remained their chief exports to Europe, though Norfolk's schooners and sloops kept up a healthy exchange of pork, lumber, and corn for the sugar and rum of the West Indies. In upland Virginia, wheat, corn, and rye were raised in the bottom lands, while cattle and sheep grazed the hills that were too steep to cultivate.

Despite the break with England in 1776, many east Virginians adhered to their old-fashioned "aristocratical" plantation ways. They saw no conflict between their republican principles of government and their enjoyment of the landed estates, the leisure, and the tradition of high good living which they had inherited. True, debts and the puritanical values of Baptists and Methodists curbed such former luxuries of planter life as horse-racing, betting, and cock-fighting, but many Virginia families nevertheless stuck to the Anglican (after 1789, Episcopal) church and the old hospitality.

The colonial era ends as George Washington departs Mount Vernon on April 16, 1789, for his inauguration in New York. Painting by John Ward Dunsmore in Fraunces Tavern, New York. *Sons of the Revolution*

An insight into the life of these post-Revolutionary eastern Virginians was given by John Sergeant Wise, who grew up in Accomack County on the Eastern Shore of Virginia, in his reminiscent *The End of An Era*:

Nowhere is the type of the original settler in Virginia so well preserved, or are to be found the antique customs, manners, and ways of the Englishman of the seventeenth century in America so little altered as in the Kingdom of Accomacke. The names of the very earliest settlers are still there. Everybody on the peninsula knows everybody else. Everybody there is kin to everybody else. Nobody is so poor that he is wretched; nobody is so rich that he is proud. The majority of the upper class are stanch Episcopalians, just as their fathers were Church of England men; and the remainder of the population are for the most part Methodists, Baptist, and Presbyterians.

The vices of the community, as well as the virtues, are equally well-recognized inheritances from their progenitors. Fighting and drunkenness are by no means absent, but theft is rare among the whites. The kinship and sociability of the population are such that the fondness of the Englishman for sports of all kinds is freely indulged. No neighborhood is without its race-boat; no court day without its sporting event of some kind; and no tavern without its backgammon board, quoits, and, in old times, its fives-court. The poorhouse has fallen into decay. When a man dies, his kin are sufficiently numerous to care for his family; and while he lives, there is no excuse for pauperism in a land where earning a living is so easy a matter . . .

Proceeding to describe a gathering of Accomack and Northampton families at the Wise plantation at Onley, he wrote:

Bright and early, activity was visible on the plantation. Under the wide-spreading oaks, long tables were improvised, covered with snowy linen, and groaning with everything good to eat. At several points under the bluffs, pits were dug where beeves and sheep and pigs were barbecued, and oysters and clams and crabs and fish were cooked by the bushel. Great hampers of food, sent from the village, or from the homes of neighbors, stood about the tables, ready for distribution when the feast should begin. The house itself, decorated with flowers and evergreens, was thrown wide open to the guests . . .

By eight o'clock in the morning, the earliest of the guests hove in sight. By ten o'clock the grandees of the county began to arrive. There were Colonel Joynes, the county clerk; Lorenzo Bell, the county attorney; the Arbuckles, the Custises, the Finneys, the Waples; the Corbins from Bowman's Folly on the seaside; the Sneads from Mount Prospect; the Upshurs from Brownsville; the Baylys from Mount Custis; and the Yerbys, the Nottinghams, the Goffigons, the Kennards, and the Smiths, from Northampton . . .

By midday the stables and stable-yards were filled; and the horses, fastened to the front-yard fence, formed a continuous line; while the creek about the grove was literally filled with small craft ranging from canoe to "pungy" . . .

While these Tidewater planters continued to live confidently, there was no hiding the fact that the political leadership they had once exercised had now passed to the newer Piedmont. This was the hilly midsection of Virginia from the fall line of the rivers westward to the mountains. In this region lived Patrick Henry, Jefferson, Madison, and — for most of his adult years — Monroe. It was the area in which Samuel Davies and George Whitefield had sowed the seeds of the Great Awakening in Virginia. More democratic and pietistic than the older Tidewater, it was also more attuned to the Jeffersonian democracy of the new age. Here Baptists and Methodists now outnumbered Episcopalians and Presbyterians. Here political office was won rather than inherited.

The Piedmont counties were also more productive in 1790 than the lowlands. Tidewater's worn-out fields could not compete with the soils of northern, central, and southern Virginia, which were newly cleared. From Tidewater families like the Carters, Burwells, Nelsons, Randolphs, Tuckers, Marshalls, Cabells, Pages, and Byrds, ambitious scions moved to upland and southern Virginia to clear new plantations.

An especially prosperous section was the southern tier of counties adjoining North Carolina. Fed by the new affluence of southside Virginia, Petersburg on the Appomattox River in Dinwiddie County became the center of Virginia's tobacco kingdom. Breeders of thoroughbreds and quarter horses raced there each fall and spring at the New Market track. Planters in the "black belt" in Brunswick, Cumberland, Dinwiddie, Greensville, King George, Lunenburg, Powhatan, and Sussex bought so many slaves that more than half the population of these counties in 1790 was Negro.

Obviously, Piedmont was more in accord with the democratic spirit of the age than the older counties. No longer did offspring of the first families dominate its life. In such counties as Powhatan, Amherst, and Albemarle, the culture of highland and lowland met and mingled. Descendants of the Huguenot settlers of 1700 and a few Germans added to the mixture. Except in the Southside counties, slaves were fewer per household than in Tidewater, though widely prevalent. Richmond and Petersburg remained Piedmont's shipping centers, but by 1790 trading posts had begun at Charlottesville, Farmville, and Danville.

An even more democratic spirit prevailed in the great Valley which bisected Virginia from Harper's Ferry to Cumberland Gap. Here, between the Shenandoah, Massanutten, Blue Ridge, and Allegheny mountain ranges, the Scotch-Irish and Germans were only two generations away from their first settlers. Except for a few landed families like the Prestons, Breckenridges, Pattons, Lewises, and Hites, every man worked for his daily bread. The mixture

New opportunities in western Virginia and its Kentucky and Ohio lands were sought after the Revolution by many Pennsylvania families, here shown stopping at Fairview Inn, Frederick, Maryland. *Maryland Historical Society*

of English and Scottish had a noticeable stimulus in such border towns as Winchester, Staunton, Lexington, and Lynchburg. Colleges and schools were quick to grow there.

Valley Germans lived so much to themselves that other settlers seldom saw them. Clustered in farms about their church and school, they ventured to New Market, Luray, Woodstock, or Harrisonburg only to trade. About 57 per cent of the population of Shenandoah and Rockingham Counties and about 33 per cent in Page and Frederick were Germanic. Speaking a *Hochdeutsch* understandable only to themselves, they depended on their best-educated members — usually their pastors — to represent them in dealings with the English-speaking world.

With tireless industry and thrift, the Germans ate well, lived modestly, and gave a tenth of their earnings to their Church. Unlike the trade-minded Scotch-Irish, they took little interest in land speculation. Their spending money came from sale of wheat to mills in Baltimore and Richmond. They made the Valley of Virginia "the granary of the world."

Neighbors laughed at the old-fashioned customs of the Germans, but their settlements were neat patches of cultivation in the hilly Shenandoah landscape. Like their kinsmen, the Pennsylvania Dutch, they preserved folkways brought from Europe: their *schwenkfelder* bread on Thanksgiving, *fastnacht* on Shrove Tuesday, and dishes of dandelion greens on Maundy Thursday to ward off fevers. They fed ashes from Good Friday's fires to keep their pigs healthy, and threw water from the baptismal font on a rose bush to insure rosy cheeks for the baptized infant. Never venturesome, they remained clustered in the northern counties of the Valley, slowly learning English and discarding old customs.

West of the Valley settlers, on the far western reaches of Virginia in 1790, was the trans-Appalachian frontier. Though it constituted a third of Virginia's acres, this rocky hinterland held only 70,000 of her 747,000 people, divided into ten huge counties — Berkeley, Greenbrier, Hampshire, Harrison, Hardy, Kanawha, Monongalia, Ohio, Pendleton, and Randolph. Nearly all of these had moved into the region after Daniel Boone in 1774 led the way through Cumberland Gap, the opening in the Cumberland Mountains which Dr. Thomas Walker had first discovered in 1750. Since the Revolution, the exodus of Revolutionary veterans into this region to claim their bounty lands had become a steady stream.

Such was Virginia as the colonial era ended. Though towns and roads were growing, life on the western frontier was still full of danger and hardship. Thus, generation after generation, the pioneer spirit was kept alive. The sun-

After 1774 an extension of the Great Philadelphia Wagon Road was blazed westward from Cumberland Gap into the Kentucky and Tennessee territories, carrying settlers coming from Pennsylvania through Maryland, Virginia and the Carolinas. *From The Wilderness Road, permission of Mrs. Robert L. Kincaid*

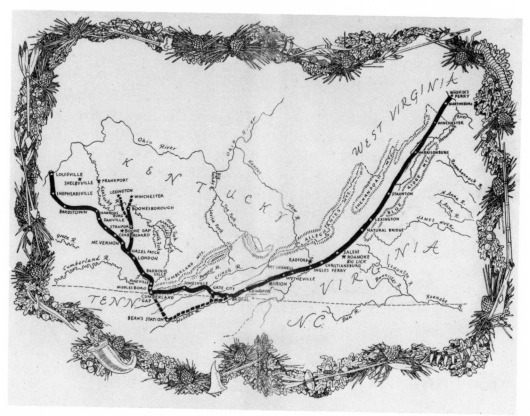

bonneted women and leather-clad men in Kentucky and Western Virginia lived much as the first Virginians had lived in 1607. Food and shelter were much the same as they had been at Jamestown. Planting corn, settlers still placed four seeds to each hill:

One for the blackbird
One for the crow
One for the cutworm
And one to grow

Salt was brought west through Cumberland Gap at $10 a bushel. Ever so slowly, as western Indian trails broadened into cart roads, Conestoga wagons brought larger loads and cut the price to $5. But the kitchen salt-gourd was still guarded as a luxury.

Thus, as a Potomac River farmer accepted the Presidency in New York, his fellow Virginians looked to a hopeful future. "The preservation of the sacred fire of liberty," Washington told the inaugural assembly, is "staked on the experiment entrusted to the hands of the American people." Across the wide expanse of his native state, thousands of planters and pioneers shared his dream for America's future.

BIBLIOGRAPHY

American Heritage Editors. *The American Heritage Book of Great Historic Places*. Narrative by Richard M. Ketchum; Introduction by Bruce Catton. New York: American Heritage Publishing Co., in cooperation with Simon and Schuster, Inc., 1957.

American Heritage Editors. *The American Heritage Cookbook, and Illustrated History of American Eating & Drinking*. New York: Simon and Schuster, Inc., 1964.

Aresty, Esther B. *The Delectable Past*. New York: Simon and Schuster, Inc., 1964.

Arnow, Harriette Simpson. *Flowering of the Cumberland*. New York: The Macmillan Company, 1963.

Babcock, C. Merton. *The American Frontier: A Social and Literary Record*. New York: Holt, Rinehart and Winston, Inc., 1965.

Bean, R. Bennett. *The Peopling of Virginia*. Boston: Chapman & Grimes, Inc., 1938.

Belden, Albert D. *George Whitefield, The Awakener*. New York: The Macmillan Company, 1953.

Blanton, Wyndham B. *Medicine in Virginia in the Seventeenth Century*. Richmond: The William Byrd Pres, Inc., 1930.

Boley, Henry. *Lexington in Old Virginia*. Richmond: Garrett & Massie, Inc., 1936.

Book of Common Prayer, with Additions and Deviations Proposed in 1928. London: Cambridge University Press.

Bridenbaugh, Carl. *Myths and Realities: Societies of the Colonial South*. Baton Rouge: Louisiana State University Press, 1952.

Bruce, Philip Alexander. *Economic History of Virginia in the Seventeenth Century*. Vol. 1. New York: The Macmillan Company, 1907.

———. *Social Life of Virginia in the Seventeenth Century*. Second Edition. Lynchburg, Va.: J. P. Bell Company, Inc., 1927.

Brydon, George Maclaren. *Virginia's Mother Church*. Vol. II. Philadelphia: Church Historical Society, 1952.

Bullock, Helen. *The Williamsburg Art of Cookery*. Fourth Edition. Williamsburg: Colonial Williamsburg, Inc., 1947.

Cartmell, T. K. *Shenandoah Valley Pioneers and Their Descendants: A History of Frederick County, Virginia*. Berryville, Virginia: Chesapeake Book Company, 1963.

Davis, Richard Beale. *Intellectual Life in Jefferson's Virginia, 1790-1830*. Chapel Hill: The University of North Carolina Press, 1964.

Duren, William Larkin. *The Top Sergeant of the Pioneers*. Emory University, Georgia: Banner Press, Publishers, 1930.

Dykeman, Wilma. *The French Broad*. New York: Rinehart & Company, Inc., 1955.

Eisenberg, William Edward. *The Lutheran Church in Virginia, 1717-1962*. Roanoke, Va.: The Trustees of the Virginia Synod, Lutheran Church in America, 1967.

Foote, William Henry. *Sketches of Virginia — Historical and Biographical*. New edition with Index. Richmond: John Knox Press, 1966.

————. *Sketches of Virginia, Historical and Biographical*. Second Series, Second Edition, Revised. Philadelphia: J. B. Lippincott & Co., 1856.

Franklin, John Hope. *From Slavery to Freedom: A History of American Negroes*. Second edition, revised and enlarged. New York: Alfred A. Knopf, 1956.

Frazier, E. Franklin. *The Negro Family in the United States*. Chicago: The University of Chicago Press, 1939.

Gewehr, Wesley M. *The Great Awakening in Virginia, 1740-1790*. Durham, N.C.: Duke University Press, 1930.

Gottmann, Jean. *Virginia at Mid-Century*. New York: Henry Holt and Company, 1955.

Greene, Lorenzo Johnston, Ph.D. *The Negro in Colonial New England, 1620-1776*. New York: Columbia University Press, 1942.

Green, B. W. *Word-Book of Virginia Folk-Speech*. Richmond: Wm. Ellis Jones, Book and Job Printer, 1899.

Hagy, James W. "Castle's Woods: Frontier Virginia Settlement, 1769-1799." Unpublished master's thesis. East Tennessee State University, 1966.

Hervey, John. *Racing in America, 1665-1865*. Vol. I. Written for the Jockey Club. New York: Privately Printed by the Jockey Club, 1944 (Scribner Press).

Hoge, Rev. John Blair. *Sketch of the Life and Character of The Rev. Moses Hoge, D.D.* Historical Transcripts No. 2. Richmond: The Union Theological Seminary in Virginia, 1964.

A Hornbook of Virginia History. Richmond: The Virginia State Library, 1965.

Howison, Robert R. *A History of Virginia from its Discovery and Settlement by Europeans to the Present Time*. Volume II. Richmond: Drinker and Morris. New York & London: Wiley and Putnam, 1848.

Ingalls, Fay. *The Valley Road*. Cleveland and New York: The World Publishing Company, 1949.

Jamestown 350th Anniversary Historical Booklets. Edited by E. G. Swem. Richmond: Garrett & Massie, 1957.

John Norton & Sons, Merchants of London and Virginia: Being the Papers from Their Counting House for the Years 1750 to 1795. Edited by Frances Norton Mason. Richmond: The Dietz Press, 1937.

Kegley, F. B. *Kegley's Virginia Frontier*. Roanoke: The Southwest Virginia Historical Society, 1938.

Kercheval, Samuel. *A History of the Valley of Virginia*. Fourth edition. Strasburg, Va.: Shenandoah Publishing House, 1925.

Leyburn, James G. *The Scotch-Irish: A Social History*. Chapel Hill: The University of North Carolina Press, 1962.

Little, Bryan. *The City and County of Bristol: A Study in Atlantic Civilization*. London: Werner Laurie, 1954.

Morison, Samuel Eliot. *The Founding of Harvard College*. Cambridge, Mass.: Harvard University Press, 1935.

Middleton, Arthur Pierce. *Tobacco Coast*. Newport News, Va.: The Mariners' Museum, 1953.

The Mount Vernon Ladies' Association of the Union. "Mount Vernon, Virginia: An Illustrated Handbook." Mount Vernon, Va.: Judd & Detweiler, Inc., 1964.

Quennell, Marjorie and C. H. B. *A History of Everyday Things in England*, Vol. II. New York: G. P. Putnam's Sons, 1965.

Rankin, Hugh F. *The Theater in Colonial America*. Chapel Hill: The University of North Carolina Press, 1960.

Regionalism in America, edited by Merrill Jensen with foreword by Felix Frankfurter. Madison: The University of Wisconsin Press, 1951.

Simkins, Francis Butler and Spotswood Hunnicutt. *Virginia: History, Government, Geography*. New York: Charles Scribner's Sons, 1957.

Smith, Elmer Lewis, John G. Stewart, and M. Ellsworth Kyger. *The Pennsylvania Germans of the Shenandoah Valley*. Allentown, Penna.: Schlechter's, 1964.

Soltow, J. H. "Scottish Traders in Virginia, 1750-1775," *The Economic History Review*, second series, Vol. XII, No. 1, 1959. Printed in the Netherlands.

Spruill, Julia Cherry. *Women's Life and Work in the Southern Colonies*. Chapel Hill: University of North Carolina Press, 1938.

Strickler, Harry M. *Massanutten, Settled by the Pennsylvania Pilgrim 1726: The First White Settlement in the Shenandoah Valley*. Strasburg, Va.: Shenandoah Publishing House, 1924.

Summers, Lewis Preston. *Annals of Southwest Virginia, 1769-1800*. Abingdon, Va.: Lewis Preston Summers, 1929.

Sweet, William Warren. *Virginia Methodism — A History*. Illustrations by Erle Prior. Richmond, Va.: Whittet & Shepperson, 1955.

Tate, Thad W., Jr. *The Negro in Eighteenth-Century Williamsburg*. A Colonial Williamsburg Publication. Charlottesville: The University Press of Virginia, 1965.

Thompson, Ernest Trice. *Presbyterians In the South, Volume One: 1607-1871*. Richmond: John Knox Press, 1963.

Trevelyan, G. M. *Illustrated English Social History: Vol. II*. London: Penguin Books, 1964.

United States Bureau of the Census. *Heads of Families at the First Census of the United States Taken in the Year 1790*. Washington: Government Printing Office, 1908.

Wagner, Anthony Richard. *English Genealogy*. Oxford: The Clarendon Press, 1960.

Wise, John Sergeant. *The End of an Era*. Edited and annotated by Curtis Carroll Davis. New York: Thomas Yoseloff, 1965.

Withers, Alexander Scott. *Chronicles of Border Warfare*. Edited and annotated by Reuben Gold Thwaites. Seventh impression. Cincinnati: Stewart & Kidd Company, Publishers, 1920.

Wright, Louis B. *The First Gentlemen of Virginia*. Charlottesville: The University Press of Virginia, 1964.

———. *Everyday Life in Colonial America*. New York: G. P. Putnam's Sons, 1965.

Some of the Leading Early Virginia Families, Listed by Region

The dominantly Anglo-Saxon character of Virginia is evident in its family names. This list of typical surnames is based on colonial county records, many of which were destroyed by fire or in the Civil War.

Jamestown and the James-York Peninsula

Adams, Alderly, Allen, Allsop, Ambler, Anderson, Archer, Armistead, Austin, Aylmer, Baker, Ballard, Banks, Barrett, Bassett, Beckley, Berkeley, Blair, Bland, Brodnax, Bowe, Bowker, Boyd, Bridges, Brown, Buchanan, Buck, Burney, Burwell, Bushrod, Byrd, Caldwell, Carter, Cary, Carys, Chamberlayne, Chiswell, Clay, Clopton, Clough, Claiborne, Cocke, Coles, Collings, Cory, Cosby, Cox, Cross, Curles, Curtis, Custis, Dale, Dandridge, Davies, Davis, Devereux, Dickson, Diggs, Dixon, Doran, Douthat, Dudley, Dunbar, Ellis, Fauntleroy, Fitzhugh, Fontaine, Foushee, Gamble, Gibbons, Goddin, Gooch, Goodwin, Grammer, Gray, Griffith, Hampton, Harwood, Hankins, Harris, Harrison, Harvie, Hay, Hebard, Henley, Henry, Heron, Hill, Hobson, Hockaday, Hogg, Holdcroft, Hopkins, Hunt, Hunter, Hylton.

Jamieson, James, Jaquelin, Jarrett, Jennings, Jones, Keeling, Kenney, Kilpatrick, Kirby, Lang, Langhorne, Leavell, LeNeve, Lewellyn, Lewis, Lightfoot, Littlepage, Ludwell, Lyons, Macakain, Macawly, Macon, Madison, Malloy, Marshall, Massie, Maury, Meriwether (Merriweather), Mitchell, Moreau, Morris, McCabe, McClung, McCloud, Nelson, Nelville, Nicholson, Norris, Norwood, Ogilvie, Oliver, Owen, Pack, Page, Parke, Payne, Pendleton, Pickett, Pollard, Pope, Power, Prince, Prosser, Radcliffe, Ragland, Randolph, Read, Reid, Richardson, Rolfe, Russell, Scherer, Scott, Seddon, Selden, Sherman, Sheild, Shields, Slater, Smith, Stratton, Syme, Taylor, Terrell, Thacker, Thorpe, Throckmorton, Thornton, Timberlake, Tinsley, Tonshee, Trueheart, Tucker, Tyler, Vaughan, Waddell, Wade, Warrington, Webb, West, White, Whittaker, Wickham, Wilkinson, Williams, Wilmer, Winn, Winston, Woodridge, Woodward, Wormeley, Wyatt, Wythe, Yardley.

The South Shore of the James

Allen, Andrews, Applewhite, Archer, Atkinson, Avis, Baker, Balfour, Ballentine, Bannister, Barker, Barnell, Barnett, Barter, Barham, Batte, Basse, Baugh, Beasley, Bennett, Berry, Berryman, Betts, Bland, Bodman, Bolling, Boyd, Boyle, Bradley, Bradshaw, Branch, Brasseur, Brett, Bridger, Brodie, Brooke, Browne, Buchan, Bullock, Burgess, Burroughs, Burwell, Butler, Cahoon, Calvert, Capps, Carey, Carroway, Carver, Cary, Cawson, Cheatham, Cheely, Chisholm, Christian, Clarke, Cocke, Codd, Cole, Coleman, Collier, Cofer, Collins, Conrad, Coupland, Cook, Covington, Crew, Cromwell, Dale,

Davis, Day, Dean, DeFord, Dickson, Dier, Digges, Donald, Downing, Drayton, Driskoll, Earle, Eaton, Edwards, Elam, Etheridge, Everard, Eyers, Farrar, Faulkner, Ferguson, Floyd, Fontaine, Forbes, Ford, Foster, Fowler, Fulghum.

Garner, Garrison, Gaskins, George, Gibbs, Gilbert, Giles, Gilliam, Glasscock, Goddin, Godfrey, Godwin, Gookin, Gordon, Gregory, Grymes, Guilliam, Gwaltney, Hall, Halleck, Hancock, Hankins, Harrington, Harrison, Hart, Hawkins, Hayes, Hedges, Hill, Hinton, Hitchcock, Hobson, Hoges, Hoge, Holliday, Holmes, Holt, Hopkinson, Horner, Horton, Hoskins, Howard, Howell, Ingles, Ironmonger, Isles, Ivy, Jackson, Jefferson, Johns, Johnson, Jones, Jordan, Judkins, Keeling, Kempe, Kemps, Kenalds, Kent, Kidder, King, Lambert, Langley, Lanshire, Latham, Lawson, Lawne, Lee, Leitch, Linch, Lind, Lloyd, Locke, Lovitt, Marsh, Marshall, Martin, Mason, Maury, Meade, Mears, McCabe, McCallum, Miller, Mills, Moor, Moore, Nash, Newland, Norfleet, Norsworthy, Nunally, Oberon, Owen.

Page, Parker, Pasteur, Pegram, Penn, Peters, Peyton, Philips, Pitt, Poole, Powell, Price, Prichard, Prince, Puckett, Radford, Rainsford, Rales, Randolph, Richardson, Robinson, Ruffin, Savedge, Savill, Sawyer, Sayer, Scarburg, Scott, Sewell, Shelton, Sheriff, Shores, Short, Show, Sibsey, Sicklemore, Sidney, Silvester, Simonds, Skipwith, Slaughter, Smith, Southall, Spencer, Stewart, Stout, Stratton, Taylor, Thorogood, Tilgham, Todd, Tower, Traylor, Turnbull, Tucker, Turner, Underwood, Urmston, Vaden, Vaughan, Veale, Wade, Waddington, Walke, Walker, Walters, Ward, Waters, Watkins, Watson, Webb, West, Wheat, Wheeler, White, Whitehurst, Will, Williams, Willis, Willowby, Wilmer, Windham, Wingfield, Wise, Wiseman, Woodhouse, Worsley, Wright, Yates, Yerby.

The Eastern Shore of Virginia

Addison, Avery, Ayres, Brown, Bowdoin, Boden, Bowman, Charlton, Corbin, Cropper, Custis, Eastham, Emmerson, Evans, Eyre, Finney, Gardner, Harmonson, Hobart, Hopkins, Joynes, Kerr, Marshall, Monroe, Nottingham, Nugent, Parker, Preston, Reese, Savage, Scarborough, Stith, Teagle, Upshur, Vare, Wise, West, Yeardley, Zimmer.

The Gloucester-Middlesex-Mathews Peninsula

Alexander, Anderson, Armistead, Bacon, Bagby, Baker, Barnard, Baron, Baronet, Bassett, Battaile, Baylor, Beale, Berkeley, Beverly, Bibber, Biggs, Billops, Bird, Blackford, Blackwell, Bland, Booker, Booth, Boucher, Bowker, Braxton, Brockenbrough, Brook, Buckner, Buford, Burge, Burress, Burwell, Byrd, Campbell, Carmichael, Carr, Carraway, Carrington, Carter, Cary, Catlett, Chamberlayne, Chapman, Charles, Chew, Chichley, Chiles, Churchill, Clarke, Clayborne, Clements, Clowder, Coakley, Cooke, Cole, Corbin, Croxton, Curtis, Custis, Dabney, Dangerfield, DeJarnette, Dick, Digges, Dixon, Dudley, Dunn, Duval, Echols, Edmund, Edmundson, Ficklin, Field, Fitzhugh, Fontaine, Forbes, Fox, Friend.

Gayle, Gray, Grayson, Gresham, Grymes, Guinea, Guy, Gwynn, Gwynne, Hansford, Hanson, Harris, Harrison, Hart, Haws, Haynes, Henry, Herndon, Hill, Holmes, Hoomes, Hopkinson, Hubard, Hubbard, Hughes, Hudgins, Innes, Jennings, Johnson, Johnston, Jones, Kean, Keeble, Kemp, Kenner, Kidd, Knopf, Knowles, Knox, Latane, Lee, Leigh, Lewis, Lightfoot, Littlepage, Lock, Lomax, Lord, Low, Lowry, Madison, Mann, Marye, Mathews, Maury, Meade, Mercer, Metcalfe, Middleton, Miller, Mills, Minor, Moncure, Monroe, Montague, Moreton, Morris, McBride, McCarthy, McDuff, McGuire, McKinney.

Nash, Nelson, Nicholson, Page, Parker, Peachy, Pearl, Pendleton, Penn, Peyton, Pollard, Pollock, Price.

Rawlins, Read, Rey, Richards, Ritchie, Roane, Robertson, Robins, Robinson, Rogers, Rothrock, Ruffin, St. Clair, Saunders, Savage, Scandrith, Scott, Selden, Sharp, Shepherd, Shuman, Singleton, Skipwith, Skyren, Slaughter, Smith, Smoot, Staige, Stephenson, Sterling, Stewart, Tabb, Taliaferro, Tayloe, Taylor, Thornton, Throckmorton, Thurston, Todd, Turner, Tyler, Typerios, Upshaw, Van Bibber, Vass, Walker, Waller, Ward, Ware, Warner, Warwick, Washington, Waugh, Webb, West, Wheatle, Whiting, Wickham, Willis, Winston, Woodford, Woodville, Wormeley, Wyatt, Yates, Young.

The Northern Neck of Virginia

Adams, Alexander, Allerton, Andrew, Andrews, Armistead, Ashton, Aubrey, Bailey, Baily, Ball, Barber, Barbour, Barnes, Barrow, Bassett, Beacham, Beale, Beckwith, Bell, Bellfield, Berkeley, Bernard, Berry, Bertrand, Beverly, Bloomfield, Boon, Boucher, Branham, Broadhurst, Brockenbrough, Bryant, Burnet, Bushrod, Campbell, Carter, Champe, Chesley, Chewning, Chidwell, Chilton, Chinn, Clapham, Clemens, Cloughton, Coffin, Cole, Colston, Conway, Corbin, Corbyn, Cornish, Cox, Crabb, Currie, Dade, Dale, Dangerfield, Dashiell, Davenport, Davies, Davis, Deane, DeButts, Delafield, Digges, Dishman, Dobyns, Donophan, Dowman, Downman.

Elliott, Eustace, Eyre, Farnefold, Fauntleroy, Fitzhugh, Fleet, Flood, Fowke, Fox, Friend, Gardner, Garner, Gaskins, Gerard, Gerrard, Giberne, Gibson, Glascock, Glyn, Goldsmith, Goodrich, Gordon, Griffin, Griffith, Grymes, Gwin, Hainy, Hamilton, Hardy, Harney, Harrison, Harvey, Hooe, Hopkins, Hornby, Hurst, Ingo, Jackson, Jennings, Jett, Johnson, Jones, Jordan, Joynes, Keith, Kelley, Kendall, Kenner, Kennor, Kibble, Kick, Kirk, Landon, Latane, Leach, Leacock, Lee, Leland, Levy, Lovall, Low, Lloyd, Ludlow, Lurino, Mackay, Markham, Marmaduke, Marshall, Martin, Massey, Matram, Merryman, Metcalf, Meuse, Micou, Middleton, Miles, Minnis, Miskall, Montague, Moore, Moseley, Mottrom, Mountjoy, McCarty, McComas, McDonald, McGuire, McKay, McNaughton.

Nash, Neale, Needler, Nelson, Newton, Norris, Nutt, Oldham, Page, Palmer, Parker, Parsons, Peachy, Pierciful, Piet, Piper, Plummer, Powell, Poythress, Prescott, Presley, Pritchard, Reynard, Richmond, Robinson, Rochester, Rogers, Rose, Rowsee, Roy, Rumney, Russell, Rust, Sanford, Savage, Scott, Sebastian, Seward, Shearman, Sherlock, Shreiner, Simpson, Slaughter, Smith, Speke, Stewart, Stuart, Stone, Swan, Taliaferro, Tarpley, Tayloe, Taylor, Temple, Templeman, Thornby, Thornton, Tibbs, Tomlin, Townshend, Traveson, Travis, Tucker, Turbeville, Tuttle, Tyler, Underwood, Upshaw, Upshur, Waddell, Walke, Ward, Waring, Washington, Williamson, Willoughby, Wilson, Woffendall, Woodbridge, Yerby, Young.

Alexandria and Northern Virginia

Adams, Adie, Alexander, Allen, Ambrose, Amburger, Alexander, Anderson, Aneux, Armistead, Ashby, Bacon, Baker, Ball, Balmaine, Band, Barbour, Barclay, Barnes, Barnette, Barrow, Barry, Baxter, Baylis, Beach, Beale, Becket, Belfield, Bell, Beller, Bennett, Bernard, Berryman, Betty, Bivings, Blackburn, Blackwell, Blaford, Blankenbaker, Bloodsworth, Booker, Booton, Bowen, Bowie, Bowman, Bradfort, Brent, Briscoe, Broadwater, Brock, Bronough, Brooke, Brown, Broyles, Bryan, Bryant, Buchan, Buchanan, Buck, Bullett, Bullinger, Bunton, Burger, Burnley, Burwell, Butler, Cacklum, Campbell, Carlyle, Carney, Carpenter, Carr, Carter, Cary, Catlett, Cave, Chambers, Chapman, Chevalle, Chew, Chichester, Chigler, Churchill, Claggett, Clapham, Clawse, Clemons, Clermont, Clore, Cobbler, Cobbs, Coffee, Cole, Colmes, Colston, Compton, Conway, Cook, Cooke, Coppage, Craik, Crigler, Crisler, Crisman, Cromley, Crow, Crump, Culpepper, Cunningham, Custis.

Dade, Dana, Dangerfield, Daniel, Darnel, Dashiell, Davenport, Davis, deButts, Deed, De la Foyalle, Deskin, Donithon, Dorrell, Douglass, Dudley, Duff, Dughen, Duncan, Dunn, Earnest, Ellzey, Elsey, Emorie, Erogg, Eskridge, Eustace, Ewell, Fairfax, Ferguson, Field, Finlayson, Fisher, Fleshman, Forbes, Ford, Fouchee, Fowke, Froman, Gaines, Gardener, Garner, Garnet, Garr, Gassell, Gibbs, Gibson, Gipson, Glassell, Gordon, Gore, Graham, Gray, Grayson, Green, Gregrie, Griffith, Grigsby, Grymes, Gunnell, Gwatkin, Hague, Hamilton, Hampton, Hardin, Harper, Harrison, Hedgeman, Hedgman, Helms, Henderson, Henning, Herbert, Heydt, Higgins, Higginson, Hill, Hite, Hoe, Hoeger, Hoffman, Hoge, Holt, Holzclaw, Hooe, Hooper, Hopper, Howard, Hugh, Hunter, Huntley.

Iredell, Irish, Jackson, James, Jennings, Johns, Johnson, Johnston, Jones, Kaifer, Keastley, Kebler, Keith, Kennon, Kerker, Kincheloe, Kirkpatrick, Knox, Lackwood, Lavid, Larne, Leavell, Lee, Lemmon, Lemon, Lewis, Lightfoot, Lindsay, Linton, Lohew, Long, Low, Ludwell, Lynton, Macatee, Machen, Mann, Manspoil, Marr, Marshall, Martin, Mason, Mass, Massey, Maury, Markham, Mauzy, Mayer, Meade, Meldrum, Mercer, Milton, Minor, M'Millon, Moncure, Moore, Morgan, Morton, Moss, Mountjoy, Motz, McCarty, McCloed, McCormick, McCoy, McCrae, McDaniel, McFarlen, McGuire, McKay, McLean, McMahan, McMahon, Neil, Nelson, Neville, Nicholas, Nisbet, Norton, Novis, O'Neal, O'Neil, O'Rear, Orr, Owsley, Page, Parker, Parlur (later Barlow), Parmel, Parsons, Patton, Paulitz, Payne, Payton, Pearson, Pendleton, Penn, Perkins, Peter, Peterkin, Peyton, Pollard, Powell, Preston, Price.

Ramsey, Randolph, Rankin, Raynhart, Rearsher, Regan, Renno, Reno, Rice, Roaker, Robert, Robertson, Rose, Ross, Rouse, Rousson, Rucker, Russell, Rust, Rutherford, Ryley, Scot, Scott, Seale, Selden, Shepherd, Sheible, Sherman, Shiraz, Shirly, Shone, Simms, Skrein, Slaughters, Smith, Snyder, Spottswood, Staige, Staunton, Stephens, Stevens, Stewart, Stolts, Stone, Stover, Stringfellow, Strother, Stuart, Tacquet, Taliaferro, Tanner, Tayloe, Taylor, Terrett, Thomas, Thompson, Thornton, Threlheld, Thurston, Tibbet, Tibbs, Todd, Towles, Travers, Triplett, Tuberville, Turley, Turner, Twyman, Tyler, Utz, Van Meter, Van Swearingen, Vaunce, Vauter, Waggener, Waite, Walker, Wall, Washington, Waters, Watkins, Waugh, Wayland, Weems, West, Whettige, White, Whiting, Whitridge, Whittle, Wickliffe, Wiley, Wilkes, Williams, Willis, Willock, Wilmer, Winston, Withers, Wood, Woodroff, Woods, Woodville, Wright, Yager, Young, Zimmerman, Zollicoffer.

Central Virginia

Ambler, Anderson, Anglen, Archer, Armstrong, Ashton, Ball, Ballou, Balmaine, Barbour, Barksdale, Barnes, Barrett, Baskerville, Battersby, Beesley, Bedford, Bentley, Berkeley, Beverly, Black, Bocock, Bodkin, Bolling, Bordon, Benjamin, Brand, Bratton, Breckenridge, Brent, Brooking, Buchanan, Bulkly, Burnley, Burnside, Burton, Bryce, Cabell, Campbell, Carlile, Carr, Carrington, Caw, Celmens, Clark, Clarkson, Clay, Cloner, Cobbs, Cocke, Cole, Coles, Conway, Cory, Cosby, Coxe, Crockett, Crump, Cunningham, Dalton, Daniel, Darneile, Davenport, Davies, Davis, Deane, Defoe, Delamontony, Dickie, Donnely, Dor, Doughen, Dunlap, Eldridge, Ellis, Eppes, Estill, Farrar, Fisher, Fleming, Foster, Fry, Garland, Gay, Gillial, Gilmer, Goolsby, Goodwin, Graham, Gray, Grymes, Hall, Hammer, Hare, Harper, Harris, Harrison, Harvie, Haskins, Henry, Heydt, Hicklen, Hickman, Hill, Hodges, Holmes, Hook, Hopkins, Howard, Hubbard, Hudson, Hughes, Hume.

Irving, Jackson, Jamiesen, Jefferson, Johnson, Jones, Jordan, Kincaid, King, LaGrand, Leake, Lee, Leland, Lewis, Lynch, MacDowell, Madison, Magruder, Marks, Marr, Marshall, Martin, Massie, Maury, Maxwell, Mayo, Mead, Meredith, Meriwether, Miller, Mills, Minor, Moore, Morgan, Morris, Morsons, Morton, Moseley, McCandless, McKay, McPherson, Muller, Napier, Nelson, Netherland, Neville, Nicholas, Oglesby, O'Neil, Page, Paulett, Peers, Pemberton, Pendleton, Perkins, Pleasants, Poindexter, Pollard, Price, Pritchett, Pullen, Pryor, Randolph, Read, Rice, Rives, Robertson, Rhodes, Roger, Ronald, Rose, Rucker, Ryan, Sampson, Saunders, Scott, Sedoon, Shaw, Shelton, Shepherd, Sims, Slaughter, Smith, Stark, Stuart, Swann, Taliaferro, Tarleton, Taylor, Terrell, Terry, Thomas, Thompson, Tims, Tinsley, Tithers, Trent, Tucker, Tunstall, Turpin, Twyman, Tyree, Underwood, Vaughan, Venable, Wade, Waddell, Walker, Wallace, Waller, Ware, Wheeler, White, Williams, Williamson, Willis, Wilmer, Wilson, Wingate, Wirt.

South Central Counties

Agee, Allen, Ambler, Amouet, Archer, Bacon, Bagby, Ballard, Banister, Barksdale, Barraud, Barry, Baskerville, Bell, Berkeley, Bernard, Betts, Blackwell, Boisseau, Bolling, Bondurant, Bonvell, Booker, Bouldin, Bridgforth, Broodman, Brunskill, Buford, Caldwell, Cameron, Car-

gill, Castleman, Chadouin, Chasteen, Chevers, Claiborne, Clay, Coleman, Conway, Cook, Cooksey, Cory, Craig, Crawford, Davis, Dawson, DeGraffenreid, Delaney, Dibrell, Dixon, Dupuy, Duvall, Edmundson, Eggleston, Ellis. Embry, Eppes, Farrar, Flournoy, Fontaine, Foushee, Fuqua, Garland, Gee, Giles, Grammar, Gray, Hall, Hardaway, Harding, Hardy, Harris, Harrison, Hatcher, Hatchett, Hill, Hobson, Howard, Jarrett, Jaqueline, Jefferson, Jennings, Jeter, Jones, Jordan, Jonette, Kello, Kidder.

LaGrande, Lanier, Lane, Lassiter, Latane, Lawson, Lee, Leigh, LeNeve, Lester, Ligon, Mahone, Markham, Marye, Mason, Massie, Mathews, Maupin, Maury, Maxey, May, Meaux, Meade, Michael, Michelle, Mileston, Moncure, Morris, Morton, Munford, Murray, McCreary, McFarland, McGuire, Nash, Niblett, Pasteur, Pemberton, Perron, Phelps, Potter, Pride, Pryor, Ragsdale, Randolph, Read, Robertson, Rochelle, Royall, Scott, Skelton, Smith, Speed, Stokes, Street, Sublett, Tabb, Talbot, Taliaferro, Taylor, Thweatt, Townes, Tucker, Twitty, Urquhart, Vaughan, Wade, Walthall, Ward, Watkins, Webb, Wiley, Williamson, Willie, Withers, Worsham, Wynne, Yates.

The Southern "Tobacco Belt" Counties

Adams, Adkinson, Adkisson, Agur, Alexander, Allen, Anderson, Andrews, Archer, Armstrong, Arthur, Atkinson, Bagby, Bailey, Baker, Balling, Barksdale, Baskerville, Bates, Bean, Bell, Bennett, Berkeley, Black, Blunt, Bondurant, Booker, Bouldin, Boyd, Branch, Brandon, Breckenridge, Bruce, Brunskill, Buchan, Bullock, Bumpass, Burgee, Burke, Butler, Byrd, Cabell, Caldwell, Calloway, Cameron, Camp, Campbell, Cannon, Cargill, Carlton, Carper, Carrington, Carson, Carter, Caven, Chamberlayne, Chandler, Chastain, Chasteen, Choice, Clark, Clement, Clouds, Cobb, Cobbs, Cocke, Cofer, Coleman, Coles, Colquett, Cook, Cooke, Copeland, Copen, Coupland, Cowan, Craddock, Craig, Crawford, Crew, Critz, Crouch, Crute, Cunningham, Currie. Dalton, Daly, Dame, Daniel, Darneille, Dashiell, Daughen, Dauson, Davenport, Davis, DeJarnette, Delany, DeShazean, Dickinson, Dillard, Dix, Dodson, Donaldson, Donelson, Dresser, Dudgeon, Dudley, Duncan.

Early, Echols, Edmund, Edmundson, Edwards, Ellis, Emmerson, Epes, Esdale, Fallen, Faris, Faulkner, Fisher, Fitzgerald, Fitzpatrick, Flournoy, Floyd, Fontaine, Foote, Foster, Foulis, Fourqueran, Frambrough, Francisco, Franklin, Freeman, Fuqua, Garden, Gardland, Garland, Garrard, Gibson, Gilbert, Gilfron, Gilliam, Gillintine, Glover, Goode, Goodon, Goodwin, Gordon, Green, Guilliam, Gurley, Haile, Hairston, Hale, Haley, Hall, Hampton, Hancock, Hanly, Hanna, Hanson, Harland, Harris, Harrison, Hart, Hatcher, Hawkins, Hay, Haynes, Helm, Henderson, Hendrick, Hill, Hilton, Hite, Holmes, Holt, Hooker, Hopkins, Humphrey, Hundley, Hunt, Hunter.

Innes, Irby, Irvine, Jackson, Jarrett, Jefferson, Jenings, Jeter, Johns, Johnson, Johnston, Jones, Jordan, Kennon, Key, Kilkronse, Kinckle, King, Kinsolving, Knowlin, Lacy, Langford, Langhorne, Lanier, Lankford, Laws, Lawson, Leigh, Leonard, Lewis, Ligon, Little, Locke, Logan, Love, Lovelace, Lowden, Lowder, Lucas, Lynch, Lyne, McAlexander, McBryde, McCraw, McDowell, McGriffin, McGuire, McIlroy, McKinney, McLary, McMahan, McNeal, McReynolds, McRoberts, Macklin, MacMillon, Madison, Mann, Marlow, Martin, Maynham, Mayo, Meade, Meredith, Meriwether, Michaux, Mickeljohn, Miller, Mitchell, Moore, Moorman, Morgan, Morris, Morton, Moseley, Mullens, Nash, Navison, Neal, Nelson, Nicholas, Nichols, Nowlin, Onsrud, Osgood, Otey, Owen, Page, Palmer, Parish, Parker, Parsons, Payne, Paynor, Peasley, Penn, Perkins, Pine, Pinston, Powell, Pride, Proctor.

Ragland, Ramsey, Randolph, Ravenscroft, Read, Rice, Richer, Robert, Robertson, Robinson, Rogers, Rowland, Royall, Royster, Russell, Ryburn, Sale, Saunders, Scott, Scruggs, Shelby, Shelton, Sims, Skelton, Skinner, Skipwith, Slaughter, Smith, Snuggs, Sprigg, Staples, Steele, Stevens, Stewart, Stith, Stoval, Stover, Stroud, Sturdevant, Swift, Sydnor, Syne, Tabb, Talbott, Taliaferro, Tarrant, Tate, Terry, Thompson, Thorp, Throckmorton, Thurston, Tinsley, Tompkins, Townes, Tredway, Trent, Tucker, Tuggle, Tunstall, Twitty, Van Bibber, Vaughan, Venable, Wade, Walker, Waller, Walton, Ward, Washington, Watkins, Webb, West, Wharton, Whitten, Whittle, Wilkinson, Wilmer, Willis, Wilson, Winbush, Witcher, Withers, Womack, Wooding, Woodson, Wynne.

The Valley of Virginia

Abercrombie, Adams, Alexander, Allen, Allison, Anderson, Arbuckle, Archer, Armstrong, Arthur, Atkins, Baldwin, Barger, Barnett, Barney, Bates, Beale, Beckner, Bell, Beverly, Black, Blackford, Blessing, Bledsoe, Borden, Bowen, Bowman, Bowyer, Boyden, Bradshaw, Breckenridge, Brooke, Brown, Buchanan, Burk, Burns, Campbell, Carlock, Carlton, Carmickle, Carpenter, Carper, Carrigan, Cartwill, Carwin, Cassell, Childress, Chillop, Christian, Clark, Clay, Cloyd, Coffey, Coherin, Cole, Coles, Copenhaver, Cosby, Crabtree, Craig, Craven, Crawford, Crocker, Crockett, Crow, Culton, Cunningham, Curren, Daugherty, Davidson, Davis, Dearly. Denton, Devereux, Dickenson, Dillman, Ditty, Doad, Doak, Donally, Douglas, Drake, Dungan, Dunlap, Dutton, Dwyn, Edmondson, Edwards, Elliott, Estill, Evans. Ewing.

Fancy, Ferris, Finley, Fitzpatrick, Fitzwater, Fowler, Fox, Frazer, Fuller, Galbraith, Gardner, Garwood, Gibson, Gillespie, Gilman, Glenn, Goodman, Goodwin, Gordon, Grayson, Greener, Greever, Griffiths, Griffy, Grigsby, Grome, Groseclose, Gross, Hale, Hall, Hammon, Harmon, Harrison, Hatfield, Haven, Haynes, Hays, Henderlite, Henderson, Henneger, Herghart, Heydt, Hellman, Hilton, Hindman, Hobson, Hoge, Holeman, Holston, Houston, Howe, Hubble, Hughart, Hohl, Humphrey, Ingles, Jackson, James, Jameson, Johnson, Johnston, Jones, Kauffman, Keller, Kerr, Kincaid, Kincannon, King, Kinney, Lafferty, Lammie, Lang, Langdon, Lark, Ledgerwood, Lee, Lester, Lewis, Lochart, Logan, Lupton, McAfee, McCallister, McCartney, McCarty, McCausland, McClanahan, McCorkle, McCray, McCue, McDonald, McDowell, McGavock, McHenry, McIlhaney, McKay, McKee, McPherson, Machen, MacKall, MacMurray, Madison, Manning, Mathews, Mauzy, Maysie, Midrock, Miller, Millroy, Mitchell, Montgomery, Moore, Morgan, Morris, Mosby, Muhlenburg, Muldrock, Murray.

Nash, Neal, Neely, Nelson, Noffsinger, Painter, Patterson, Patton, Payton, Persinger, Phillips, Pickens,

Pierce, Poague, Preston, Pugh, Randolph, Rayburn, Reynolds, Richardson, Rinehart, Roads, Robertson, Robin, Robinson, Roller, Ruddell, Ruffin, Russell, Sayer, Scott, Selzer, Sevier, Sholl, Simmons, Simpson, Skidmore, Slaughter, Slemp, Sly, Smith, Staley, Stalnaker, Starnes, Steenbergen, Stevens, Stevenson, Stover, Stribling, Strickler, Strother, Stuart, Sylvester, Tackler, Tapp, Taylor, Telford, Terry, Thompson, Thomson, Tingler, Tosh, Trigg, Turner, Vancie, Vanover, VanSandt, Waddell, Walker, Ward, Warwick, Wassum, Watson, White, Whittey, Wickham, Williams, Willis, Wills, Wilson, Wolfe, Wood, Woods, Woolsey, Wright.

Southwestern Virginia

Acklin, Adams, Alderson, Allen, Ballard, Bane, Barnett, Baskerville, Baugh, Beason, Beattie, Beckley, Bell, Berry, Beverly, Black, Blackburn, Blackmore, Blacks, Blevins, Bourn, Bowen, Bowlen, Boyd, Breckenridge, Brown, Bruce, Bryant, Buchanan, Burke, Bush, Bustard, Calfer, Calhoun, Campbell, Carrico, Carr, Carter, Champ, Chapman, Charlton, Church, Clendenin, Clyburg, Colley, Collier, Colvill, Compton, Cooper, Cornutt, Coulton, Counts, Cowan, Cox, Craig, Craven, Crawford, Creeche, Crieger, Crockett, Crouch, Crow, Curran, Datson, David, Davidson, Davis, Dean, Deel, Denny, Dickinson, Dickey, Dickson, Doak, Duncan, Dunlap, Dysart, Eaton, Edmondson, Elder, Emyart, Evans, Ewing, Faires, Faley, Ferguson, Fields, Findley, Fisher, Floyd, Folie, Fone, Fraser, French, Frisbee, Fugate, Fulkason, Fuller, Gardner, Garrison, Gibson, Gillespie, Glass, Graham, Gray, Grayson, Green, Greer, Grey.

Hale, Hamilton, Hamlin, Hancock, Harlan, Harman, Harmon, Harold, Hash, Hay, Hayes, Helvy, Herbert, Hibbits, Hobbes, Hoge, Hogg, Hollins, Hope, Hore, Houck, Houndshell, Howell, Hubbard, Hubert, Huston, Inglass, Ingletone, Inglish, Ison, Jacob, Johnson, Johnston, Jones, Joseph, Keel, Kelly, Kennedy, Kerheart, Killgore, Kincannon, Kinkead, Kinser, Kirk, Larne, Laughlin, Law, Lean, Lee, Lestly, Lewis, Liggett, Lindsay, Lipps, Livingston, Lory, Love, Lowry, Lundy, Lynch, MacDonald, McCamont, McCullock, McCullough, McErwin, McFarland, McGavock, McIntyre, McMullin, McTaylor, Mairs, Mallory, Martin, Mastin, Mathews, Mathias, Maxwell, Mendenhall, Miles, Miller, Moffett, Montgomery, Moore, Morescoe, Morgan, Morrison, Munch, Muncy.

Nash, Neece, Neff, Neville, Newell, Nuckols, Orr, Osborn, Owen, Patterson, Pearis, Peck, Peery, Peters, Phipps, Pickerell, Pinkley, Pogue, Pollock, Polly, Pope, Porter, Porterfield, Powell, Ramey, Rasnick, Ratliff, Rawley, Refuss, Renfer, Richmond, Roberson, Roberts, Robinette, Robinson, Rodgers, Rose, Ross, Russell, Rutherford, Salyers, Sanders, Sartin, Saunders, Sayers, Shanow, Shaver, Shelby, Short, Simpson, Slemp, Smith, Snidow, Snodgrass, Snody, Southair, Southerland, Stailey, Staley, Stalnaker, Starnes, Stedman, Steel, Stevens, Stone, Straw, Stredham, Sturgill, Summer, Swift, Tate, Taylor, Thomas, Thompson, Todhunter, Tracey, Trimbull, Vain, Vance, Walker, Walling, Wampler, Ward, Webb, Wells, West, Wharton, Wherry, White, Whitten, Williams, Willoughby, Wills, Winn, Wood, Woods, Worrell, Wright, Wylie, Young.

Index

Illustrations are shown in italics.